puzzle pieces

Classroom Guidance Connection

**Gwen M. Sitsch
& Diane S. Senn**

ISBN 1-889636-42-8

Library of Congress Number
2001098324

Cover Design by Elaine Callahan/e graphics
Layout by Elaine Callahan/e graphics
Computer Illustration by Elaine Callahan/e graphics
Book Review by Sandy Ragona & Teresa Prier
Project Editing by Susan Bowman & Renee Wildman

10 9 8 7 6 5 4
Printed in the United States

P.O. Box 115 • Chapin, South Carolina 29036
(800) 209-9774 • (803) 345-1070
Fax (803) 345-0888 • Email YL@sc.rr.com
www.youthlight.com

ACKNOWLEDGEMENTS:

SPECIAL THANKS

Thank you to the faculties and students of Lake Murray Elementary and Crowders Creek Elementary who have warmly welcomed us into their classrooms over the past years. Also thank you to our students' parents who shared their support and appreciation for the lessons taught to their children. The enthusiasm of our faculties, students, and parents for the classroom guidance lessons gave us the incentive to share the lessons with others through this publication.

Thanks to the counselors in South Carolina, Georgia, and Texas who have received with such genuine interest the ideas that have been shared at our workshops in their state. Your asking, "Do you have these in a book?" encouraged us to follow through with putting the lessons in writing.

Thanks to the staff at YouthLight, Inc., for their patience as this book took form and grew.

Thanks to Mike and Shuler Sitsch who gave up many hours of family time so that this book could be completed.

Thanks to Stan, Bryan, and Lindsay for their continued support and confidence in me and belief in what I do.

And, most importantly, we give honor and thanks to God without whom none of this would be possible.

DEDICATION

To my husband, Mike, who helps me fit pieces together when the puzzle seems too difficult. You always build me up and without your support and encouragement, none of this would be possible. And to my son, Shuler, who is a "counselor's kid" and copes with it like a champ! You are the most blessed gift your dad and I have ever received.

To my parents, Thomas and Kay McAlhany, who sacrificed much so that I could be what God had planned for me. You "put me together right" and in turn I can share what you taught me with other children.

—Gwen

To all the children who I have had the privilege to guide through their elementary years. Your bright faces and eagerness to learn has been the motivating force that keeps me going.

To my husband who is always accepting and supporting of my professional adventures. And to my children, Bryan and Lindsay – the treasures in my life—who continue to be my cheerleaders.

—Diane

TABLE OF CONTENTS

DECISION MAKING *con.t*

COPING

SCHOOL-TO-WORK

Introduction

There is a story about a father who was trying to keep his young son occupied while he got some jobs done around the house. The son kept interrupting and so the father decided he would give his son a job that would take a while to get done. He tore a picture of the world from a magazine, cut it into many puzzle pieces and gave it to his son. "When you're done with this puzzle, come get me."

Less than five minutes later, the son comes to the father and says that he's done. The father, feeling very frustrated but a little curious, follows his son and finds that the picture of the world is put together exactly as it should be. The father is overwhelmed. "Son, that was a very hard puzzle. How did you put the world together so quickly?" he asks. The son giggles. "Oh, dad. I didn't put the world together…that would be too hard. But I noticed that there was a picture of some children on the back and I figured that if I put the children together right, then the world would come out right too."

Putting children together "right." That mission lies at the heart of everyone who works with children. Often children come to school "broken"—broken hearts, broken spirits, broken coping skills. Those children need extra support to help them heal.

But all children need help learning skills that will help them be more successful learners, more understanding friends, more effective communicators, more creative problem-solvers, and more responsible citizens. This book is designed with that goal in mind.

Puzzle Pieces contains lessons in five areas of affective development:

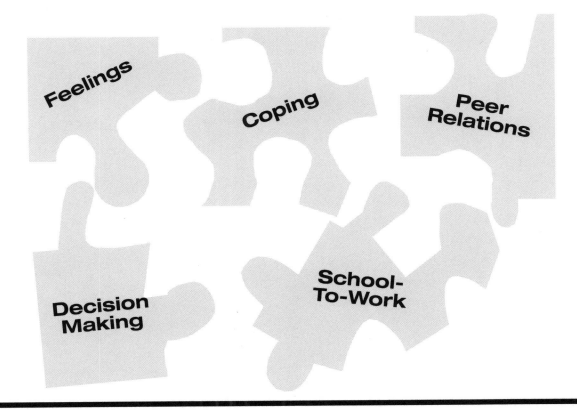

HOW DO YOU USE THE LESSONS?

The lessons can be used either as a unit or each can stand alone. Some counselors use a topic per grade level and teach all the lessons in that given topic. Some choose to cover each topic in each grade level, and therefore choose a lesson or two in each area that best fits the needs of the students.

Tuning into students' needs can best help you determine what will work for your school. If your school population is very stable and most students stay with you for their entire elementary school experience, you may choose a topic for each grade level. If your school is transient, you may choose to teach many different topics in a school year. Ask yourself the following questions in deciding "What do I teach when?"

- Around what topics do the majority of referrals from teachers in the grade level center?
- What are the common concerns of the students according to grade level?
- What are the developmental needs of the students in the grade level?

We encourage you to make a yearly plan for your guidance lessons at the beginning of each year. Three plans are provided as samples. Two are topical grade level plans. The first uses peer relations as the topic and the second uses the "bug" theme throughout a year to teach about feelings. The third sample uses many different topics for a grade level. A blank template is also provided for your use in making a yearly plan.

Sample Second Grade Guidance Plan
Peer Relations

Lesson No.	Week Of	TOPIC	LESSON	Guidance Competencies*
1	Sept. 11	Personal Behavior	Attractors and Repellers	
2	Oct. 1	Making a Reputation	Personal Pan Pizza	
3	Oct. 23	Choosing Friends: Individual Differences	M & M® Belief	
4	Nov. 13	Empathy	An Odd Dot	
5	Dec. 11	Making New Friends	Social Entry	
6	Jan. 22	Conflict Management	Heart Talk	
7	Feb. 12	Good Manners	Great Manners Bingo	
8	March 5	Peer Pressure	How Far Would You Go?	
9	March 26	Working in Groups	Cooperation	
10	April 23	Personality	Animal Friends	

If your school district or state has competencies or standards as a part of your comprehensive developmental guidance program, list the competencies addressed in this column.

Sample First Grade Guidance Plan
Feelings

Lesson No.	Week Of	TOPIC	LESSON	Guidance Competencies*
1	Sept. 11	Labeling Feelings	Identifying "Bug" feelings	
2	Oct. 1	Expressing Feelings	What Bugs You?	
3	Oct. 23	Physical Signs of Feelings	Bugs Inside You	
4	Nov. 13	Teaching Feeling Rules	De-Bugging	
5	Dec. 11	Positive Expression of Feelings	Healthy Ways to De-Bug: Pounding and Drawing	
6	Jan. 22	Positive Expression of Feelings	Healthy Ways to De-Bug: Chill Time and "I Feel"	
7	Feb. 12	Positive Expression of Feelings	Healthy Ways to De-Bug: Physical Activities	
8	March 5	Positive Expression of Feelings	Healthy Ways to De-Bug: Writing	
9	March 26	Positive Expression of Feelings	Healthy Ways to De-Bug: Thinking Positive Thoughts	
10	April 23	Positive Expression of Feelings	De-Bugging Review	
1	May 14	Handling a Bully	Bully Bugs	

If your school district or state has competencies or standards as a part of your comprehensive developmental guidance program, list the competencies addressed in this column.

4

Sample Fourth Grade Guidance Plan

Lesson No.	Week Of	TOPIC	LESSON	Guidance Competencies*
1	Sept. 11	Feelings	Stress Monsters	
2	Oct. 1	Coping	Introduction to Coping	
3	Oct. 23	Coping	Umbrella of Self-Confidence	
4	Nov. 13	Peer Relations	How Far Would You Go?	
5	Dec. 11	Peer Relations	An Odd Dot	
6	Jan. 22	Decision Making	Web of Support	
7	Feb. 12	Decision Making	Think, Say, Do	
8	March 5	School-to-Work	Organizational Ladders	
9	March 26	School-to-Work	How Smart Are You?	
10	April 23	School-to-Work	Career Clusters	

*If your school district or state has competencies or standards as a part of your comprehensive developmental guidance program, list the competencies addressed in this column.

Yearly Classroom Guidance Plan

Grade_____   School Year_____

Lesson No.	Week Of	TOPIC	LESSON	Guidance Competencies*

*If your school district or state has competencies or standards as a part of your comprehensive developmental guidance program, list the competencies addressed in this column.

The lessons are developed to be easy to use with minimal preparation yet provide active, beneficial learning for the student. Learning does not easily occur by just sharing the information in a lesson one time. The information needs to be continually reinforced for the student to learn. Therefore, we have added components to the lessons to provide for this reinforcement. The following are the different components offered for each lesson:

The Lesson: The basic lesson lists the suggested grade levels, a brief description of the lesson, lesson objectives, estimated time, a list of materials needed, and step-by-step procedures for teaching the lesson.

Summary Poster or Visual Reminder: A summary poster or a suggested visual reminder is given for each lesson to leave in each classroom as a reminder and reinforcement of the lesson. You may choose to ask the classroom teacher to designate a bulletin board or wall space for classroom guidance lesson information. At the end of each classroom guidance lesson, add the visual or summary poster to this area. Encourage the students to review the summary poster and make reference to the previous summary posters and visuals in future lessons.

Variations/Modifications/Extensions: There are two to four suggested activities given to follow-up, extend and/or vary the lesson. The activities may be used as part of the classroom lesson or may be used for a follow-up activity.

Journal Entry: A response journal can be set up for the students to write or draw their thoughts, reactions, and/or responses to the lesson. Each lesson includes a sentence starter or question for the student journal. The journal entries can be brief information written or drawn on half sheets of paper. You may choose to have the students make their journals during your first visit. For example, if you are planning on visiting each class 10 times during the year, then have the students fold three pieces of paper in half, staple them together and decorate the front. The journal writing or drawing may also be an extension of your class lesson or used as a follow-up activity.

Parent Letters: Parent letters are provided for each lesson. These can be sent home with each student. These letters summarize the lesson and provide information on ways parents can reinforce the lesson objectives at home. The letters are a great public relations tool for you as a counselor. They keep parents "in the know" about guidance activities and your role in the education of their child. More importantly, however, the letters provide information for the parent to help reinforce the learning at home. In order for children to learn and be their best, the school and the parent must develop and nurture a close relationship and work together.

HOW DO I PULL IT TOGETHER TO CONNECT WITH STUDENTS?

In order to connect with the students in a class lesson three things need to happen. Students need to...

**Hear the information,
Remember it,
and Do it!**

For students to **Hear the information,** we need to:

- Capture the students' attention with the use of visuals, props, and creative and entertaining lessons. Included in the book are a variety of techniques to capture their attention.

- Ask for the students' attention. Ask the students to be listening with their whole body: their eyes, their ears, and their brain. Ask them to be sitting up straight and still, with their eyes looking at you, their ears ready to hear, and their minds ready to think about what is being taught. Practice with and encourage the students to give gentle head nods to show that they are listening. If these listening skills are not already established, then you may choose to teach these listening skills first.

For students to **Remember It,** we need to:

- Display a prop or summary poster for continual visual reinforcement. A display prop or summary poster is provided or suggested for each lesson in the book.

- Send home a parent information letter summarizing the class lesson and providing home suggestions for reinforcement of the lesson. The parent letter provides a good source of information for the parent, and the success rate of the student learning the skill is increased when home and school are working together. We suggest that you reproduce any student activity sheets on the back of the parent letter. Parents are more likely to look at information from school if it contains some work by their child.

  Information included in the parent letter may also be useful for the students. If the letter contains a good summary or a listing of information that would be helpful for the students, encourage the students to borrow the letter back from their parent. Suggest that they display the letter in their room, on the refrigerator, or in their notebook as a reminder. Included in the book are parent letters for each class lessons.

- Ask the students to summarize the previous lesson or lesson(s). Challenge them to remember what they have learned.

- Utilize extended activities for reinforcement. Share an activity with the classroom teacher to use for follow-up. Suggested variations and extensions are given for each lesson.

- Use journaling as another way for the students to summarize and personalize the lesson. Suggested journal entries are given for each lesson.

For our students to **Do It,** we need to:

- Ask the students at the end of each lesson a question such as: "How can this help us in our day-to-day life?" "How can we apply this to the real world?" "How can this help us at school, at home, with our friends?"

- Summarize the previous lesson(s) and ask students to give examples of how they used what they learned at the beginning of a new lesson. Have students share examples and compliment them for putting their learning into practice. (If the class is hesitant about sharing their personal experiences, change the question to "What might be some examples of someone putting into practice what we learned last week?"). Challenge the students to continue to put what they are learning into practice.

Share with the students the three important ingredients listed above that are necessary to learn something – Hear the Information, Remember It, and Do It. Talk to the students about what each of these three phrases mean.

To reinforce these three phrases with the students, share and teach hand motions to go with these phrases. Hand motions:

Hear It – hands behind the ears

Remember It – pointer finger pointing to your mind

Do It – both hands, palms up, stretched out

Have students practice the hand motions, recalling the three components.

We hope you will be able to utilize the information in this book as well as other resources to strengthen and reinforce the part of our guidance program that impacts all of our students – classroom guidance.

feelings

Colorful Feelings

GRADE LEVEL(S): K-2

DESCRIPTION:
This lesson helps students explore feelings by relaying the concept that feelings can remind us of colors. This gives students something concrete to relate to the abstractness of feelings.

OBJECTIVE(S):
• Students will recognize and identify four feelings: happy, sad, mad, and scared.
• Students will develop listening and expression skills.

ESTIMATED TIME: 30 minutes

MATERIAL(S) NEEDED:
• Various colored sheets of construction paper (laminate for long-term use)
• *My Many Colored Days* by Dr. Seuss
• Bag of Skittles® (or other brightly colored candies)

PROCEDURES:

1. Hold up the sheets of different colored construction paper one at a time and ask the students to tell you things that the color reminds them of.
2. Tell the students that one thing that no one mentioned when they thought of colors was feelings. Tell them that you're going to read them a book that talks about how feelings can remind us of colors.
3. Read *My Many Colored Days* by Dr. Seuss and discuss the feeling that Dr. Seuss associates with each color mentioned.
4. Place the construction paper used previously around the room. Call out a feeling and have the students stand beside the color that the feeling named reminds them of. Use the feelings happy, sad, scared, mad.
5. Show the students a bag of Skittles® and explain that they are like what is in the bag of Skittles®. Ask them if they think there's just one color in the bag or more than one. Open the bag and show them that there are lots of feeling colors in the bag. Explain that they are like that—they don't just have one feeling inside. They have lots of feelings and that each feeling is O.K.
6. Give each student one of each color Skittle® to eat.

 **Colorful Feelings**

SUMMARY POSTER OR VISUAL REMINDER:
Add a Skittles® wrapper to the Summery Poster (see page 15).

VARIATIONS/MODIFICATIONS/EXTENSIONS:
- Tell your art teacher about this lesson so that s/he can take the opportunity to reinforce this concept with the students.
- Discuss various expressions that use colors to depict feelings such as "I was so mad I saw red," "I was green with envy," or "I feel blue today."
- Give each student a sheet of white paper. Call out a feeling and have each student select the color that represents that feeling to him/her. Then ask the student to color in how much of their life is that feeling on the white paper. Do this with several feelings. At the end of the activity, the student's sheet should be completely covered with color. (NOTE: This is also an excellent idea to do with an individual student to help him/her explore feelings.)
- You may want to use *The Magic Coloring Book of Feelings* to demonstrate how colors are like feelings. This book was developed by Bowman and Frank and available through YouthLight, Inc.

JOURNAL ENTRY

Draw and color a rainbow. Label each color with the feeling that you think of when you see that color. Then draw and color a picture of how you feel today.

CLASSROOM GUIDANCE NEWS

Dear Parent,

Today in classroom guidance we focused on recognizing and identifying feelings. Young children often confuse feelings. When they are sad about something, they may display these feelings in an angry way. When they say they are "bored," what they may actually mean is that they are lonely and wish they had a playmate.

It is important to constantly encourage your child's feelings vocabulary. When you are talking to your child about an experience you have had, say, "I felt proud," or "I was confused." Be a role model for expressing feelings. You will be laying the building blocks for many skills such as impulse control, interpersonal relationships, and conflict management.

Today's activity compared feelings to colors. You've heard or said such expressions as "I was so angry I saw red," or "I'm green with envy," or "I'm feeling blue." Students had an opportunity today to choose their feeling colors. We read a story entitled *My Many Colored Days* by Dr. Seuss and discussed how feelings can remind us of certain colors. These colors are different for each of us. Some see red as an angry color while others see red as a happy color. Students moved about the room standing on different colored squares of construction paper to show their happy, sad, mad, and scared colors. Discuss with your child what your "feeling colors" are.

It is a pleasure working with your child. As always, please feel free to call me with questions or concerns you may have about your child, your child's school experience, or our elementary guidance and counseling program.

In partnership,

Colorful Feelings

PLACE SKITTLES® WRAPPER HERE

I have many different feelings inside me.

15

Musical Feelings

GRADE LEVEL(S): K-2

DESCRIPTION:
This lesson helps students further explore feelings by relaying the concept that feelings can "sound" like different things. The use of musical instruments gives students something concrete to attach the abstract idea of feelings.

OBJECTIVE(S):
• Students will recognize and identify four feelings: happy, sad, mad, and scared.
• Students will develop listening and expression skills.

ESTIMATED TIME: 30 minutes

MATERIAL(S) NEEDED:
• A book about feelings such as **Today I Feel Silly** by Jamie Lee Curtis, **How Do I Feel** by Norma Simon, or **Glad Monster, Sad Monster** by Ed Emberley and Anne Miranda
• Picture cards of individuals showing the feelings happy, sad, mad, and scared (samples are provided on the summary poster on page 19).
• A variety of musical instruments (cymbals, triangle, tambourine, sand blocks, etc.) If you don't have these in your collection, ask your music teacher to borrow some.

PROCEDURES:
1. Ask the students how they feel. Many will respond with feelings like "fine" and "good." Explain that "good" is not a feeling. Have the students relay some things that have happened to them since they got up and each time ask how they felt. Assist the students with feeling word responses.
2. Introduce the feeling book that you've chosen to read. Have the students listen for feeling words and identify the one(s) on each page.
3. Show picture cards and have the students identify the feeling. Allow them to share how they could tell the feeling (facial expressions, body language, etc.)
4. Explain that feelings can sound like certain things. Ask the students if they have ever heard music that has made them feel happy or scared. Show the musical instruments. Distribute the instruments so that as many children as possible can have one. Call out a feeling and have the students make their instrument sound like that feeling. Have them pass the instrument on to another student and continue calling out feelings until all the students have had a turn with at least one instrument.

 **Musical Feelings**

SUMMARY POSTER OR VISUAL REMINDER:
The feeling faces poster on page 19.

VARIATIONS/MODIFICATIONS/EXTENSIONS:
- You may choose to actually play excerpts from musical pieces that sound happy, sad, scared, or mad.
- Tell your music teacher about this lesson so that s/he can take the opportunity to reinforce this concept with the students.
- Discuss how we can use music to help us when we feel sad or scared.

JOURNAL ENTRY

 Think about the songs you know.
Write about a song that has a happy sound.

Musical Feelings

CLASSROOM GUIDANCE NEWS

Dear Parent,

Today in classroom guidance we focused on recognizing and identifying feelings. Understanding feelings is essential to helping students appropriately express feelings. The ability to express feelings is a building block for many skills such as conflict management, anger management, impulse control, interpersonal skills, and healthy lifestyles.

Often young children speak of feeling "good" or "bad" about something. Help your child expand his/her feelings vocabulary beyond these two words. Give your child's feelings names such as happy, sad, mad, or scared. When your child is relaying an exciting event that happened to them, say something like, "You were happy when your name was called for being a good listener." When your child is talking to you about a conflict s/he had with a friend, say, "You were mad when your friend called you a name." When you're reading a story with your child, discuss the character's feelings.

In our lesson today, the students had practice identifying four feelings: happy, sad, mad, and scared. The students heard a story about these feelings and we discussed how you can sometimes tell a person's feelings by the look on his/her face or the way he/she is holding his/her body. The students then had a concrete experience with feelings. Each student had an opportunity to play a musical instrument and make that instrument "sound" like a certain feeling. We made mad music, sad music, scared music, and happy music (well, I'm not sure you'd call it music, but...)

It is a pleasure working with your child. As always, please feel free to call me with questions or concerns that you may have about your child, your child's school experience, or our elementary guidance and counseling program.

Sincerely,

Musical Feelings

HAPPY

SAD

MAD

SCARED

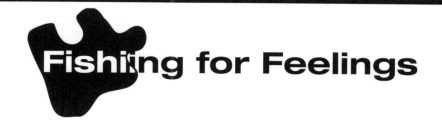

Fishing for Feelings

GRADE LEVEL(S): 1-2

DESCRIPTION:
This lesson is designed to strengthen and extend the students' feelings vocabulary. Students are actively involved as they "fish" for a variety of feelings.

OBJECTIVE(S):
- Students will recognize and identify feelings.
- Students will cooperate with others.

ESTIMATED TIME: 30 minutes

MATERIAL(S) NEEDED:
- A pail
- Paper fish cutouts in various sizes (see page 23). Write feeling words on each large and medium size fish and assign a point value to the fish. Large fish are worth 10 points, medium size fish are worth 5 points, and small fish are worth zero points (laminate for long-term use.) Suggested feeling words are: mad, worried, sad, scared, lonely, happy, proud, excited, glad, embarrassed, jealous, pleased, and loved.
- Paper clips to attach to paper fish so that the magnet on the fishing pole attracts a fish
- Child's fishing pole with a magnet attached to the end of the line
- Plastic pail (do not use metal) or a large box covered with blue paper to represent water
- Fish stickers (optional)
- Goldfish crackers (optional)

PROCEDURES:
1. Ask the students to share the variety of feelings inside them when they get ready to do something for the first time such as riding a bike without training wheels, coming to school, getting up to bat, riding an amusement park ride, etc. Discuss that sometimes it's hard to understand our feelings because they seem to get all jumbled up inside of us.
2. Explain that today's lesson will help them understand the many different feelings they have inside them.
3. One by one, show the paper fish. Have the students name the feeling. Explain that the number on the fish is the point value their team will receive if they "catch" this fish. After you show each fish, place it into the pail or box. Jumble the fish in the pail and reiterate that sometimes our feelings get jumbled inside us.
4. Divide the students into two fishing teams. Demonstrate how to place the fishing pole into the pail or box to catch a fish. Explain that each time a fish is caught, the feeling word will be read and the "fisher" will describe a time he/she experienced that feeling. Then, the student's team will be awarded the number of points assigned to the fish caught. The fish is then

put back into the pail and mixed so the same fish does not lie on top. When a small fish is caught, no points are given, no feeling is discussed, and the fish is put back into the pail. Since the student threw the fish back, he/she gets another turn. If any student makes excessive noise or laughs at someone who catches a low-point fish, that students' team loses 5 points. Have the students take turns fishing and sharing. When everyone has had a turn, the team with the most points wins.

5. OPTIONAL: After the game is over, award the "winners" with fish stickers and give all students some Goldfish crackers to eat as a prize for playing the game well.

6. As students are eating their crackers, have them list as many feeling words as they can recall.

SUMMARY POSTER OR VISUAL REMINDER:

Catch of the Day summary poster on page 24.

VARIATIONS/MODIFICATIONS/EXTENSIONS:

- Teachers can use this activity as a writing center. Students go to the writing center, catch a fish, and write about a time they had the feeling that is written on the fish.
- Use this activity in individual counseling. Take turns with the student discussing the feelings.

JOURNAL ENTRY

Think about your day. Write about all the different feelings you have had since you woke up this morning.

CLASSROOM GUIDANCE NEWS

Dear Parent,

I enjoyed being in your child's class today. In our lesson today we explored the names of many different feelings. Research on emotional intelligence shows that the ability to label feelings is one of the basic characteristics necessary for social success. Children often display undesirable behaviors (fighting, temper tantrums, disrespect) simply because they do not have the feelings vocabulary to properly express what they are feeling. Being "feelings smart" helps children in a number of ways. It aids with communication with peers and adults; it helps with self-control; it leads to a better understanding of oneself and others; and it helps children express themselves in positive ways.

Students had fun today "Fishing for Feelings." As we fished, each child had an opportunity to discuss things that made him/her feel sad, mad, scared, happy, proud, embarrassed, jealous, etc.

If you would like more information on the importance of being "feelings smart," I would encourage you to read Dr. Daniel Goleman's book ***Emotional Intelligence: Why It Can Matter More than IQ.*** Another resource is Lawrence Shapiro's ***How to Raise a Child with a High EQ.***

I look forward to the months ahead in classroom guidance. Please feel free to call me with any concerns or questions that you may have about your child, your child's school experience, or our elementary guidance and counseling program.

In partnership,

Fish Patterns

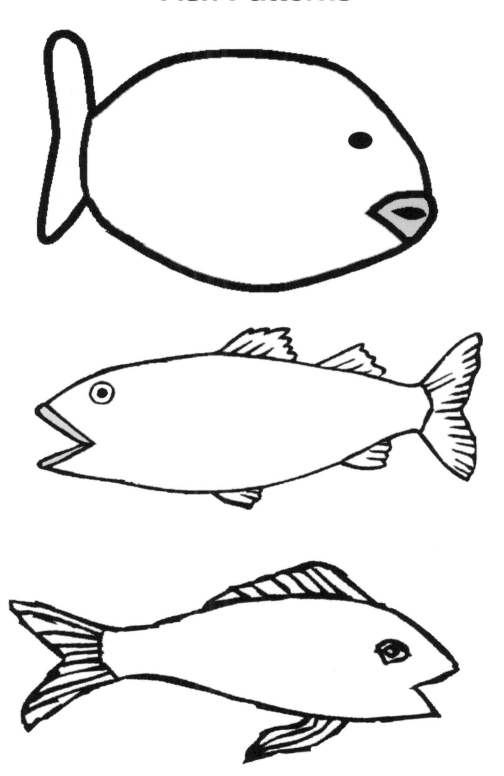

Fishing for Feelings

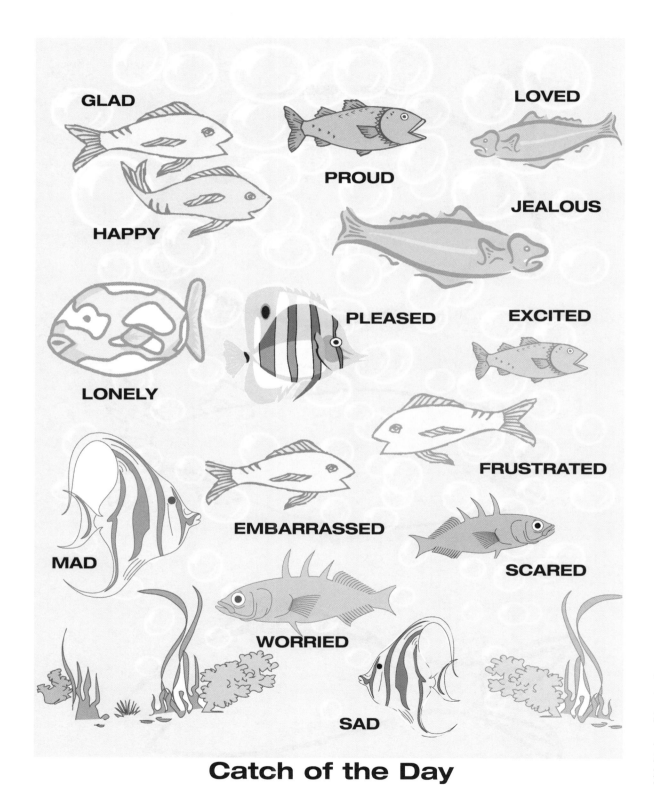

GLAD

LOVED

PROUD

JEALOUS

HAPPY

PLEASED

EXCITED

LONELY

FRUSTRATED

MAD

EMBARRASSED

SCARED

WORRIED

SAD

Catch of the Day

Dealing With Mad Feelings

GRADE LEVEL(S): 1-3

DESCRIPTION:
Children often think that anger is a "bad" feeling. They may have gotten in trouble for inappropriately expressing their angry feelings or may have had an adult say "Don't be angry." This lesson helps students understand that they can appropriately express anger.

OBJECTIVE(S):
• Students will identify times they feel angry.
• Students will identify four ways to deal with anger.
• Students will recognize the difference in a feeling and an action.

ESTIMATED TIME: 30 minutes

MATERIAL(S) NEEDED:
• Quick action water solidification powder (available through magic shops or at garden or floral shops) in a clear baggie labeled "OK Ways to Handle Mad Feelings"
• 2 paper cups
• Pitcher of water
• Pan
• Pencil
• Large clear baggie labeled "OK Ways to Handle Mad Feelings" with pictures from the summary poster found on page 29 cut out, laminated, and placed inside
• Large sheet of laminated construction paper labeled "OK Ways to Handle Mad Feelings"

PROCEDURES:
1. Tell the students that today's lesson will be about dealing with angry feelings. Have them share things that make them angry.
2. Ask the students how many of them have ever gotten in trouble because they were mad. Explain that anger itself does not get you in trouble, but what you do with anger can get you in trouble. Tell this story:

One day Melissa got a call from her best friend Yvonne. While they were talking Yvonne started making fun of the bad grade that Melissa got on her spelling test. Melissa asked Yvonne to stop making fun of her, but Yvonne kept on teasing Melissa. Melissa got mad. Finally she'd had enough. She slammed down the receiver on the phone to hang up on Yvonne. When she slammed down the receiver, she broke the phone. Just then Melissa's mom walked into the room. She saw the phone and asked what happened. Melissa explained how she got mad and hung up on Yvonne and accidentally broke the phone. Melissa's mom said that Melissa could not use the phone again for a week.

3. Ask: Did Melissa get in trouble? Did she get in trouble because she was angry? Help students understand that Melissa's angry feeling did not get her in trouble, but what she did with her angry feeling got her in trouble.

4. Pour water from the pitcher to fill one of the paper cups. Explain that the cup represents the student and that the water is angry feelings. Tell the students that we all have angry feelings inside us and that the feelings are okay as long as we know what to do with the feelings. Explain that this cup represents a person who has not learned what to do with angry feelings. Begin poking holes in the cup with the pencil, keeping the pan underneath the cup to catch the water. Tell the students that the holes are things that make them angry such as being teased, losing a game, etc. Explain that if you don't know what to do with angry feelings, you can make a mess just like you did with the cup of water.

5. Repeat the process in step four again but before punching the holes in the cup, add some of the water solidification powder from the bag labeled "OK Ways to Handle Mad Feelings." Explain that this time this person has learned some things he/she can do when he/she gets mad. Be sure that the water solidification powder has time to work before punching the holes in the cup (this usually takes just a few seconds, but be sure you practice first.) This time as you poke the holes in the cup, no water will escape. Ask the students what you did differently, and explain that knowing how to handle mad feelings will keep you from making a mess of things when you get angry.

6. Using the pictures in the large baggie labeled "OK Ways to Handle Mad Feelings" thoroughly discuss each of these four ways. As you discuss each, tape it to the construction paper labeled "OK Ways to Handle Mad Feelings."
   • Talk to someone about it.
   • Do something you enjoy.
   • Count to 10.
   • Think about the problem in a different way.

7. If time allows, have the students fold a sheet of drawing paper in half. On one half, have them draw a picture of something that makes them feel mad. On the other half, have them draw what they plan to do the next time they feel mad.

SUMMARY POSTER OR VISUAL REMINDER:
Leave the "OK Ways to Handle Mad Feelings" poster for the class.

VARIATIONS/MODIFICATIONS/EXTENSIONS:
• Have the students search through magazines to find pictures of people doing things that are appropriate ways to express anger. Make a class collage.
• Teachers may wish to add a class job entitled "Consultant." This person's job is to help a student who is angry think of things he/she can do to express the anger.
• Discuss with the students the harmful effects of holding anger inside.
• Caution the students about unhealthy ways people may use to deal with angry feelings such as cigarettes, alcohol, or drug use.

Dealing With Mad Feelings

JOURNAL ENTRY

Draw or write about a time that you handled your mad feelings in an OK way. Describe how you felt after you did so.

OK WAYS TO HANDLE MAD FEELINGS

✔ _____

✔ _____

✔ _____

✔ _____

Dealing With Mad Feelings

CLASSROOM GUIDANCE NEWS

Dear Parent,

Today our lesson focused on handling mad feelings. Many times, children (and adults) think of mad feelings as being "bad." When asked if they get in trouble for being mad, most children respond with a resounding, "Yes!" It is important for students to understand that the feeling never gets them in trouble; it's their reaction or response to the feeling that may be inappropriate. Feeling mad is unpleasant, but OK. It's what you do with the feeling that counts.

Students saw a demonstration today about what can happen if mad feelings are not handled in an appropriate way. Be sure to ask your child what happened to the water in the cup when we added some ingredients from the "OK Ways To Handle Mad Feelings" bag.

We discussed constructive ways to deal with angry feelings. Learning to cope with anger is a crucial part of maintaining effective social interactions. One way students learned to cope with anger is to talk to someone who cares about their feelings. When your child comes to you to discuss being angry at a sibling, friend, or even at you, it is important to remember to listen to your child's feelings—both what is being said and what is not being said. Instead of asking questions, reflect what your child is saying to you, "You feel upset when your brother goes into your room." Avoid putting the blame back on your child with statements like, "Well, he only does that because you go in his room." Listen.

Other ways to handle angry feelings that we discussed include doing something you enjoy to get your mind off of the problem, changing the way you think about the problem, and counting to ten before doing anything to ensure that you don't make a bad choice.

It is a pleasure working with your child. As always, please feel free to call me with questions or concerns that you have about your child, your child's school experience, or our elementary guidance and counseling program.

Sincerely,

Dealing With Mad Feelings

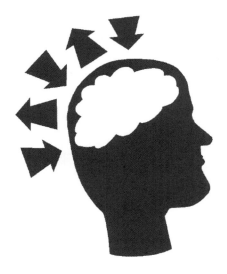

THINK ABOUT THE PROBLEM IN A DIFFERENT WAY

DO SOMETHING YOU ENJOY

1 2 3 4
5 6 7
8 9 10

COUNT TO 10 BEFORE DOING ANYTHING

TALK TO SOMEONE ABOUT YOUR FEELINGS

29

Dealing With Sad Feelings

GRADE LEVEL(S): 1-3

DESCRIPTION:
This lesson helps students understand that while everyone has sad feelings, staying sad is a choice. Students see a concrete demonstration of the difference in focusing on a problem and focusing on working to feel better about the problem.

OBJECTIVE(S):
• Students will identify times they have felt sad.
• Students will identify specific things they can do when they feel sad.
• Students will recognize the relationship between thoughts and feelings.

ESTIMATED TIME: 30 minutes

MATERIAL(S) NEEDED:
• Two sentence strips: one reads "CLEAR THINKING," the other "MURKY THINKING"
• Story and pictures on pages 34-37
• Two large clear jars or jugs about half filled with water
• Food coloring
• Two bottles: one labeled "Clear Thinking" and filled with bleach, the other labeled "Murky Thinking" and filled with water tinted to look like bleach
• "When I Feel Sad" activity sheet on page 38

PROCEDURES:
1. Ask the students to explain the difference in swimming in a pool and swimming in a pond or lake. Focus on the idea that in a pool, you can see the bottom because the water is clear; in a pond or lake, you cannot see the bottom because the water is not clear. Introduce the word "murky."
2. Explain that sometimes the way we think is just like water—sometimes we think clearly and sometimes we think murky.
3. Read the story on page 34 entitled Angie's Story. Discuss using the following questions:
    What was Angie's problem?
    How did Angie feel?
    What did Angie choose to do with her feelings?
4. Tell the students that Angie was choosing to think in a murky way. Illustrate murky thinking with this demonstration: In one of the clear plastic containers of water, add drops of food color to make the water dark as you explain that Angie's day was going just fine until her friends were mean to her. Then her day got "messed up" because she was feeling sad. Taking

the bottle labeled "Murky Thinking" pour some of that liquid into the container explaining that she chose to think in a murky way by focusing on the problem. Because of her murky thinking, she remained sad. Show that the water remains murky.

5. Read the story on page 36 entitled Tomika's story. Ask the following questions:
    What was Tomika's problem?
    How did Tomika feel?
    What did Tomika choose to do with her feelings?

6. Explain that Tomika was choosing to think in a clear way. Do the same illustration as above except add liquid (bleach) from the "Clear Thinking" bottle (you'll have to add some and stir it and then add and stir until the water becomes clear again.) Explain that because of the way Tomika was thinking, the problem did not ruin her whole day. The problem is still there, but she chose to do things that got her mind off the problem so that they can have a good day in spite of her sad feelings.

7. Say sentences that reflect either clear thinking or murky thinking. Have the students identify if these sentences are examples of clear or murky thinking. Some sample sentences include:
    a. I'll never learn to tell time.
    b. Even though tennis is hard, I'm trying my best.
    c. This is too hard for me.
    d. Nobody likes me.
    e. I have a few really great friends.
    f. My brother may be smarter than me, but my parents love me just the same as him.

8. Reemphasize that students choose how they are going to think about a problem. They can use clear thinking or murky thinking.

9. Have the students complete the "When I Feel Sad" activity sheet. Work through the top part together and then have the students do their drawing independently.

SUMMARY POSTER OR VISUAL REMINDER:

You Can Choose summary poster found on page 39.

VARIATIONS/MODIFICATIONS/EXTENSIONS:

*   Work with the classroom teacher to make a list of the options available for all the students in the class when they are feeling sad.
*   Have the students make happy/sad rocks. Give each student a rock and have them draw a happy face on one side and a sad face on the other. Students can keep the rocks on their desk (with the teacher's permission) to indicate whether they are having a happy day or a sad day. Encourage the students to recognize when others are having a sad day and work to help that student use clear thinking to feel better.

JOURNAL ENTRY

Draw or write about a time that you handled a sad situation using "Clear Thinking."

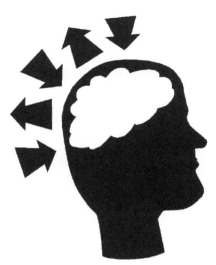

CLASSROOM GUIDANCE NEWS

Dear Parents,

Your child had classroom guidance today. We have been learning about feelings. Today students learned ways to deal with sad feelings.

Students heard a story about being rejected. This is certainly something that most children have experienced or will experience in childhood. This is an experience that evokes sad feelings in a child (or an adult.) In the story, however, two girls respond to the feeling in different ways.

We discussed two ways that people choose to think about problems. One way is using "murky thinking." When one uses murky thinking, s/he allows the problem to adversely affect one's whole day or attitude. The other way to think about a problem is using "clear thinking." This simply means keeping the problem separate from the other events in a day. Clear thinking will keep a setback from ruining an entire day.

Students were encouraged to remember about "murky thinking" and "clear thinking" the next time that they have sad or lonely feelings. Students drew some "clear thinking" activities that they could do when they are sad. You may choose to use the terms "murky thinking" and "clear thinking" in dealing with your child when problems occur with friends, school, siblings, etc.

It is important for young children to learn to think about problems in ways that don't keep them on a downward spiral. As a parent, you can help your child do this by keeping events in perspective and by listening to your child's feelings when they share them with you.

It is a pleasure to work with your child. As always, please feel free to call me with any questions or concerns that you may have about your child, your child's school experience, or our elementary guidance and counseling program.

Sincerely,

THE ROCK
Angie's Story

"That's it, Angie! Get out of here," said Angie's older sister Jan. "We've been working on this puzzle for an hour and every time you try to put in a piece you knock the other pieces off the table. This is too hard for you. Now leave us alone."

Angie was only trying to help. She liked being with Jan and her friends. It made her feel more grown up. But her friends joined in saying, "Yeah, Angie, leave us alone. This puzzle is not for little kids. I'm sure you have a little kid puzzle in your room that you could do."

Angie's feelings were hurt and she felt tears stinging her eyes as she walked out of the door. She kept walking right outside and into the woods in her backyard. Angie liked exploring in the woods. But today she didn't feel like exploring. She just wanted to get away from Jan and her mean friends.

As Angie walked through the woods, she came upon a big rock she'd never seen before. The rock was so large that Angie could sit on it like a chair. Angie sat on the rock and as she did she let go of the tears she'd been holding back.

"Jan treats me so nice when her friends aren't around," Angie thought. "But when her friends come over, she acts like she hates me. She's always treating me like a baby. I'm not a baby; after all, Jan's only 3 years older than me. But she hates me and so do all of her friends." And the more Angie thought, the harder she cried.

"I wish that I could make Jan feel as bad as I feel now. But Jan never feels bad. She's good at everything. I think even Mom and Dad like her better. She gets better grades than me, she's better at piano and sports, and she always remembers to do her chores. I'm not good at anything, even putting dumb old puzzles together."

Angie sat on the rock for a long time and thought her sad thoughts. The more she thought, the sadder she got. Finally, she heard her mother call her home. Angie got up off the rock, gave it a kick, and walked home.

THE ROCK
Tomika's Story

"We've told you a million gazillion times, Tomika. NO! You can't play with us. We already have enough people on our soccer team. If we let you play, the teams won't be even. Besides, we've seen you play soccer before and you can't play. You run slow and you miss the ball more than you kick it. Why don't you go home and play the piano or something like that?"

And off Kayla ran to join the soccer game leaving Tomika standing there with tears stinging her eyes. Every time Tomika asked to play with Kayla and her friends, she got the same answer— "No." Tomika couldn't understand it. Sometimes Kayla could be so nice to her like when they were working on a science project together or when she called to find out a homework assignment. But when it came to playing with Tomika, Kayla always said no.

Tomika started a slow walk home. As she walked she wondered what it was about her that made Kayla hate her so much. Along the path Tomika was walking on, she came to a large rock. Tomika had seen the rock before. It was big enough to sit on. Tomika climbed upon the rock and looked around. As she did, she got a great idea—this rock would make a great pretend chair in her pretend house. And with that thought, Tomika got busy. She jumped down off the rock and found another smaller rock and placed beside her "chair." This would be her table. She gathered some sticks and placed them together to look like a doormat. On and on she worked finding things to place in her new "house." Tomika lost track of time and was so busy pretending that she forgot all about Kayla.

Tomika didn't know what time it was when she heard her father call, "Tomika, it's time to come home." "Coming, Daddy, " Tomika said as she raced home with thoughts of what she could do to her pretend house tomorrow afternoon.

Dealing With Sad Feelings

WHEN I FEEL SAD

You can choose what you will do when you are sad. You can use MURKY THINKING and let the sad feelings ruin your whole day.

Or you can use CLEAR THINKING and find something else to do or think about that takes your mind off the sad feelings.

Put a ✔ by the things that you would do when you have sad feelings.

_____ Talk to someone who cares.

_____ Go for a bike ride.

_____ Write about your feelings in a journal.

_____ Play with your pet.

_____ Draw

_____ Play with your favorite toy.

_____ Listen to music.

Below draw a picture of something else that you can do when you have sad feelings.

© YouthLight, Inc. (Handout)

 **Dealing With Sad Feelings**

"You Can Choose"

Dealing With Worry

GRADE LEVEL(S): 1-3

DESCRIPTION:
Worry is a feeling that young students experience but often do not know how to label or express. Many times adults invalidate a child's worry. This lesson helps define worry, offers ways to deal with it, and gives students an opportunity to share things that worry them.

OBJECTIVE(S):
• Students will define worry.
• Students will identify times they feel worried.
• Students will identify healthy ways to deal with worry.

ESTIMATED TIME: 30 minutes

MATERIAL(S) NEEDED:
• Worry bee pattern found on page 43.
• Recording of the song, "Don't Worry, Be Happy" (optional)

PROCEDURES:
1. Ask the students if they have ever felt bad but had a parent, nurse, or doctor say that they were not sick. Have the students share stories.
2. Write the word "worried" on the board. Tell the students that sometimes our bodies can feel sick if we hold worried feelings inside. The most common ailments include headaches, stomach aches, and feeling tired.
3. Define worry for the students as a feeling that comes when you think about something negative that might happen. Give examples such as:
   • Thinking about striking out when you get to bat.
   • Thinking that no one will like you in your new class.
   • Thinking about going to the dentist to get a filling.
4. Ask the students to share some things that they have worried about in the past.
5. Discuss three ways to get rid of worry. Write each on the board as you discuss. These include:
   • Talk to someone you trust.
   • Say positive things to yourself.
   • Do something you enjoy.
6. Have the students make "worry bees" using the pattern on page 43. On one wing have the students draw or write something about which they worry. On the other wing, have the students draw or write about something they plan to do when they are worried. If available, while the students are working, play the song "Don't Worry, Be Happy."

SUMMARY POSTER OR VISUAL REMINDER:

"Don't Worry, 'Bee' Happy" poster on page 44.

VARIATIONS/MODIFICATIONS/EXTENSIONS:

- Display the worry bees on a bulletin board entitled "Don't Worry. Bee Happy."
- If available, read the book *What If It Never Stops Raining* by Nancy Carlson or *Wemberly Worried* by Kevin Henkes.
- To further extend the concept of what worry can do to you physically, discuss how the body can be affected when worry causes stress. This can manifest itself in various ways. Examples include:
  - Headache
  - Crying easily
  - Knots in your shoulders
  - Cramp in your neck
  - Tiredness
  - Butterflies in the stomach
  - Clenched jaw
  - Tightened fists

JOURNAL ENTRY

Draw or write about a time that you were worried but found a good way to handle it.

CLASSROOM GUIDANCE NEWS

Dear Parent,

Today in classroom guidance, students learned ways to deal with their worries. As adults, we may think of childhood as a worry-free time. You may watch your child play and think that s/he doesn't have a care in the world. But, just like adults, children worry. They feel stress. Children at the ages of seven and eight strive to be liked and appreciated by their teachers and parents. They are becoming more independent and taking on more tasks, so they may feel worried about finishing things or they may become frustrated because they don't yet know how to use their time wisely. Seven and eight-year-olds have a fear of being singled out and are self-conscious and easily embarrassed. They fear not being able to do well in school or in sports.

Your child made a "worry bee" today. Please ask your child to see his/her worry bee. You will notice that your child wrote or drew about something that makes him/her feel worried on one wing and then wrote about how s/he plans to deal with these feelings of worry. We spent much time discussing what to do when one feels worried. Ideas included talking to a grown-up that you trust, doing some positive self-talk, and doing an activity that you enjoy to get your mind focused on something else.

As a parent, you can't always protect your child completely from worry or stress, nor should you. The following hints may help you help your child cope with worry or stress.

- **Gradually expose your child to problems.** Avoid over-protecting your child. Tell your child the truth about situations in age-appropriate ways.

- **Resist the urge to rescue your child.** Allow your child to solve his/her own problems starting with simple ones and then more complex ones. Allow him/her to experience the "negative" emotions that accompany problems. For example, don't try to immediately replace a lost or deceased pet to keep a child from being sad.

- **Teach healthy "self talk."** Encourage your child to say things to him/herself that are optimistic, rational, and self-encouraging.

- **Teach your child to allow him/herself adequate time for recovery from periods of over-stress.** Many children feel a let down after a big event. Teach your child to tune into what his/her body is saying and take rest when needed.

- **Teach your child to filter stressors.** Have your child ask him/herself, "Is this worth worrying about?" "Is it really important?"

As always, please feel free to call me with questions or concerns that you have about your child, your child's school experience, or our elementary guidance and counseling program.

Sincerely,

Worry Bee

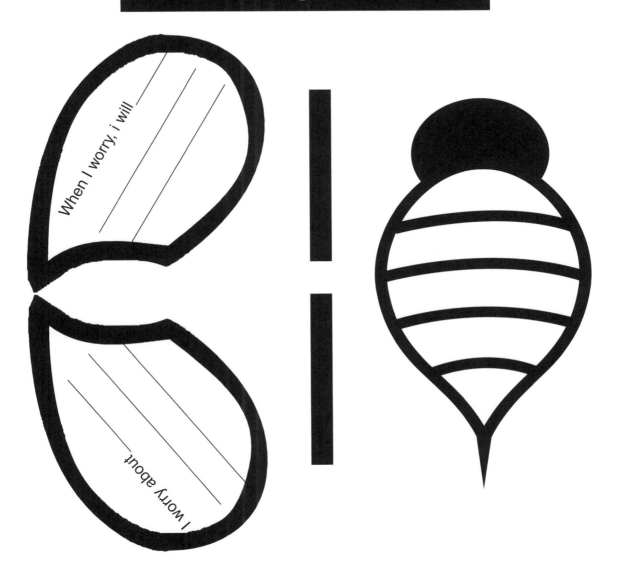

DIRECTIONS FOR ASSEMBLING:

1. Write or draw something you worry about on the wing that reads "I worry about."
2. Write or draw what you will do the next time you worry about that on the wing that reads, "When I worry, I will."
3. Cut out the body of the bee.
4. Cut out the wings of the bee.
5. Glue the wings on either side of the bee with your writing facing out.
6. Cut out the stingers. Glue them to the top of the bee's head. Roll them around a pencil to make them curl.
7. Color your Worry Bee.

43

Dealing With Worry

Talk to someone
you trust.

I know
I can
do this!

Say positive things
to yourself.

Do something
you enjoy.

Don't Worry "Bee" Happy

Stress Monsters

GRADE LEVEL(S): 2-5

DESCRIPTION:
There are two kinds of stress—good stress, called eustress, and bad stress, called distress. Students have most probably heard the phrase "stressed out." This lesson will help students identify stressors as well as positive ways to handle negative stress.

OBJECTIVE(S):
• Students will distinguish between good stress and bad stress.
• Students will recognize bad stress in their own lives.
• Students will identify positive ways to deal with bad stress.

ESTIMATED TIME: 30 minutes

MATERIAL(S) NEEDED:
• A balloon
• Drawing paper for each student
• Don't Let the Stress Monster Get You Down activity sheet found on page 48

PROCEDURES:
1. Tell the students about a student who has recently had some physical ailments: headaches, feeling nervous, tummy jittery, being "crabby." Explain that this student hasn't been "sick" but that he/she hasn't felt well either.
2. Ask the students to share how they may have had similar feelings. Explain that our feelings inside, if not understood and dealt with, can sometimes lead to us having physical symptoms.
3. Show a balloon and blow it up more and more. Ask what would eventually happen. Ask the students if they can think of other things with this same concept.
4. Write the word "stress" on the chalkboard. Define it as a feeling of being uptight and nervous.
5. Explain two types of stress: positive and negative. Positive stress can provide energy to get a job done. For example, you're getting ready to perform in a contest or game that you feel confident about. Negative stress can keep you from doing your best or from even trying at something.
6. Discuss these ways to turn negative stress into positive stress:
   • Talk to a good listener.
   • Do an activity you enjoy that is healthy and/or productive.
   • Make a list of steps to get a goal accomplished.
   • Know your warning signs and stay tuned into yourself for them.

7. Describe stress as a monster that may be out to get you. Have the students draw their stress monster and then throw it into the garbage. Then have them complete the sentence on the activity sheet about a way that they know that they can get rid of their stress.

SUMMARY POSTER OR VISUAL REMINDER:
Ways to Get Rid of a Stress Monster summary poster found on page 49.

VARIATIONS/MODIFICATIONS/EXTENSIONS:
- Make a class list of "Common Stressors in Fourth Grade" (or whatever grade you're teaching.) Then make a list of ways to relieve each of the stressors. For example, a common stressor may be "tests." A relief for the stressor may be studying.
- Have the students trace a body outline of themselves. Then have them identify places in their bodies where they feel stress (butterflies in the stomach, clenched jaw, etc.)

JOURNAL ENTRY

Write about the healthy activities you do to balance the stress in your life.

 **Stress Monsters**

CLASSROOM GUIDANCE NEWS

Dear Parent,

Today's classroom guidance lesson focused on stress management. The word "stress" is used frequently these days. We often refer to ourselves as feeling "stressed out." As parents, we have many obligations that often leave us feeling stressed—children, household duties, careers, children's extra-curricular activities, our own extra-curricular activities, etc. Children also feel stress, and while the things that cause them to feel stress may seem petty to us as adults, they are as real to them as our adult stresses are to us. Growing up is not easy—think back to some of your own experiences as a pre-teen. These pressures were real to you then and the stresses your child faces today are real to him/her. Schoolwork is demanding. Friends are becoming more and more important, and day-to-day, off-again/on-again friendships greatly affect a child's feelings.

Today in classroom guidance we compared stress to a balloon: if you continue to inflate—put more stress into yourself—and not release any pressure, you will eventually "explode." We discussed two kinds of stress, good stress and bad stress. Stress, in its positive aspect, can help you to concentrate, focus, perform and can often help you to reach peak effectiveness. Many people, in fact, do their best work when under pressure. However, stress in its negative form keeps you "geared up" and unable to relax even after meeting a challenge. Bad stress inhibits productivity and effectiveness. When stress becomes a constant, on-going cycle, one's health and well-being can suffer. Negative stress can be linked with physical ailments like restlessness, headaches, appetite change, muscle aches, colds, digestive upsets, and more.

As a parent, you cannot protect your child from stress. But you can help him/her deal with stress in a healthy way. Below are some ways we discussed during classroom guidance today:

- Talk to a good listener.

- Do an activity you enjoy that is healthy and/or productive (exercise, draw, write, paint, play, etc.)

- Make a list of steps to get a goal accomplished (the goal may not be as hard to reach as you have it pictured in your mind.)

- Know your warning signs and stay tuned into yourself for these.

As parents, discuss ways that you positively deal with stress with your child. Talk about stressful times and how you handle them. Your actions speak volumes to your child.

As always, please feel free to contact me with any questions or concerns that you may have about your child, your child's school experience, or our school's elementary guidance and counseling program.

Sincerely,

Don't let the *STRESS MONSTER* get you down!

I can tell when I'm feeling stress because I _____

_____

_____

_____

_____

One way that I plan to deal with my feelings of stress is _____

_____

_____

_____

_____

_____

Stress Monsters

- **Talk to a good listener.**
- **Do an activity you enjoy that is healthy and/or productive.**
- **Make a list of steps to get a goal accomplished.**
- **Know your warning signs and stay tuned into yourself for them.**

Indentifying "Bug" Feelings

GRADE LEVEL(S): 1-3

DESCRIPTION:
In this lesson, bugs are used as a catalyst for a discussion about feelings and how some feelings "bug" you. This lesson can stand alone or be used as the first lesson in a series of lessons on handling "bugs." The other lessons in this series are included in this book and include:

What "Bugs" You (see page 61)
Bugs Inside You (see page 66)
"De-Bugging" (see page 73)
Healthy Ways to "De-Bug" (There are five lesson on this. See pages 78, 84, 88, 91, 96.)
"De-Bugging" Review (see page 100)
Bully Bugs (see page 111)

OBJECTIVE(S):
• Students will identify pleasant feelings.
• Students will identify unpleasant feelings.
• Students will develop listening and expression skills.

ESTIMATED TIME: 30 minutes

MATERIAL(S) NEEDED:
• Bug Feelings summary poster found on page 60
• Bug Bingo Cards found on pages 54-57 (There are four different cards. Each card has a different bug in the bottom left hand corner for ease in identifying the card.)
• Bug Call Cards found on page 58
• Bug and Smiley markers found on page 59

PROCEDURES:
1. You may choose to take a bug puppet or a large picture of a bug in with you to tell this story about Harry the Bug.

   Harry has had a horrible week. One day he was playing with his friend and his friend decided he didn't like Harry anymore. So he flew away from Harry and wouldn't come back. Harry was sad. He went home to talk to his parents about it, but before he could say anything, they started fussing at him because he forgot to clean up his room. They told him he couldn't go out to play for a whole week. Harry was mad. He hated staying in his room. A few days later on his way home from school, he was thinking about how he didn't have anyone to play with and wasn't paying attention to where he was flying. He looked up and saw the light of a BUG ZAPPER! Harry was scared. He knew that bug zappers were dangerous! He turned just in time to avoid the bug zapper. But then he didn't know where he was. He was lost. Harry got worried. "What if I never find my way

home?" he thought. Just then he saw his ex-friend. Harry wanted to ask for his help, but he was nervous. What if his friend refused to talk to him? He asked anyway. His friend said, "Follow me," and showed him the way home. He didn't stick around to play, but at least Harry was home. He wishes he had someone to play with.

2. Have the students name all the feelings that Harry had in the story. Discuss what happened to cause each feeling.

3. Make two columns on the board—one for feelings you enjoy having and the other for feelings you do not enjoy having. Have the students name as many feelings as they can to go in either category.

4. Discuss how easy it is for you when you're having feelings you like, but how difficult it is when you are having feelings that you don't like. Explain that these feelings can really "bug" you—just like a bug that won't go away. They stick around and just annoy you and keep you from enjoying things. Use examples of ways that bugs "bug" us—at picnics, when we're sleeping and they're buzzing around our ear, when they are biting us, etc.

5. Show the Summary Poster "Bug Feelings." Have the students read each of the words on the list. Explain that these are feelings that just stick around and annoy us if we don't do something about them. If you are using this as the first of a series of lessons on feelings that "bug" you, explain that this year the students will be learning about handling these "bug" feelings.

6. Play a game of "Bug Bingo." Give each student a card, some bug markers, and some smiley markers. Using the Bug Call Card, call out the letter and feeling. If the feeling is a "bug" feeling, have the students cover it with a bug marker. If it is a feeling you enjoy, have them cover it with a smiley face maker. The first student to get 3 bugs in a row, up and down, across, or diagonally wins. Play several games if time allows.

SUMMARY POSTER OR VISUAL REMINDER:
Bug Feelings summary poster found on page 60.

VARIATIONS/MODIFICATIONS/EXTENSIONS:
- Name a situation that could happen to students (someone breaks ahead of you in line, you forgot your homework, it rained when you wanted to go outside and play with your friend, your pet died.) Have the students draw a bug representing the size of that "bug feeling" and share the feeling they would have.
- Name a feeling word. Have the students "buzz" if it is a "bug feeling" and smile if it is a positive feeling.

JOURNAL ENTRY

Choose a "bug" feeling. Write about something that has happened that gave you that feeling.

CLASSROOM GUIDANCE NEWS

Dear Parent,

I enjoyed being in your child's class today for classroom guidance. Today we discussed the difference in feelings that are pleasant and feelings that are unpleasant. We termed unpleasant feelings "Bug Feelings." We made a list of the identified bug feelings. Students had fun playing a game of Bug Bingo.

Research on emotional intelligence shows that the ability to label feelings is one of the basic characteristics necessary for social success. Children often display undesirable behaviors (fighting, temper tantrums, disrespect) simply because they do not have the feelings vocabulary to properly express what they are feeling. Being "feelings smart" helps children in a number of ways. It aids with communication with peers and adults; it helps with self-control; it leads to a better understanding of oneself and others; and it helps children express themselves in positive ways.

At home, I encourage you to use feeling words as often as the opportunity presents itself with your child. For example, when your child is telling you about not getting chosen to be the class helper, you might say, "You felt sad when you didn't get picked." Or when you are frustrated with your child for not packing his book bag, you might say, "I feel mad because you did not pack your book bag." When you are relaying an experience at work, you might say, "I felt nervous because I wasn't ready to talk to my boss yet."

It is a pleasure getting to know your child through our classroom guidance program. Please feel free to call me with questions or concerns that you may have about your child, your child's school experience, or our elementary guidance and counseling program.

Sincerely,

B	U	G
mad	scared	worried
happy	**FREE BUG**	nervous
proud	silly	loved

B	U	G
silly	happy	loved
glad	FREE BUG	proud
sad	scared	worried

B	U	G
mad	proud	loved
sad	FREE BUG	silly
scared	happy	glad

B	U	G
loved	scared	nervous
glad	**FREE BUG**	worried
happy	proud	mad

Bug Call Cards

(Cut these cards apart and put them in a bag. Draw out one at a time and call out for students when playing Bug Bingo.)

B	U	G
B happy	**U** happy	**G** happy
B glad	**U** glad	**G** glad
B silly	**U** silly	**G** silly
B proud	**U** proud	**G** proud
B loved	**U** loved	**G** loved
B mad	**U** mad	**G** mad
B sad	**U** sad	**G** sad
B worried	**U** worried	**G** worried
B scared	**U** scared	**G** scared
B nervous	**U** nervous	**G** nervous

BUG AND SMILEY MARKERS

Cut apart and give each child five of each maker. Putting five of each in a plastic bag and distributing bags saves time.

Bug Feelings

 **sad**

 **mad**

 scared

 **worried**

 **nervous**

What Bugs You?

GRADE LEVEL(S): 1-3

DESCRIPTION:
This lesson can stand alone or be used as a follow-up to the lesson "Identifying Bug Feelings."
The lesson focuses on helping students express things that make them feel sad, scared, mad,
nervous, or worried. Students also learn that they can feel more than one feeling at a time.

OBJECTIVE(S):
- Students will develop listening and expression skills.
- Students will identify events that make them experience unpleasant feelings.
- Students will recognize that they can have more than one unpleasant feeling at a time.
- Students will recognize that there are varying degrees of unpleasant feelings.

ESTIMATED TIME: 30 minutes

MATERIAL(S) NEEDED:
- The book *Alexander and the Terrible, Horrible, No Good, Very Bad Day* by Judith Viorst
- Plastic bugs (at least one big and one small one)
- Mixed Bugs activity sheet found on page 64

PROCEDURES:
1. If you used the Identifying Bug Feelings lesson, review "bug" feelings. If not, briefly discuss how some feelings "bug" us—they make us feel uncomfortable and are not fun feelings to have. Discuss these feelings: sad, mad, scared, worried, and nervous.
2. Read *Alexander and the Terrible, Horrible, No Good, Very Bad Day* aloud. Many students will have already heard this book. Ask the students to listen for "bug" feelings as you read the story. Discuss the different feelings Alexander has throughout the book. Refer throughout the book to the "Bug Feelings." (You may want to use the Summary Poster from the Identifying Bug Feelings lesson.)
3. After reading the book, discuss some of the things that made Alexander feel mad, sad, scared, worried, and nervous.
4. With the students sitting in a circle, pass around a plastic bug. Have each child share something that "bugs" them and then have the other students identify the "bug" feeling.
5. Discuss how sometimes we have more than one bug feeling at a time. For example, Alexander felt sad and mad when Paul said that he wasn't his best friend anymore.
6. Work together to do the "Mixed Bugs" activity sheet found on page 64.

SUMMARY POSTER OR VISUAL REMINDER:
Name the Things That Bug You summary poster found on page 65

What Bugs You?

VARIATIONS/MODIFICATIONS/EXTENSIONS:

- Use a bug puppet to tell a story similar to *Alexander and the Terrible, Horrible, No Good, Very Bad Day* in place of reading the story to the students. Think of "terrible, horrible" things that could happen in a day for a bug (not being allowed to feast on a leaf with other bugs, almost getting zapped by a bug zapper, getting swatted at, etc.)
- Have the students think of two different bugs and draw these bugs as one bug (i.e., a dragon beetle.) Then have them think of two feelings that they have felt at the same time.
- Ask the teacher to place a bug catcher in the room. Hang this like a basketball hoop. Encourage the students to write or draw things that happen during their day that "bug" them and place these in the bug catcher. This may prevent tattling that goes on during the day and can alert the teacher to more severe problems. If a bug catcher is not available a can or basket decorated with bugs could also be used.

JOURNAL ENTRY

Write about something that really bugs you.
Be sure to include the "bug feeling" words in your writing.

 **What Bugs You?**

CLASSROOM GUIDANCE NEWS

Dear Parent,

Today in classroom guidance we identified things that "bug" us. We all have things that cause us to feel sad, mad, scared, nervous, or worried. It is important that young children learn to identify how events make them feel.

Students had a great time listening to the story *Alexander and the Terrible, Horrible, No Good, Very Bad Day* by Judith Viorst. We discussed that many times we may have more than one "bug" feeling at a time. For example, when a child forgets his/her homework he/she may feel mad and worried at the same time. Students completed an activity sheet entitled "Mixed Bugs." Be sure to ask your child to see the sheet.

At home you can encourage your child to express his/her feelings using feeling words. When your child is obviously upset, ask him/her to tell you what has happened. Then allow time to discuss the feeling(s) your child is having. Avoid saying, "You shouldn't feel that way," when your child identifies a feeling. And, most importantly, always take the time to listen to your child's experiences. When you detect that your child is mad, avoid the tendency to say, "I don't want to hear about it. Just go to your room."

I truly enjoy working with your child. As always, please feel free to call me with any questions or concerns that you may have about your child, your child's school experience, or our elementary guidance and counseling program.

Sincerely,

MIXED BUGS

Many times when something bothers you, you will have more than one "bug" feeling at a time.

Read about each student below. Choose two words from the BUG BOX to complete the sentence.

1. Jamie wanted Chris to play with her. Chris said that she had chores to do and couldn't play. Later Jamie sees Chris riding bikes with Buddy.

    Jamie feels _____ and

    _____.

BUG BOX

mad

sad

scared

worried

nervous

2. Chuck's parents told him to be home at 5:00. He was so busy playing with his friend that he lost track of time. He realizes it's now 5:30. He's been late many times before and his parents told him that if he was late again, he would not be allowed to play outside for a week.

    Chuck feels _____ and

    _____.

3. Juan is playing his first game of baseball. He's never batted in front of so many people before.

    Yuan feels _____ and _____.

 **What Bugs You?**

 TATTLING

FORGETTING HOMEWORK

 BREAKING IN LINE

 A BROKEN TOY

BEING LEFT OUT

Name The Things That Bug You

Bugs Inside You

GRADE LEVEL(S): 1-4

DESCRIPTION:
This lesson introduces the concept that unpleasant feelings such as sad, mad, scared, nervous, and/or worried can lead to physical symptoms. Students will learn that their bodies react and respond to these feelings in a variety of ways.

OBJECTIVE(S):
• Students will identify where they experience specific feelings in their bodies.
• Students will understand the difference in being sick and feeling stress.

ESTIMATED TIME: 30 minutes

MATERIAL(S) NEEDED:
• Bug jar (available at discount toy stores) or a glass jar with a lid with holes in it
• Outline of body (provided on page 69) enlarged to poster size
• Physical symptom pictures on page 70
• Bugs Inside Me activity sheet on page 71

PROCEDURES:
1. Ask the students if they have ever heard of being sick referred to as "having a bug." Discuss that sometimes we use that phrase when we have a stomach virus or a cold.
2. Discuss another kind of "sick." Explain that sometimes when we hold our "bug" feelings inside (sad, mad, scared, nervous, and/or worried) those feelings can make us feel sick. Show a bug jar. Ask what it's for. Discuss what would happen if we caught a bug in there and never let it out. It may start to feel bad. Holding the bug in the jar only makes it feel worse. Explain that this is the same with our feelings. If we hold our bug feelings inside, they can make us feel bad. Explain that today students will learn where the bug feelings can be experienced in our bodies.
3. Display the poster size outline of a body. Starting from the top of the body, tape each of the physical symptons (found on page 70) of having "bug feelings" to the body one at a time and discuss which "bug feelings" can go along with each symptom.

Throbbing head (all feelings)
Heavy eyes (sad, worried)
Tingly nose (sad)
Face on fire (mad)
Bad taste in mouth (nervous, worried, scared)
Nervous cough (nervous, scared, worried)
Clenched jaw (mad, worried, nervous)
Knot in chest (nervous, worried, scared)

Skipping heart (mad, nervous, scared)
Sweaty palms (nervous, scared)
Tight fists (mad, nervous)
Butterflies in stomach (all)
Wobbly knees (worried, nervous, scared)
Pins & needles feelings (nervous, worried, scared)

4. Give each student a BUGS INSIDE ME worksheet (found on page 71). Work through this together.

5. Explain to the students that bug feelings only hurt your body if you hold the feelings inside. Therefore, it is important to get the bugs out in an OK way. If you are not following this lesson up with lessons on ways to "De-Bug" discuss some of the OK ways to get the feelings out such as doing something you enjoy, drawing, talking with someone you trust, or pounding clay.

SUMMARY POSTER OR VISUAL REMINDER:

Where You Feel Bug Feelings summary poster on page 72

VARIATIONS/MODIFICATIONS/EXTENSIONS:

- Show students an "Anger Management Biofeedback Card" (available through YouthLight, Inc.). Discuss how our body has its own built-in level of feelings. Pass the card around and have the students share how their bodies tell them they are feeling: For example, mad, some anger or relaxed. Explain how the color changes according to body temperature.
- Have the students act out feeling each of the "bug feelings." Have the other students point out how their bodies are showing they are feeling "bugged."

JOURNAL ENTRY

 Choose a "bug" feeling. Write about what happens to your body step-by-step when you start to feel this feeling.

Bugs Inside You

CLASSROOM GUIDANCE NEWS

Dear Parent,

Today in classroom guidance we discussed how our bodies send us signs of unpleasant or "bug" feelings. We all have our bodily warning signs. For example, your face or neck may start to turn red when you're mad. Or when you're nervous, your heart may start racing or you may feel queasy in your stomach.

Today students learned about several different warning signs. They identified their own warning signs on an activity sheet entitled "Bugs Inside Me." Be sure you ask your child to see his/her activity sheet. Discuss his/her warning signs and take time to share your own. You may say, "Have you ever noticed how my neck gets red when I start to get mad? That's one of the ways my body lets me know I'm getting angry."

Your child may have complained of being sick when you knew he/she was not truly sick. It's important to help your child understand the difference in being sick and having a feeling that is making him/her feel sick. You may say, "I hear you saying your stomach hurts. I'm wondering if you've been thinking about spending the weekend with Aunt Susan while I go to my meeting this weekend." Your child may or may not understand that the two are linked, and you have the perfect opportunity to talk to your child about his/her feelings.

Please feel free to call me with any questions or concerns that you have about your child, your child's school experience, or our elementary guidance and counseling program.

Sincerely,

OUTLINE OF BODY

Enlarge on poster board and laminate.

PHYSICAL SYMPTOMS

Reproduce, cut apart, and laminate for durability

 **THROBBING HEAD**

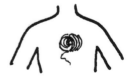 **KNOT IN CHEST**

 HEAVY EYES

 **SKIPPING HEART**

 **TINGLY NOSE**

 **SWEATY PALMS**

 **FACE ON FIRE**

 **TIGHT FISTS**

BAD TASTE IN MOUTH

 BUTTERFLIES IN STOMACH

 **NERVOUS COUGH**

 **WOBBLY KNEES**

 CLENCHED JAW

 PINS & NEEDLES FEELINGS

BUGS INSIDE ME

- Mark an "M" on the parts of the body where you feel MAD feelings.
- Mark an "S" on the parts of the body where you feel SAD feelings.
- Mark a "W" on the parts of the body where you feel WORRIED feelings.
- Mark "SC" on the parts of the body where you feel SCARED feelings.
- Mark an "N" on the parts of the body where you feel NERVOUS feelings.

Bugs Inside You

WHERE DO YOU FEEL BUG FEELINGS?

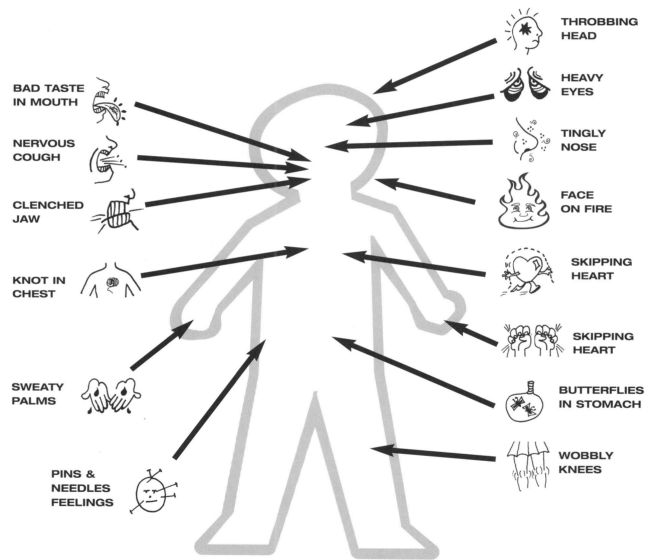

BAD TASTE IN MOUTH

NERVOUS COUGH

CLENCHED JAW

KNOT IN CHEST

SWEATY PALMS

PINS & NEEDLES FEELINGS

THROBBING HEAD

HEAVY EYES

TINGLY NOSE

FACE ON FIRE

SKIPPING HEART

SKIPPING HEART

BUTTERFLIES IN STOMACH

WOBBLY KNEES

De-Bugging

GRADE LEVEL(S): 1-3

DESCRIPTION:
This lesson deals with teaching students rules for dealing with unpleasant feelings such as mad, sad, scared, worried, and nervous. The analogy of getting rid of bugs, or "de-bugging" is used as students learn "De-Bug Rules."

OBJECTIVE(S):
- Students will identify feelings.
- Students will identify healthy and safe ways to make themselves feel better when they feel sad, mad, scared, worried, and/or nervous.
- Students will recognize the difference in a feeling and an action.

ESTIMATED TIME: 30 minutes

MATERIAL(S) NEEDED:
- A bug jar or glass jar with a lid with holes punched in it
- De-Bug Rules summary poster found on page 77
- De-Bugging activity sheet found on page 76

PROCEDURES:

1. Ask the students how many of them have ever gotten in trouble because they were mad, sad, scared, worried, or nervous. Share the following story to explain that feelings don't get you in trouble.

   When I was in elementary school I had a best friend. One day we were talking on the telephone and my friend said something I didn't like. I felt sad about what she was saying and mad at her for saying it. I decided I wanted to get back at my friend so I was going to hang up on her. Only when I hung up, I slammed the phone down and the phone broke.

2. Ask, "Did I get in trouble for being sad and mad at my friend?" "What did I get in trouble for?" Emphasize the difference in the feeling and the action.

3. Explain that when we have feelings that bug us, we need to let them out in an OK way. This is called "De-Bugging" just like when you have bugs in your house you get rid of them in a safe way. Tell the students that they will be learning "De-Bug Rules" today.

4. Discuss Rule #1: **I will not hurt myself.** Use the bug jar to explain how one way of hurting yourself is by holding all your feelings inside. If you taught the lesson "Bugs Inside You," refer to the ways bug feelings come out in your body. If you did not teach this lesson, discuss some of the physical signs of holding feelings inside like a queasy stomach, headaches, clenched fists, tight jaw, etc.

5. Discuss De-Bug Rule # 2: **I will not hurt property.** Explain that property means things. Give

examples of ways that people hurt property—slamming a door, breaking a pencil, etc.

6. Discuss De-Bug Rule #3: **I will not hurt others.** Discuss the two ways we hurt others—with our bodies and with our words. Allow students to offer examples such as pushing, hitting, shoving, calling names, teasing, etc.

7. Display the "De-Bug Rules" summary poster in the room (see page 77).

8. Work through the DE-BUGGING worksheet together (see page 76).

SUMMARY POSTER OR VISUAL REMINDER:

De-Bug Rules summary poster on page 77

VARIATIONS/MODIFICATIONS/EXTENSIONS:

• Name ways that people De-Bug and have the students make a thumbs-up if it is an OK way to De-Bug and a thumbs down if it is a not OK way to De-Bug.

• Discuss how people sometimes drink alcohol, smoke cigarettes, or take medicines not prescribed by a doctor to make them feel better and why this is not an OK way to De-Bug.

• Have the students identify one healthy way to De-Bug and write or draw about this way.

JOURNAL ENTRY

Write or draw a picture of a time you got in trouble for letting your feelings out in a not OK way. Then write what you could have done differently.

De-Bugging

CLASSROOM GUIDANCE NEWS

Dear Parents,

Today in classroom guidance your child learned three rules for "De-Bugging" referred to as "De-Bug" rules. Many times we have feelings that "bug" us such as sad, mad, scared, worried, and/or nervous. Learning to let these feelings out in an appropriate way is a life skill that all children and adults must learn and practice. "De-Bug Rules" are:

1. I will not hurt myself.

2. I will not hurt property.

3. I will not hurt others.

We discussed each of these rules in detail today. One of the main ways that people hurt themselves is by holding in their feelings. These feelings then come out in physical ways such as queasy stomachs, headaches, tight jaws, etc. Many people think it is OK to slam a door or throw something that breaks. While this may make you feel better momentarily, there are always consequences for such actions. Not only are you still mad or sad, but you have broken property. Finally, we discussed the two ways we may hurt others: with our bodies as well as our words. Neither are OK ways to deal with "bug" feelings.

At home it is important that you discuss with your child the difference between a feeling and an action. You may say, "It's OK to feel mad at your little sister, but it's not OK to hit her." When your child must suffer a consequence as a result of something he/she did because he/she was feeling "bugged," always make the distinction that the child is being punished for what he/she did, not for the feeling. You may find it helpful to post "De-Bug Rules" in your home or to discuss them in a family meeting.

I enjoy working with your child in classroom guidance. As always, please feel free to call me with questions or concerns that you may have about your child, your child's school experience, or our elementary guidance and counseling program.

Sincerely,

DE-BUG RULES
Feeling mad, sad, scared, worried, or nervous is OK.
But remember these important rules:

I will not hurt myself.
I will not hurt property.
I will not hurt others.

Draw a line through all of the not OK ways to De-Bug.

Circle all the OK ways to De-Bug.

Kick a door

Draw a picture

Run away

Call someone a name

Talk to a parent

Kick someone

Kick a football

DE-BUG RULES

I will not hurt myself.

I will not hurt property.

I will not hurt others.

Healthy Ways to De-Bug
Squeezing and Drawing

GRADE LEVEL(S): 1-3

DESCRIPTION:
This lesson introduces two appropriate ways to release unpleasant feelings: squeezing soft objects like a pillow or clay and drawing.

OBJECTIVE(S):
• Students will identify feelings.
• Students will identify rules for dealing with unpleasant feelings.
• Students will identify two appropriate ways to "de-bug."

ESTIMATED TIME: 30 minutes

MATERIAL(S) NEEDED:
• ABCs of De-Bugging poster (sample is shown on page 83)
• A plastic bag of clay (a recipe for making clay is on page 82)
• Drawing paper for each child

PROCEDURES:
1. If you used the lesson entitled "De-Bugging," review the De-Bug Rules. Ask the students some of the things they feel like doing when they are mad, sad, scared, worried, or nervous. Discuss how some are OK and some are not OK and why.
2. Tell the students that they are going to learn two things that they can do that will not get them in trouble when they are feeling "bugged." Tell these stories:

One day a potter, who is a person who makes pottery, was busy working at her wheel. She had almost finished a beautiful vase when her hand slipped and her vase fell off the pottery wheel. The potter was very sad because she had worked so hard. She was also very angry. She picked up the clay off of the floor and put it back on the pottery wheel. But she didn't feel like working anymore. She was too "bugged." She noticed that her fists were drawn up into balls. They were tight. So she opened up her fists and began to squeeze the clay. She squeezed it very tight and let it ooze between her fingers. It didn't hurt her because the clay was soft. It didn't hurt the clay because clay doesn't have feelings and can't be broken. She kept squeezing the clay. She squeezed until her fists didn't feel like being tight anymore. She noticed that she felt better and was ready to start her vase again. Only this time, she was extra careful not to let it slip off the wheel!

An artist was busy working in his studio. He was almost finished with a picture he was painting when someone came into the studio. He walked away from his picture and when he came back his picture was a mess. His cat had knocked the picture over and also knocked

paint over that had spilled onto his picture. The artist felt sad because he had worked so hard on the picture. He was mad at his cat for making the mess. He took his paintbrush and started making long, angry strokes on the picture. The picture started to look angry. He kept painting and painting. He painted all his angry feelings into the picture. The picture looked even more angry, but the artist started feeling less angry. He decided he may have made a masterpiece and called it "Angry Cat."

3. Show the ABCs of De-Bugging poster (found on page 83). Explain that you are going to put this in the class for the class to add ideas to when they think of great ways to De-Bug. The goal is to get at least one for each letter of the alphabet. If you plan to use any of the other lessons on Healthy De-Bugging found in this book, tell the students that you will add others as you come for other guidance lessons.
4. Discuss how the potter handled her mad feelings by squeezing clay. Under "s" write "squeeze clay". Give each class a plastic zipper bag of clay for their room (see directions for making clay on page 82.) If time allows, give each student a small piece of the clay and allow them to squeeze it. Discuss why it is OK to squeeze clay, but not OK to squeeze a pet or a person's arm.
5. Allow the students to share their "angry" pictures.
6. Review the two ways students learned to De-Bug today—squeezing clay and drawing.

SUMMARY POSTER OR VISUAL REMINDER:
The ABCs of De-Bugging (found on page 83)

VARIATIONS/MODIFICATIONS/EXTENSIONS:
- Read the book ***Painting the Fire*** by Liz Farrington and Jonathan Sherwood.
- Have each child create something out of clay that makes them mad, sad, scared, worried, or nervous. Then have them reshape the clay into something that makes them happy.
- Provide a Graffiti Wall for drawing. Attach a large piece of paper to a wall in the classroom. When the students have "bug" feelings, they can go draw pictures on the Graffiti Wall.
- As a science project, allow the students to make the clay (recipe on page 82).
- Show and discuss the video ***Ten Things to do Instead of Hitting*** available from Sunburst, Inc. This video provides several stopping points for you to do the worksheets that accompany the video. You can show part one with this lesson, and parts two and three with the lesson on Chill Time and I Feel. Or you can show the video in its entirety as a follow-up lesson to this or any of the other Healthy Ways to De-Bug lessons.

JOURNAL ENTRY

Write about how you feel when you squeze clay. Tell what happens to your "bug" feelings as you squeeze clay.

Write about the colors that you think show mad, sad, scared, nervous, and worried feelings. Tell why you chose these colors.

CLASSROOM GUIDANCE NEWS

Dear Parent,

Today in guidance we discussed two ways to deal with unpleasant feelings. We call these unpleasant feelings "bug" feelings. Getting rid of the feelings is called "de-bugging." Therefore we focused on two ways to de-bug.

We began the lesson by reviewing De-Bug Rules. These include: **1) I will not hurt myself; 2) I will not hurt property**; and **3) I will not hurt others.** The two ways of de-bugging that students learned today include squeezing clay and drawing. Students learned that it's OK to squeeze something like clay that cannot be hurt or hurt themselves. They also learned that they can draw their angry feelings into a picture.

At home, you may want to provide some type of clay (Play-Doh® will work) or other soft substance for your child when he/she is feeling "bugged." Squeeze the clay with your child as he/she puts the "bug" feelings into the substance. A pillow will also work. Provide paper, pencils, crayons, pens, markers, etc. for your child as well. Have him/her draw a picture of what made him/her feel "bugged." Or allow them to simply scribble angry marks onto a paper.

These healthy ways of de-bugging will produce a happier child as well as a safer child. Children who know what to do with "bug" feelings are less likely to resort to acts that hurt.

As always, please feel free to call me with any questions or concerns that you may have about your child, your child's school experience, or our elementary guidance and counseling program.

Sincerely,

RECIPE FOR CLAY

2 1/4 cups non-self-rising wheat flour
1 cup salt
1 tablespoon powdered alum
4 tablespoons vegetable oil
1 1/2 cups boiling water
food coloring or poster paints

1. Combine flour, salt, and alum in a bowl. Add vegetable oil.
2. Stir in boiling water. Stir vigorously with a large spoon until mixture holds together.
3. Knead the dough until it is smooth.
4. Divide the dough into several lumps. Add a few drops of food coloring or poster paint to each lump and knead to mix the color of the dough.

Makes about 3 cups. Stored in an airtight container, the clay will keep a long time.

Healthy Ways to De-Bug

This is a sample of the poster for all of the lessons on Healthy De-Bugging. Recreate this on a large chart tablet or poster board. Laminate and write on the chart with an overhead transparency marker so that it can be reused year after year. As you introduce a new concept or as students think of things that they can do to de-bug, they write it beside the corresponding letter.

THE ABCs OF DE-BUGGING

A	N
B	O
C	P
D	Q
E	R
F	S
G	T
H	U
I	V
J	W
K	X
L	Y
M	Z

Healthy Ways to De-Bug
Chill Time and "I Feel"

GRADE LEVEL(S): 1-3

DESCRIPTION:
This lesson introduces two other ways to appropriately deal with unpleasant or "bug" feelings: taking time to cool off and using an "I feel" statement.

OBJECTIVE(S):
- Students will identify feelings.
- Students will develop expression skills.
- Students will explain the phrase "chill time" and understand that it means time to cool off when you're feeling mad, sad, scared, worried, or nervous.
- Students will practice using "I feel" statements to express their feelings.

ESTIMATED TIME: 30 minutes

MATERIAL(S) NEEDED:
- Summary poster of The ABCs of De-Bugging (sample found on page 83)
- De-Bug Sentence poster found on page 87

PROCEDURES:
1. Remind the students about De-Bug Rules if you have taught the lesson entitled "De-Bugging." Also review any ways to De-Bug that have been written on the ABCs of De-Bugging poster. Explain that today they will learn two other ways to handle "bug" feelings.
2. Ask the students if they have ever said or done something before they even realized they said or did it. Say: *Doing something without thinking is called acting on impulse. Acting on impulse means that you do something without thinking. Some impulses are natural and help keep you safe. For example, when you touch something hot, you pull your hand away very quickly. This is an impulse. You don't really think about it; you just do it. Another example is if you hear a loud noise when you're in a very quiet place, you may jump. This is an impulse. Some impulses however, can get you into trouble, especially if you do something without thinking because you feel "bugged."* Ask the students for examples. These may include hitting someone, calling a name, screaming at someone, throwing something, etc.
3. Discuss chill time. Explain that this is stopping and giving yourself time to think so that you do not do something you should not. During a chill time, you should get your mind busy doing something else while you're taking some deep breaths. Suggest counting to 10 slowly; model. Show the ABCs of De-Bugging poster and write "count to 10" under "c". Also suggest saying your ABCs backwards—model and write under "A" on the ABCs of De-Bugging poster. Allow students to practice each of these.
4. Discuss how difficult it can be to talk to someone with whom you feel "bugged." Many times, if you say the wrong thing, it can make you and the other person feel even more "bugged."

Healthy Ways to De-Bug

Tell students that you are going to teach them a magic "De-Bug Sentence" that they can use anytime someone is doing something they don't like. Teach the "I feel" message using these steps:

Say the person's name: "_____,"
"I feel (use a feeling word) _____."
"because (describe the behavior) _____."
"Please (describe what you want them to do) _____."

5. Write this under "I" on the ABCs poster for "I feel message."

6. Role play using the "De-Bug Sentence." Some sample role play situations include:
   • A classmate breaks ahead of you in line.
   • A friend laughs at an answer when you get it wrong.
   • Someone makes fun of a picture you drew.
   • Your friend borrows something from you then loses it.
   • Your sister breaks your favorite toy.
   • Your teacher tells you that you must make a speech in front of the whole school.
   • Your parents are going away for a weekend and you are concerned about where you are going to stay.

SUMMARY POSTER OR VISUAL REMINDER:
Two posters are needed for this lesson:
• The ABCs of De-Bugging found on page 83
• De-Bug Sentence found on page 87

VARIATIONS/MODIFICATIONS/EXTENSIONS:
• Have the students draw pictures or make a list of other things they could do during chill time besides counting to ten or saying the ABCs backwards.
• Have the students write or draw situations that happen in school or at home where using the De-Bug sentence might work.
• Each day, ask teachers to spend about five minutes allowing the students to say a De-Bug sentence if something has happened to them that has made them feel "bugged" at school.

JOURNAL ENTRY

Write a De-Bug Sentence using the "I feel" for each of these feelings: sad, mad, scared, worried, and nervous.

CLASSROOM GUIDANCE NEWS

Dear Parent,

Today in classroom guidance students learned two ways to handle unpleasant or "bug" feelings. Students learned about "chill time." We discussed how people often act on impulse when they are feeling mad, sad, scared, nervous, or worried. Many times acting on impulse leads a person to do something inappropriate such as hitting, name-calling, or destroying property. Students learned that they need to stop and think to give themselves time to cool off; thus, the term "chill time." During chill time, students learned that they can count to 10, breathe deeply, and/or say the ABCs backwards. All of these things give a person time; time to think so that they don't act on impulse.

Students also learned a way to verbally express bug feelings without hurting someone else's feelings. We called this a De-Bug sentence. It is also referred to as an "I feel" sentence. There are four parts to a De-Bug Sentence. These are:

Say the name of the person to whom you are talking.

Say, "I feel" and put in one feeling word (mad, sad, scared, nervous, worried).

Say "because " and state why in a short way.

Tell the person what you want beginning with the word "Please."

An example might be, "Mike, I feel sad because you laughed at my picture. Please don't laugh at my work."

Using a De-Bug sentence is very effective. I encourage you to use it at home when speaking to your child. "I feel frustrated because you haven't put away your toys. Please put them away," is a more appropriate expression of your feelings than yelling at your child, ridiculing, screaming, or nagging.

My goal is to give your child as many possible ideas about the proper expression of feelings as possible. Feeling "bugged" is natural, therefore teaching what to do with these feelings is essential. Please feel free to call me with questions or concerns that you may have about your child, your child's school experience, or our elementary guidance and counseling program.

Sincerely,

Healthy Ways to De-Bug

De-Bug Sentence

Name _____

I feel _____

because _____.

Please _____

_____.

Healthy Ways to De-Bug
Physical Activity

GRADE LEVEL(S): 1-3

DESCRIPTION:
This lesson introduces doing something physical to release energy generated by some "bug" feelings such as mad, nervous, or scared. It also explains how physical activity, even though difficult when you are sad or worried, can produce more pleasant feelings.

OBJECTIVE(S):
• Students will identify feelings.
• Students will recognize that bug feelings such as mad, nervous, and scared produce energy inside you.
• Students will discuss how difficult it can be to get yourself up and moving when you feel sad or worried.
• Students will identify physical activities that help them feel better when they have unpleasant feelings.

ESTIMATED TIME: 30 minutes

MATERIAL(S) NEEDED:
• The ABCs of De-Bugging Summary Poster (sample on page 83)
• The book *The Grouchy Ladybug* by Eric Carle
• Drawing paper for each child

PROCEDURES:
1. If you have used a bug puppet with students use the puppet to tell this story. If you choose not to use a bug puppet, tell this story about a friend of yours:
   This little bug (or a friend of mine) is very bugged. Her little cousin who was visiting went into her room and took apart the 500 piece jigsaw puzzle that she had almost finished. It had taken her almost 2 weeks to get it to where it was. She was so mad that she just wanted to DO something. She felt like hitting, but knew that was a not OK way to de-bug. So she went outside and rode her bike. The harder she pedaled, the better she felt. She could feel all her anger energy going into the pedals of the bike. Before long, she was enjoying the feel of the breeze in her hair and forgot all about being mad at her cousin. By the time she got home, she was calmed down enough to talk to her mom about what happened.
2. Discuss how some bug feelings like mad, nervous, and scared produce energy inside you. You feel like you want to do something. Other bug feelings like sad and worried make you feel like you do not want to do anything. Ask "what happens if you just sit around and do nothing when you feel sad or worried; what happens if you do something like riding your bike even if you don't feel like it?"

3. Tell the students that today you will focus on doing something with your body when you feel bugged. Ask the students to predict what can happen when you do that.
4. Read *The Grouchy Ladybug* by Eric Carle. Discuss how each time the ladybug wanted to fight, she left and did something else instead. Flying from place to place took energy and that helped get her mind off her anger.
5. Work on the ABCs of De-Bugging. Have the students name some physical activities that they can do both in school and in other places that can help them de-bug. If their letter is not taken, add their ideas to the list.
6. Have each child draw a picture of a physical activity they enjoy. Allow time to share.

SUMMARY POSTER OR VISUAL REMINDER:
Use The ABCs of De-Bugging (sample poster found on page 83)

VARIATIONS/MODIFICATIONS/EXTENSIONS:
- A ladybug puppet adds a great deal to the reading of *The Grouchy Ladybug*.
- Play a game naming physical activities. Each student has 15 seconds to name a physical activity that has not been named. Go around in a circle. When a student exceeds the time limit or names an activity that has already been named, he/she is out. Keep the game going until one student is left.
- Give each student a small bouncing ball. Have them bounce the ball and name something that bugs them with each bounce. Discuss putting all your energy into the ball.
- Play a game of charades allowing the students to act out physical activities they could use to "de-bug."

JOURNAL ENTRY

Write about your favorite physical activity.
Write how you feel when you do this activity.

CLASSROOM GUIDANCE NEWS

Dear Parent,

Today students learned another way to handle unpleasant feelings. We have discussed unpleasant feelings and termed them "bug" feelings. Some examples include mad, sad, scared, nervous, and worried.

Some "bug" feelings such as mad, scared, and nervous create energy inside you. When you feel these feelings, you want to DO something. Sometimes people do inappropriate things like hitting or throwing things which lead to consequences. Other "bug" feelings like sad and worried can make you feel like doing nothing. Doing nothing, sitting and moping, watching TV, thinking only about the problem can make you feel even worse.

Physical activity is a great way to "de-bug." When you have that energy inside you that makes you feel like doing something, do something healthy. When you have no energy, physical activity creates energy inside you that can help you think more clearly about the problem that is creating the "bug" feelings inside you. Examples of physical activity include riding a bike, playing basketball, dancing, cleaning house, organizing a closet, bouncing a ball, and washing a car.

At home it is important to provide your child ways to release his/her energy that may be created by some "bug" feelings. It is equally important to encourage your child to engage in physical activity when he/she may be feeling sad or worried. One way to do this is to engage in the activity with your child.

Please feel free to call me with any questions or concerns that you may have about your child, your child's school experience, or our elementary guidance and counseling program.

Sincerely,

Healthy Ways to De-Bug
Writing

GRADE LEVEL(S): 1-4

DESCRIPTION:
This lesson emphasizes writing as a means of releasing "bug" feelings such as sad, mad, scared, nervous, or worried.

OBJECTIVE(S):
- Students will identify feelings.
- Students will develop expression skills.
- Students will use writing as a method of expressing unpleasant feelings.

ESTIMATED TIME: 30 minutes

MATERIAL(S) NEEDED:
- Book cover found on page 95
- ABCs of De-Bugging Summary Poster (sample found on page 83)
- *Rosie's Story* by Martine Gogoll

PROCEDURES:

1. Read this poem and tell the students it was written by a friend of yours.

BUG FEELINGS

I feel sad.
I wish I was glad.
Feeling sad feels bad.
I wish I had
Listened to my dad
And not used his favorite pad
To draw a picture of my friend Thad.

Explains that your friend wrote that poem when her dad sent her to her room after she drew on all of his paper. Tell students that your friend shared with you that while she was writing the poem, she put all her feelings and energy into the writing. After a while she started to feel better, even silly, about the poem she wrote. And then she apologized to her dad for disobeying.

2. If you have used previous lessons on Healthy Ways to De-Bug, remind the students that they have been learning about ways to de-bug—to get rid of feelings that bug you. Review the de-bug rules and bug feelings. Tell the students that they will learn another way to de-bug in today's lesson.

3. Read *Rosie's Story* by Martine Gogoll. Following the story, discuss how Rosie used writing to help her express her feelings, just as your friend did with her poem. Emphasize that when you're writing about your feelings, it's private and you don't have to share it with anyone. You don't even have to worry about spelling, capital letters, or punctuation. What you do is just write anything that comes into your head about your feelings.

4. Model writing about feeling worried on an overhead projector, the board, or a chart tablet. You might write something like this:

    I feel worried today because I have to go to the dentist. I usually don't mind going, but I remember that the last time I was there, the dentist told me that he thought I had the beginning of a cavity and that if it looked any worse when I came back that he was going to have to fill it. I hate getting fillings. The shot hurts and that makes me feel scared and nervous. Then after that your mouth feels weird because you can't feel anything and you talk funny. I hope I don't have to get a filling today.

    While modeling the process, emphasize that you're putting your thoughts down as they come. In doing this type of writing, you don't have to worry about writing rules like capital letters and punctuation. This is a personal writing so no one else will read it or grade it.

5. Add "Write about your feelings" on the ABCs of de-bugging under the "w."

6. Assist students in making "BUG BOOKS" for students to use as personal journals. These books are easily made by using the cover page provided on page 95. Directions for making the books are:
    *   Reproduce the cover page on card stock or white construction paper. This works best because it is more durable. However, plain white paper will work also.
    *   Use either the card stock, construction paper, or plain white paper for the back.
    *   Between the front and back, put notebook paper or other lined writing paper.
    *   Staple the book together.
    *   Allow the students to color and decorate the front of their Bug Book.

7. Encourage the students to keep these in their desks at school and to use it when things bug them.

SUMMARY POSTER OR VISUAL REMINDER:
The ABCs of De-Bugging poster (sample found on page 83)

VARIATIONS/MODIFICATIONS/EXTENSIONS:
*   Students may make more than one Bug Book—one for school use and one for home use.
*   Have the students write a poem about a "bug" feeling. They may choose to do an acrostic by writing their name vertically and either thinking of something that "bugs" them that begins with each letter of their name or writing a healthy way to "de-bug" with every letter of their name.

Samples may be:

J oggers who run on the sidewalk when I'm riding my bike
A lways having to clean my room
M aking a bad grade
I ce cream cone melts
E armuffs

J ump rope
A ct like a frog and leap
M ake something from blocks
I magine I'm riding a roller coaster
E xercise

JOURNAL ENTRY

Write about a small thing that got you bugged.
Then write about a big thing that made you feel bugged.

CLASSROOM GUIDANCE NEWS

Dear Parent,

Today in classroom guidance we discussed another healthy way to release unpleasant feelings. We've referred to this as "de-bugging." De-bugging means doing something to get rid of feelings that "bug" you like sad, mad, scared, nervous, or worried.

Today we discussed using writing as a way of releasing "bug" feelings. Students heard a story entitled *Rosie's Story* by Martine Gogoll. In this story, Rosie is teased because she has red hair and freckles. But when Rosie writes a story to share with the class about a boy named Rusty who is being teased, her classmates start to realize how Rosie must feel.

Writing is a wonderful avenue for releasing feelings. I modeled writing about my feelings for the students. When doing this kind of personal writing, students were encouraged to let their thoughts flow to the paper. Normal rules of writing such as capitalization, spelling, and punctuation do not apply when writing about your personal feelings. This is only for you to see.

Allow your child to have some type of journal or notebook at home in which he/she can write about his/her feelings. Avoid the temptation to read this; remember it is personal. When your child is feeling "bugged" you can say, "You could write about your feelings in your journal" (or bug book or whatever you call it at your home.)

Please feel free to call me with any questions or concerns that you may have about your child, your child's school experience, or our elementary guidance and counseling program.

In partnership,

MY BUG BOOK

By _____

Healthy Ways to De-Bug
Thinking Positive Thoughts

GRADE LEVEL(S): 1-3

DESCRIPTION:
This lesson provides students another way to deal with "bug" feelings which is to change their thinking about events that make them feel "bugged." Students will enjoy making an "ah-ha" box and placing positive messages in them.

OBJECTIVE(S):
- Students will identify feelings.
- Students will recognize the relationship between thoughts and feelings.
- Students will create positive messages about themselves.
- Students will recognize their strengths and abilities.

ESTIMATED TIME: 30 minutes

MATERIAL(S) NEEDED:
- Small box with a cover for each student (Ask department stores for donations. Many will donate these especially if you offer to thank them in a school newsletter that goes home to parents. It's free advertisement for that store!)
- An assortment of jewels, sequins, stickers, buttons, etc. with which students can decorate their "ah-ha" boxes
- Ah-ha message strips found on page 99 (one set for each child)

PROCEDURES:
1. Ask the students if they have ever wished they could be someone else. Perhaps they wished they looked like someone else or could do something someone else could do. Allow time for students to share.
2. Explain to the students that many times when we wish we were someone else, it is because we may feel bad about ourselves. Sometimes we become focused on thinking about ways we wish we were different or things we cannot yet do. At these times we can feel really "bugged." Ask the students to suggest some of these "bug" feelings.
3. Discuss how our thoughts lead to our feelings. Write this on the board:
   Thought ➔ Feeling ➔ Action
4. Explain to students that when they are feeling bad about themselves that there is something that they can do to themselves. They can change their thinking which will change their feeling. One way to do this is to give themselves "Ah-Ha!"s. Explain that an "Ah-Ha" is a thought or message that makes you feel good about yourself. These may be messages about things you're good at, messages about your personality, or messages about how special things you do that make others happy.

Healthy Ways to De-Bug

5. Discuss how when you're feeling bugged, it's sometimes hard to think of these messages. So in order to help, students are going to make "Ah-Ha" boxes to put special messages in. Give each child a small box (a jewelry box or other appropriate boxes.) Give a supply of things to decorate the box with such as sequins, jewels, stickers, etc. Have the children decorate the box as much as they like to symbolize a very special treasure box.

5. After the students are done, give each child a set of Ah-ha messages strips found on page 99. These messages are:

   I can _____.

   _____loves me no matter what I do.

   I am good at _____.

6. Have the students place these strips in their "Ah-ha" box. Explain to the students that when they are having a hard time getting rid of a thought that's causing them a bug feeling, they can open their "Ah-Ha" box, take out a message and read it and think about that thought for a while. Encourage the students to frequently add to their "Ah-Ha" box as they think of other positive things about themselves.

7. Add "Think Positive Thoughts" or "Use your Ah-ha box" on the ABCs of de-bugging poster.

SUMMARY POSTER OR VISUAL REMINDER:
The ABCs of De-Bugging poster (sample found on page 83)

VARIATIONS/MODIFICATIONS/EXTENSIONS:
- Several weeks before this lesson, send a note home asking parents to write down several positive things about their child. Ask them to keep them a secret and have the teacher collect these for you. During the lesson, after the students have written their positive message strips and placed them in their boxes, distribute the messages the parents sent in. If a student's parents do not send in any, ask the teacher or another staff member who knows the child well to write some messages for distribution during this time.
- Encourage the students to write "Ah-ha" messages to other students in the class. Teachers may even take a special time each week for writing "Ah-ha" messages. Encourage teachers to write messages for students to place in their boxes all through the year.
- Have students make "I can's" from empty soup cans that they decorate with pictures of eyes. The students fill their "I" cans with things they can do well that is written/drawn on pieces of paper.

JOURNAL ENTRY

Write a letter to yourself. Begin your letter "Dear Me." Tell yourself all the wonderful things you love about yourself. Tell yourself what to do the next time you feel "bugged."

 **Healthy Ways to De-Bug**

CLASSROOM GUIDANCE NEWS

Dear Parent,

Today in classroom guidance we discussed the relationship between our thoughts and our feelings. Our feelings are created by the thoughts we have about certain events. Students learned that the process is:

Thought → Feeling → Action

When we're feeling "bugged" about something, one way to handle it is to try to change our thoughts about the event that's giving us the "bug" feeling. Today students stored up some positive thoughts in their "Ah-ha" boxes. Each student decorated a box and wrote some positive messages about him/herself to place in the box. Students were encouraged to put more positive messages about themselves in the box frequently. They were instructed to open up the "Ah-ha" box and read the positive messages whenever they feel "bugged."

You may like to do a similar activity at home. Make a box for each family member and have other family members write positive things about each person to place in the individual boxes. Add to them often. For example, when your child cleans his/her room without being asked, you might write "You are responsible" and place it in his/her box.

When your child is feeling "bugged" talk with him/her about what is making him/her feel that way. Help your child try to change his/her thoughts about the event in an effort to help change the feelings.

As always, please feel free to call me with any questions or concerns that you may have about your child, your child's school experience, or our elementary guidance and counseling program.

Sincerely,

Ah-Ha Message Strips

I can _____

_____.

Ah-Ha Message Strips

_____loves me no matter what I do.

Ah-Ha Message Strips

I am good at _____

_____.

De-Bug Review

GRADE LEVEL(S): 1-3

DESCRIPTION:
This lesson is designed to be used if you have done the previous lessons on De-Bugging. Students create a De-Bug Book that is a cumulative review of the many ways that they have learned to get rid of "bug" feelings.

OBJECTIVE(S):
Students will identify healthy ways to deal with unpleasant feelings.

ESTIMATED TIME: 30 minutes

MATERIAL(S) NEEDED:
A copy of "A Dozen Ways to De-Bug" for each student beginning on page 103. Reproduce the pages front/back as they are in the order given. For example, pages 103 and 104 should be reproduced front and back and placed on the bottom of the stack for folding.

PROCEDURES:
1. Share the following rap song about De-Bugging (of course you will need the appropriate attire—shades and a cap).

DE-BUG RAP

I used to get bugged
all scared, mad, and sad,
nervous and worried;
I was feeling pretty bad.

I held it all inside
or I let it just explode.
Those old bugs
were a very heavy load.

Then I learned some rules
about ways to de-bug
without getting into trouble
or becoming a thug.

Being mad or sad's OK
but hurting is not.
Gotta get it out
keeping it inside makes you rot!

So now I ride my bike
or I write a mad story.
Or I talk to a friend
whenever I worry.

I use de-bug sentence
it begins with "I feel."
Saying it lets others know
my feelings are real.

Sometimes I need time
just to cool off.
I say my ABCs backwards
That's pretty tough.

There are hundreds of ways
to de-bug, my friend.
I could keep on going,
but this is the end.

2. Explain to the students that they have learned a lot about de-bugging too. Today they will make a book called ***A Dozen Great Ways to De-Bug.*** Show the book and distribute one to each student. Instruct the students to draw and/or write a different "de-bugging" idea on each page. They may refer to the ABCs of De-Bugging Poster if there is one in their class.

3. Allow a little time for the students to share some of their ways they included in their book.

SUMMARY POSTER OR VISUAL REMINDER:
The ABCs of De-Bugging (sample found on page 83)

VARIATIONS/MODIFICATIONS/EXTENSIONS:
• You may choose to have a puppet sing the De-Bug Rap.
• Hold a "De-Bug" party where students can share their books with other classes and/or staff members.
• Place the "De-Bug" books in the media center for a week for other students and staff members to read.

JOURNAL ENTRY

 Write a story about someone who got "bugged" and then "de-bugged."

CLASSROOM GUIDANCE NEWS

Dear Parent,

Today in classroom guidance students wrote a book entitled "A Dozen Great Ways to De-Bug." Contained in the book are ideas that your child has about ways that he/she can feel better when they feel "bugged." Please be sure that you ask your child to see his/her book.

It is very important for your child to have many ideas about how to appropriately deal with unpleasant feelings. You may choose to post a list in your home of ways to deal with these feelings. When you do something to deal with a feeling, tell your child about it. For example you may say, "Today at work I got very angry with a co-worker because she didn't finish something on time. I was so mad, I needed some time to cool off. So I went outside and walked around our building three times. Exercising and the fresh air made me feel better. When I went back inside, I said to my co-worker, 'I feel frustrated because those schedules are due to my boss in two hours. Would you please work on them and have them to me by that time?'"

Remember, children tend to model behaviors they see exhibited most often in the significant people in their lives. When your child sees and hears about you dealing with your "bugs" appropriately, it makes a great impact on him/her.

Please feel free to call me with questions or concerns that you may have about your child, your child's school experience, or our elementary guidance and counseling program.

Sincerely,

A Dozen Great Ways to De-Bug

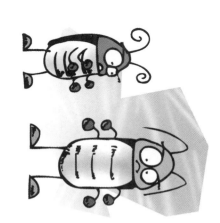

Written and Illustrated

By

De-Bug Number 12

12

De-Bug Number II

Feeling

mad

sad

worried

scared

or
nervous

can really "bug" you.

When you feel "bugged" it's important
to do something about it so that you feel
better. Here are a dozen (that's 12)
GREAT ways to "de-bug."
Don't believe me? Try them!

De-Bug Number 10

De-Bug Number 1

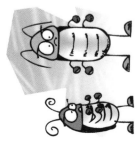

De-Bug Number 9

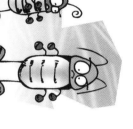

De-Bug Number 2

De-Bug Number 8

8

De-Bug Number 3

De-Bug Number 7

De-Bug Number 4

De-Bug Number 6

6

De-Bug Number 5

Bully Bugs

GRADE LEVEL(S): 1-3

DESCRIPTION:
This lesson helps students understand how to recognize a bully as well as how to deal with a bully. It uses the analogy of bugs by explaining to students that some bugs just annoy us, but other bugs can really hurt us if we do not do something about them.

OBJECTIVE(S):
• Students will define a bully.
• Studenst will identify three types of bullies.
• Students will explain how to deal with a bully.
• Students will describe how they feel when around a bully.

ESTIMATED TIME: 30 minutes

MATERIAL(S) NEEDED:
• Clip at least three pictures of children from a magazine. Be sure you get girls and boys. All of the children should look pleasant and kind.

PROCEDURES:
1. Ask the students to think of different kinds of bugs. Write some of their ideas on the board. Say this to students: *Some bugs, like a fly or a beetle, may just annoy us. Just like some feelings annoy us. However, other bugs can really hurt us. A black widow spider or a bumblebee, for example. We might call these bugs "Bully Bugs."*
2. Ask the students to tell what they think of when they hear the word "bully." Ask them to picture a bully in their minds. Then have them describe the person they pictured. Ask if the person was a male or female (students overwhelmingly choose a male culprit.)
3. Show the pictures of people you clipped from the magazines and ask if they are bullies. Explain that you can't always tell by looking at someone if they are a bully or not. Tell the students that all of the people you showed them are bullies. Bullies may even be someone you think of as a friend.
4. Give the definition of bullying: when someone unfairly hurts you over and over again. Discuss the difference in one-time teasing and bullying emphasizing the "over and over again."
5. Explain that there are three kinds of bullying. Show one of the pictures and explain that this person is a "muscle bully." Muscle bullies use their bodies to hurt others. Allow the children to give examples of things muscle bullies do.
6. Show another picture and explain that this person is a "mouth bully." Mouth bullies use words to hurt people. Allow the students to give examples.
7. Show the third picture and explain that this person is a "friend snatcher bully." Friend snatch-

ers hurt relationships with other people by doing things like starting rumors, controlling, gossiping, etc. Explain each to the students.

8. Ask the students how bullies make you feel. Explain that bullies can give you "bug" feelings. Bullies especially make you feel scared, worried, or nervous.

9. There is only one way to handle a bully: TELL. Discuss the difference in tattling and telling. Tattling is telling something just to get someone in trouble or just to get your own way or to make you look good and the other person look bad. Telling is talking to someone about a problem because you or someone else may be or have been hurt.

10. Write the words tattling and telling on the board. Read these examples and have the students stand beside the word that describes whether the examples are tattling or telling. Ask students to also identify if the behavior is bullying and to give a reason for their answer.

- Mandy was waiting in line in the cafeteria. Sandra was behind her in the line. As the line moved forward, Sandra tripped on her shoelace and bumped into Mandy. Mandy slipped on some chocolate milk that someone had spilled on the floor and landed "kerplunk!" on her bottom. Mandy was embarrassed. She pointed her finger at Sandra and yelled at Mrs. Epting, the lunchroom monitor, "That girl pushed me down on purpose!" Sandra was sent to the principal's office.

- Every day on the playground Bert went to play on the slide. Every day Bert saw a big girl holding a little girl down under the slide and heard her calling the little girl names. The little girl tried to stay away from the slide, but whenever she walked by the big girl would grab her or follow her and call her names. Bert decided to tell his teacher about what the big girl was doing.

- Donna ran to hide in the bathroom. She was crying. Her class went to art, but Donna stayed behind. A little while later, her teacher heard noises in the bathroom. She knocked on the door and Donna opened it. The teacher noticed that Donna had been crying. She asked Donna what was wrong and Donna made up something about not feeling well. The teacher asked her if there was something else. Donna thought for a while and then said, "It's Robert. Every day he's been taking my lunch money and then saying that he'll beat me up if I don't give it to him or if I tell."

- The class was working on a special writing project. Jeremy looked over and saw Bridget and Elsa passing notes. "Mrs. Yao," he screamed. "Bridget and Elsa are passing notes!"

11. If your school has a no-bully policy, discuss the school consequences of bullying. You may choose to discuss what happens to bullies in society and how laws protect people against bullying.

SUMMARY POSTER OR VISUAL REMINDER:
No Bully summary poster found on page 115

VARIATIONS/MODIFICATIONS/EXTENSIONS:

• Have the students make No-Bully posters to put around the school.
• Hold a Bully Education seminar for staff and/or parents. Have the students write about how bullies make them feel and share some of these writings at the seminar.

JOURNAL ENTRY

Write a story about someone who was bullied and how he/she handled the situation.

CLASSROOM GUIDANCE NEWS

Dear Parent,

Today in classroom guidance we discussed dealing with a bully. We used the analogy of bugs to describe bullies. Some bugs just annoy us like flies and beetles. Other bugs, like bumblebees or black widow spiders, can really hurt us. We called those "bully bugs" to help students understand bullies.

The definition of bullying that students learned is this: when someone unfairly hurts you over and over. Bullying can take three forms. Students learned about these three types of bullies:

Muscle bullies: Use their bodies to hurt you

Mouth bullies: Use their words to hurt you

Friend snatcher bullies: Hurt your friendships with others

Students learned that there is only one appropriate way to deal with a bully and that is to TELL. We discussed the difference in tattling and telling. Tattling is talking to someone just to get someone else in trouble or to get your own way. Telling is talking to someone about a problem because you or someone else may be hurt.

Listen to your child if he/she is reporting bullying to you. Resist the temptation to tell your child to "just ignore" the bully or to ask, "Well, what did you do to them first?"

When your child reports something to you, it is important that you encourage him/her to tell the appropriate authority. If bullying occurs in a school situation, the school can only deal with it if we are aware of it.

As always, please feel free to call me with any questions or concerns that you may have about your child, your child's school experience, or our elementary guidance and counseling program.

In partnership,

Bully Bugs

NO BULLIES!

Bullying: when someone unfairly hurts you over and over.

Bullies may be:
Muscle Bullies
Mouth Bullies
Friend Snatcher Bullies

To deal with a Bully — TELL.

Peer Relations

Animal Friends

GRADE LEVEL(S): K-3

DESCRIPTION:
This lesson uses various animals to describe desirable and undesirable personality traits. These traits are compared to the traits that are desirable in a friend.

OBJECTIVE(S):
- Students will recognize the relationship between their behavior and forming friendships.
- Students will explore the consequences of their actions.

ESTIMATED TIME: 30 minutes

MATERIAL(S) NEEDED:
Animal puppets, stuffed animals, or animal picture cards (see pages 121-123) of the following:
- Monkey
- Shark
- Snake
- Turtle
- Lamb or sheep
- Teddy bear

PROCEDURES:
1. Explain to the students that the way they behave can affect the way others feel about them. Tell them that you are going to use animals to help them understand this concept today.
2. Show the monkey. Explain that monkeys are silly all the time. Monkeys do not know that there are times to be silly and times to be serious. Explain that people who act like monkeys do the same thing—they are silly all the time. They never take things seriously. While they may be funny, they can sometimes get on your nerves. Ask the students if they think they would like a "monkey friend?"
3. Repeat with the other animals using these analogies:
    - **Shark:** Sharks are on the attack. They bite and hurt. "Shark friends" don't care about your feelings. They will say or do anything without thinking about if it hurts you or not.
    - **Snake:** Some snakes are good, some are not. You never know if they are good snakes or bad snakes. You can't trust a snake. "Snake friends" can't be trusted either. They may like you one day and hate you the next. They may tell your secrets or make fun of your secrets.
    - **Turtle:** Turtles stay inside their shells, especially when they are scared. They may be nice, but we can't tell much about them because they are usually in their shells. "Turtle friends" keep to themselves. They may be shy, but they will not join in games. They like being by themselves.

Animal Friends

- **Lamb:** Lambs follow one another—that's why shepherds tend to the flocks. They really do not think for themselves; they do what the other lambs and sheep do. "Lamb friends" may seem nice because they do what you want to do, but they never have their own ideas. They just follow along with anyone who comes along.
- **Teddy bear:** While a teddy bear is not a real animal, a teddy bear is there for you whenever you need it. It listens and comforts.
4. Explain to the students that if they want to have good friends, they must first be a good friend. Challenge the students to be a "teddy bear friend" for a week and see what happens.

SUMMARY POSTER OR VISUAL REMINDER:
What Kind of a Friend Are You summary poster on page 124

VARIATIONS/MODIFICATIONS/EXTENSIONS:
- Have the students think of other animals that display traits of a good friend.
- Have the students list or draw pictures of things a "teddy bear friend" might do that are friendly.
- Have the students choose one "teddy bear friend" thing to do and write a plan for doing it.

JOURNAL ENTRY

Think about your week and write or draw about how you have been a good "teddy bear friend" during the week.

 **Animal Friends**

CLASSROOM GUIDANCE NEWS

Dear Parent,

Today in guidance students learned about the relationship between their actions and their friendships. Using animals, we discussed desirable and undesirable personality traits—traits that make friends and traits that drive friends away. Some of the undesirable traits students discovered are overly silly (monkey), aggressive (shark), untrustworthy (snake), lack of confidence (turtle), and continually following (lamb.) The desirable traits of a friend include being there when you need them and listening (teddy bear.)

Your child is at an age when he/she needs much guidance in understanding how his/her actions affect others. Watch as your child plays with another child. Compliment the actions that you see that are desirable. Assist your child in understanding why some behaviors are undesirable and how they may drive a friend away.

As always, please feel free to call me with questions or concerns that you may have about your child, your child's school experience, or our elementary guidance and counseling program.

Sincerely,

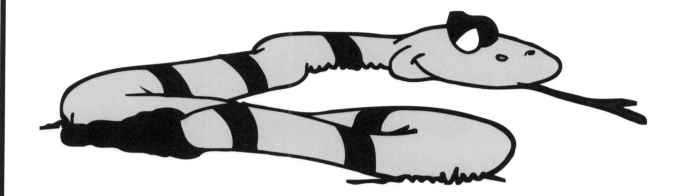

Animal Friends

"What Kind of a Friend are You?"

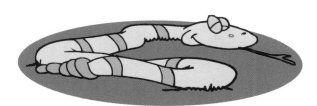

Attractors and Repellors

GRADE LEVEL(S): 2-5

DESCRIPTION:
This lesson compares the properties of a magnet to personal behavior. Students are actively involved as they play Attractor and Repellor Tic-Tac-Toe.

OBJECTIVE(S):
• Students will explore the consequences of actions of self and others.
• Students will develop an awareness of the importance of personal responsibility.
• Students will recognize the relationship between personal behavior and forming friendships.

ESTIMATED TIME: 30-45 minutes

MATERIAL(S) NEEDED:
• Set of strong magnets
• Chart Tablet
• Attractor and Repellor Tic-Tac-Toe card for each child found on pages 128-131 (laminate for longer use)
• At least five each of the + and – signs for each child found on page 133 (for easier distribution and collection, prior to class put one Tic-Tac-Toe card and 5 each of the + and – in a zip-top baggie for each child)
• Attractor and Repellor call cards found on page 132 (cut apart and place in a paper bag)

PROCEDURES:
1. Discuss how everyone makes a choice about their own behavior. Explain that as you teach, each child is choosing where he/she will look, if he/she will listen, etc.
2. Emphasize how personal behavior affects how other people see you and if they are going to want to be your friend.
3. Show magnets and demonstrate the two properties. First show the students how the magnets can attract and stick together. Explain that people's behavior is sometimes like that—there are things that people do that make others want to be around them. Then demonstrate how the magnets repel. Explain that sometimes a person's behavior is like that—it pushes people away and makes them not want to be around that person.
4. Divide the chart tablet into two sections vertically. On one side write the word "Attractors" and on the other write the word "Repellors." Have the students first name things that people do that attract other people. Be sure that the students are more specific than "Be nice." If general statements like this are offered, ask "What nice thing can someone do to make other people want to be around them?" Repeat with the "Repellors."
5. Distribute the Tic-Tac-Toe cards and + and – symbols. Explain that this game is played like Tic-Tac-Toe. The first person to get three +s or three –s in a row, calls out "Attractor Tic-Tac-

Toe" or "Repellor Tic-Tac-Toe." As you call out one of the actions on the cards, students look for that action on their card, and, if they have it, decide if it is an attractor behavior or a repellor behavior. Attractor behaviors are covered with +s because they add to friendships and repellor behaviors are covered with –s because they take away from friendships.

SUMMARY POSTER OR VISUAL REMINDER:

Leave the chart tablet page of attractor and repellor behaviors that were listed during the lesson.

VARIATIONS/MODIFICATIONS/EXTENSIONS:

* If possible, coordinate the timing of this lesson with the class science study of the property of magnets.
* Read aloud **The Very Angry Day that Amy Didn't Have** by Lawrence Shapiro. Discuss the attractor and repellor behaviors in the story and the consequences of these behaviors.

JOURNAL ENTRY

Think about your week and write about the "Attractor" behaviors you have shown to others to be a good friend.

CLASSROOM GUIDANCE NEWS

Dear Parents,

Today's lesson focused on the personal decisions that we each make about how we treat other people—our personal behavior. I used the analogy of a magnet and the properties it has. A magnet can either attract other magnets to it, or it can repel other magnets from it. People are the same way. The things that we do can either attract others to want to be around us, or they can push people away and make them not want to be around us. Therefore, it is very important to think about a behavior or action before doing it. In class, we made a list of "attractor behaviors" and "repellor behaviors" and played Attractor and Repellor Tic-Tac-Toe. Emphasis was placed upon the idea of treating others in the way that you would like to be treated.

While helping your child develop friendships, it is important to assist him/her in seeing how his/her behavior affects what others think of him/her. Catch your child when he/she does something desirable and be sure that your child knows how impressed you are with that behavior. When your child is having difficulty in a relationship with a peer, listen to the problem, reflect the feeling he/she is having, and have him/her come up with possible strategies to try to help with the relationship.

As always, please feel free to call me with any questions or concerns about your child, your child's school experience, or our elementary guidance and counseling program.

Sincerely,

ATTRACTOR AND REPELLOR TIC-TAC-TOE CARDS

Talks to you	**Tattles on you**	**Pushes you**
Teases you	**Hugs you**	**Cuts in front of you**
Says hello	**Laughs at you**	**Smiles at you**

Helps you	**Ignores you**	**Gives you a hug**
Plays with you	**Tells you a joke**	**Plays a joke on you**
Shares with you	**Makes fun of you**	**Says hello**

ATTRACTOR AND REPELLOR TIC-TAC-TOE CARDS

Listens to you	**Smiles at you**	**Cheers you up**
Hugs you	**Calls you a name**	**Plays with you**
Lets you borrow a pencil	**Makes a mean face**	**Tells a lie about you**

Asks you to play	**Leaves you out of a game**	**Teases you**
Tells you a secret	**Ignores you**	**Laughs at you**
Listens to you	**Interrupts you**	**Lies to you**

129

ATTRACTOR AND REPELLOR TIC-TAC-TOE CARDS

Helps you	**Talks to you**	**Cheers you up**
Gives you a hug	**Lies to you**	**Plays a joke on you**
Ignores you	**Asks you to play**	**Makes fun of you**

Tells you a joke	**Laughs at you**	**Smiles at you**
Leaves you out of a game	**Tattles on you**	**Says hello**
Teases you	**Listens to you**	**Shares with you**

ATTRACTOR AND REPELLOR TIC-TAC-TOE CARDS

Tells you a joke	**Teases you**	**Listens to you**
Laughs at you	**Gives you a hug**	**Asks you to play**
Says hello	**Plays a joke on you**	**Ignores you**

Says hello	**Asks you to play**	**Teases you**
Lets you borrow a pencil	**Smiles at you**	**Shares with you**
Plays a joke on you	**Lies to you**	**Ignores you**

ATTRACTOR AND REPELLOR CALL CARDS

DIRECTIONS FOR USE:

Cut the call cards apart. Put them in a bag or container. When playing the game, draw a card out, read the behavior, and have the students decide if it is an attractor or repellor behavior. If it is an attractor, students cover the behavior with a + symbol. If it is a repellor, students cover the behavior with a -.

Asks you to play	Makes a mean face
Calls you a name	Makes fun of you
Cheers you up	Plays a joke on you
Cuts in front of you	Plays with you
Gives you a hug	Pushes you
Helps you	Says hello
Hugs you	Shares with you
Ignores you	Smiles at you
Interrupts you	Talks to you
Laughs at you	Tattles on you
Leaves you out of a game	Teases you
Lets you borrow a pencil	Tells a lie on you
Lies to you	Tells you a joke
Listens to you	Tells you a secret

+ and – cards

+	+	+	–	–	–
+	+	+	–	–	–
+	+	+	–	–	–
+	+	+	–	–	–
+	+	+	–	–	–
+	+	+	–	–	–
+	+	+	–	–	–
+	+	+	–	–	–
+	+	+	–	–	–
+	+	+	–	–	–
+	+	+	–	–	–
+	+	+	–	–	–
+	+	+	–	–	–

Bandages for Friendships

GRADE LEVEL(S): K-1

DESCRIPTION:
This lesson uses the visual of a bandage to explain the importance of apologizing when you hurt someone's feelings. This lesson, used with the lessons beginning on pages 138, 144 and 152, provides strategies for conflict management.

OBJECTIVE(S):
• Students will demonstrate conflict management skills.
• Students will recognize the effect of their behavior on others.

ESTIMATED TIME: 20 minutes

MATERIAL(S) NEEDED:
• *Matthew and Tilly* by Rebecca Jones
• Bandage for each child
• Apology summary poster found on page 137

PROCEDURES:
1. Ask how many students have ever had a problem with a best friend. Allow the students to share these experiences.
2. Read aloud **Matthew and Tilly** by Rebecca Jones. Explain that this is a story about best friends who sometimes do not like each other very much.
3. Discuss how Matthew and Tilly worked out their problem—they apologized. Discuss the meaning of the word apologize—saying "I'm sorry" when you have done something to hurt someone's feelings.
4. Show the Apology summary poster. Discuss why there is a bandage on the card. Use a real bandage to help discuss how bandages don't make scrapes go away, but they do make them feel better. Compare this to saying the words "I'm sorry." The words do not make whatever happened go away, but they do make you and the other person feel better.
5. Give each child who would like one a band-aid to remind them to say "I'm sorry" when they do something to hurt someone else's feelings.

SUMMARY POSTER OR VISUAL REMINDER:
Apology summary poster found on page 137

VARIATIONS/MODIFICATIONS/EXTENSIONS:
• Ask the teacher to set up a special place in the room for you to place this poster as well as any other posters or materials you plan to leave in future lessons. Teachers may want to label this "The Problem Solving Corner" or some other creative name. Students should be encour-

aged to go to this special place when they are having conflicts with other students in the class.

• Have the students draw pictures of times when they have needed to apologize to someone.

JOURNAL ENTRY

At times we have problems getting along with our friends and sometimes we may say or do something that is not nice. When we do something wrong we need to apologize or say, "I'm sorry." Draw or write about a time when you said, "I'm sorry," and then draw or write about how you felt afterward.

CLASSROOM GUIDANCE NEWS

Dear Parent,

Today in classroom guidance we discussed the value of apologizing. Students heard a story entitled **Matthew and Tilly** by Rebecca Jones. This is a story of best friends who sometimes "get sick of each other." Matthew and Tilly learn that the words "I'm sorry" can heal their friendship.

Students shared times that they had their feelings hurt by a friend. I used a bandage to discuss the effect that the words "I'm sorry" have on hurt feelings. Just like a bandage does not make a cut or scrape go away completely, it does make the hurt a little better. The same is true with the words "I'm sorry." These words do not make a hurt or a mistake go away, but they do make you and the other person feel better.

Some children do not like to apologize. However, you should encourage your child to recognize his/her mistakes and take responsibility for his/her actions. Saying "I'm sorry" and then working to make a wrong better are ways to encourage such responsibility.

As always, please feel free to call me with questions or concerns that you may have about your child, your child's school experience, or our elementary guidance and counseling program.

Sincerely,

Bandages for Friendships

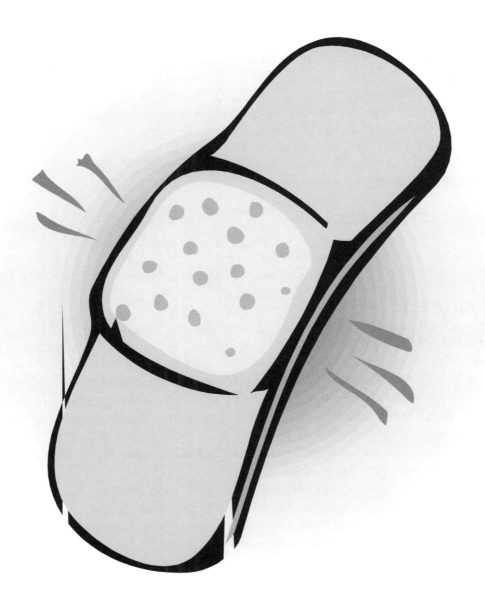

I'm sorry!

Heart Talk

GRADE LEVEL(S): K-2

DESCRIPTION:
This lesson in conflict management teaches children "heart talk" which is using "I" messages to help work out conflicts or problems that come up with their friends.

OBJECTIVE(S):
- Students will demonstrate conflict management skills.
- Students will identify and express feelings.
- Students will make "I feel" statements.

ESTIMATED TIME: 20 minutes

MATERIAL(S) NEEDED:
- Puppet
- Heart Talk summary poster found on page 143
- Heart Talk pillow with Heart Talk message attached (directions on page 142)

PROCEDURES:
1. Begin with a dialogue between you and your puppet:

   Puppet: (Looks around with an angry face.)

   Counselor: What's going on with you?

   Puppet: Well, the other day I was in the block center. I had built this wonderful block tower when along comes Henry running by and he knocked my tower flat that I was making. I got up and yelled at him about what he had done and then I pushed him down.

   Counselor: Sounds like you were really mad.

   Puppet: Yeah. But what really bothers me is that I was the one that got in trouble, not Henry. I guess being mad gets you in trouble.

   Counselor: Oh, (name of puppet) I would have felt mad too if my tower that I had worked so hard on had gotten messed up. I don't think feeling mad is what got you in trouble. I think it was your actions or what you chose to do when you were mad that got you in trouble.

   Puppet: Oh…well what could I have done?

   Counselor: Why don't we get some help from the students in our classroom as to what you could have done to handle your mad feelings so that you would not have gotten into trouble. (Turn to the students eliciting responses. Have the puppet agree with the appropriate responses repeating the answers.) (Name of puppet,) I came to visit the students today to share a special way to talk about our feelings. Would you like to listen? *(Puppet nods "yes". Place the puppet in a seat nearby, posed in a good listening position and encourage the puppet to be a good listener.)*

Heart Talk

2. Compliment the students for sharing such good ways for the puppet to handle his/her mad feelings. Share with them that the mad feeling is okay to have but that we need to find positive ways to handle mad feelings. Explain that today students are going to learn a new way to talk about how they feel and to tell someone how they feel. Tell them they will learn something they can do when they are angry, mad, furious, or sad that WON'T get them in trouble.

3. Ask the students to share things that have happened with friends, brothers/sisters, or classmates that have made them mad or sad.

4. Explain that when things like this happen, it is important to use "heart talk." Explain that heart talk means telling the person how you feel in your heart. Hold up the heart pillow and explain that the heart not only reminds us to tell the person how we feel inside, but also that we need to tell them in a caring way. Use this model for teaching students heart talk:

I feel _____ because_____.

Please _____.

5. Replay the puppet's problem using "heart talk." An example is, "I feel furious because you knocked down my tower. Please be more careful." Explain that the "Heart Talk" messages are especially helpful if someone may have done something by accident—it gives them a chance to explain.

6. Have the students role play using heart talk. Have them hold the pillow as they share the message. Also alert others that when someone comes to you holding the heart pillow and wanting to tell them something, they need to be good listeners. Some scenarios for role play may include:
   - Your friend says that the picture you drew is ugly.
   - Your sister takes your favorite book without asking.
   - Your classmate cuts in front of you in line.
   - Your friend calls you a mean name.
   - Your brother makes fun of your new shirt.

SUMMARY POSTER OR VISUAL REMINDER:

Heart Talk summary poster found on page 143

VARIATIONS/MODIFICATIONS/EXTENSIONS:

- If time or funds prohibit you from providing a heart pillow, omit showing the pillow and teach the lesson without the pillow. Use the summary poster in its place.
- Brainstorm as many feeling words as students can think of and make a chart of these words to help students form the appropriate "I feel.." statements.
- Encourage staff to use "I feel" statements when dealing with student conflicts. Role modeling this concept goes a long way toward making it a part of student's conflict management techniques.

Heart Talk

JOURNAL ENTRY

At times we have problems or conflicts with our friends. Sometimes a friend may say or do something that makes us feel sad or mad. When this happens, we can tell them in a nice way how we feel. We can use Heart Talk. Draw or write about a problem that you have had where you could have used Heart Talk to help you. Then write the Heart Talk message you could have used.

CLASSROOM GUIDANCE NEWS

Dear Parents,

Has your child ever gotten in trouble because he/she did not respond appropriately to angry or sad feelings? Have you yourself ever said or done something you later regretted when you were angry or sad?

Today's lesson was about "heart talk." Heart talk is using your words to tell another person how you feel. Also referred to as "I" messages, these statements help defuse conflicts and leave the door open for further communication. Heart Talk is a simple two-sentences:

I feel _____ **because** _____ .

Please _____ .

Each class was provided with an actual heart pillow with the above message printed on a heart card. This pillow helps the child to word the message correctly, to serve as a reminder to talk in a caring way, and also alerts the listener to listen to what is being asked of him/her. Our students will be practicing using Heart Talk in class over the next few weeks. Heart Talk may be used when someone cuts in front of a student in line, or when someone laughs at or teases another student. Heart Talk will not solve every conflict, but it provides a start for working out a problem.

Please model heart talk when dealing with your child. "I feel frustrated when you leave your toys on the floor. Please put them away," or "I feel sad when you call your brother names. Please use kind words" are examples of ways that you can use heart talk in your home. Being a role model for this conflict management technique is essential to your child doing the same.

Thanks for your continued support. As always, please feel free to call me with questions or concerns that you may have about your child, your child's school experience, or our elementary guidance and counseling program.

Sincerely,

 **Heart Talk**

Heart Talk Message and Heart Pattern for Pillow

Materials needed:
- Red fabric
- Sewing thread
- Batting for pillow
- Red card stock or construction paper
- Single hole punch
- 1" ring

Directions:
1. Cut, sew, and fill a heart shaped pillow using the heart pattern below.
2. Copy the HEART TALK message front and back on red card stock or construction paper from the summary poster.
3. On the reverse side of the paper heart, write "Heart Talk."
4. Single hole punch the top of the HEART TALK message.
5. Add ring through the hole punch on the HEART TALK message and then sew the ring to the corner of the pillow.

Heart Talk

HEART TALK

I feel _____

because _____ .

Please _____ .

It's Mine

GRADE LEVEL(S): K-2

DESCRIPTION:
This lesson in conflict management teaches students the value of sharing.

OBJECTIVE(S):
- Students will demonstrate conflict management skills.
- Students will identify the importance of sharing.

ESTIMATED TIME: 20 minutes

MATERIAL(S) NEEDED:
- *It's Mine* by Leo Lionni
- Pictures of Should or Should Not Share found on pages 147-150
- Share summary poster found on page 151

PROCEDURES:
1. Tell this story to the students: *I got a box of candy in the mail this week from my friend. It's my favorite candy—chocolates with peanut butter in the center. My husband/wife/friend came home and I showed him/her the box of candy. After supper I got the box of candy out and sat on the couch while we were watching TV and ate the chocolates. My husband/wife/friend got a funny look on his/her face and went into the other room to read. He/She has been acting quiet ever since. I'm really not sure what's wrong.*
2. Ask the students if they know what may be wrong and allow time for them to offer some ideas. If not mentioned, discuss that my husband/wife/friend probably wanted me to SHARE the candy. Say that you did not even think about that; you were not trying to be mean, you just like the candy so much that you forgot to ask him/her if he/she would like some.
3. Show the book *It's Mine* by Leo Lionni. Ask the students if there has ever been a time that they did not want to share with someone. Discuss.
4. Read the book and discuss.
5. Explain that it is important to share things that we can share. Have the students offer examples. However, there may be some things that are not safe to share. Have the students offer examples.
6. Show pictures of items that should or should not be shared (found on pages 147-150.) Categorize and discuss.

SUMMARY POSTER OR VISUAL REMINDER:
Share summary poster found on page 151

It's Mine

VARIATIONS/MODIFICATIONS/EXTENSIONS:

• Take something like cookies, stickers, or pencils to class and share them with the students. You may even choose to give 2 to some and none to others and allow the students to share with those who do not have any.

• Have the students draw pictures or list things that they have and are willing to share. Display the drawings or lists on a bulletin board with the title, "Sharing is Caring."

JOURNAL ENTRY

Write or draw about something that you shared with a friend.
Tell about how you felt after you shared.

 **It's Mine**

CLASSROOM GUIDANCE NEWS

Dear Parent,

Today in classroom guidance we discussed the conflict management technique of sharing. Students heard a story entitled *It's Mine* by Leo Lionni where they learned that sharing has many benefits. We discussed that sharing adds to friendships. We also discussed that, while we should share as often as possible, there are some things that we should not share such as toothbrushes, medicines, cups, etc.

Encourage your child to share as often as possible. If your child has siblings, I am certain that the subject of sharing is ever-present in your household. If your child is an only child, be sure that you watch as your child has friends over or as your child interacts with other children. Compliment him/her as you see sharing occur.

It is a pleasure teaching your child. As always, please feel free to call me with questions or concerns that you may have about your child, your child's school experience, or our elementary guidance and counseling program.

Sincerely,

SHOULD OR SHOULD NOT SHARE?

SHOULD OR SHOULD NOT SHARE?

SHOULD OR SHOULD NOT SHARE?

SHOULD OR SHOULD NOT SHARE?

It's Mine

Share

Work It Out!

GRADE LEVEL(S): K-1

DESCRIPTION:
This lesson continues the series on conflict management. It teaches students two skills: taking turns and chance—using "luck" games to help make small decisions.

OBJECTIVE(S):
• Students will demonstrate conflict management skills.
• Students will use taking turns and chance as conflict management skills.

ESTIMATED TIME: 20 minutes

MATERIAL(S) NEEDED:
• Puppet
• Chinese yo-yo
• Take Turns summary poster found on page 155
• Chance summary poster found on page 156

PROCEDURES:
1. Discuss the meaning of the word arguing.
2. Using the puppet, tell this story (you can use your own names):
   Chris's friend Rory, who is her soccer friend, came over to play inside games because of the weather. They both wanted to play on the computer but there's only one computer and only one person can play at a time, so they started arguing. No one got to play and Rory went home mad and Chris is mad too.
3. Have the students suggest how Chris and Rory could have worked out their problem. If not mentioned, show the Take Turns card. Explain why there is a see-saw on the card—a see-saw only works if you take turns going up and down. Show the Take Turns summary poster.
4. The puppet says that she knows the next problem—who goes first. Explain the Chance card. Chance means "luck." Games like "one potato, two potato," "eeney, meeney, miney, mo," or flipping a coin, paper rock scissors are luck games. Show the Chance summary poster.
5. Show the Chinese yo-yo and ask who would like to do it. Have the students think of how they can work out this problem—taking turns and then choosing a Chance way of deciding who goes first such as choosing names out of a basket, who has the next birthday, etc.
6. Students each get a turn with the Chinese yo-yo.

SUMMARY POSTER OR VISUAL REMINDER:
Take Turns and Chance summary posters on pages 155 & 156

It's Mine

VARIATIONS/MODIFICATIONS/EXTENSIONS:

- Have the students make a list of times during the week they took turns or could have taken turns.
- Have the students make a list or draw pictures of situations they could use "chance" to help them solve the problem.

JOURNAL ENTRY

Draw or write about a time that taking turns or using chance to decide who goes first could have help you and a friend work out a conflict.

It's Mine

CLASSROOM GUIDANCE NEWS

Dear Parent,

Today in classroom guidance we discussed two conflict management techniques—taking turns and chance. Chance means letting luck make a decision. Flipping a coin, Paper/Rock/Scissors, and "one potato, two potato" are examples of chance.

As children play together, conflicts are bound to occur. That's why teaching simple conflict management techniques is so important. The goal is to make students independent in working out little conflicts like who goes first or taking turns.

As you watch your child play with friends, notice what happens when they disagree. Compliment your child later about ways that he/she handled a conflict or instruct them later about how they could have worked out a conflict.

As always, please feel free to call me with questions or concerns that you have about your child, your child's school experience, or our elementary guidance and counseling program.

Sincerely,

Take Turns

Chance

Great Manners Bingo

LEVELS: Grades 2-4

DESCRIPTION:
Good manners are an important part of relating to others. This lesson provides a fun way to introduce and review good manners.

OBJECTIVES:
- Students will be aware of the importance of using good manners.
- Students will be exposed to a variety of good manners.

ESTIMATED TIME: 30-45 minutes

MATERIALS NEEDED:
- Great Manners Bingo cards – 1 per student (see pages 160-180)
- Copy of the calling cards – cut apart (see pages 181 & 182)
- Small squares of paper, beans, etc. to cover spaces on the Bingo cards
- Stickers or small prizes if you choose

PROCEDURES:
1. Compliment the students as they are settling for the lesson. Point out to the class several good manners you saw students using such as: looking at you to let you know they are ready, sitting quietly ready to begin the lesson, or perhaps someone used a polite word when speaking or helped someone clear their desk. Share with the students that today we are going to be talking about good manners.
2. Ask: "What does it mean to have good manners?" Elicit such responses as: being nice to others, polite, respectful, etc.
4. Ask: "Where should you use good manners?" The students may perhaps begin to name many different places. End with the statement that manners are important everywhere.
4. Ask: "When should you use good manners?" Come to the conclusion that manners are important all the time.
5. Ask: "Why should you use good manners?" Elicit such responses as to be nice to others, to get along with others, so others will like you and think/know you are nice, and because it's the right thing to do!
6. Ask: "Since it seems to be a pretty good thing to have, how do we get good manners?" Students may share such responses as from parents, teachers, from watching others, or perhaps learning the hard way from mistakes.
7. Tell the students that they are going to play a bingo game to help them think about good manners. Share with them that many of the manners in the game they may already know about and use, some may be manners they know about but have forgotten to use, and there may be one or two manners that are new to them. Tell the students that if they come across a man-

ner they have not heard before, remember it so that it can be decussed after the game.

8. Distribute the game cards and pieces to cover the spaces. Explain the rules of the game that when a manner is called out that is on their card they are to cover the space. Use the cut apart calling card saying the letter, number, and reading the manner. Use this time to discuss the manner having the students briefly share. They have bingo when they have straight in a row down, across or diagonally. They may call out "Great Manners" when they have bingo. Explain that in this game all are winners if they learned something new or are reminded about doing something right. You may choose to hand out stickers or something small if they have bingo.

9. As you play several games, use the calling cards that have not been called yet so that all the manners can be discussed. After several games have been played, ask the students to share something new they may have learned or something they plan to start doing that they have not been.

SUMMARY POSTER OR VISUAL REMINDER:

"You Are A Winner With Great Manners" summary poster on page 183

VARIATIONS/MODIFICATION/EXTENTIONS:

Ask the students to be on the lookout for their classmates using good manners. When they see a good manner have them say to the classmate "Bingo!" At the end of the day or week talk with the class about the good manners they may have seen.

JOURNAL ENTRY

 Choose a good manner that you feel is important.
Tell about the manner and why it is important.

Great Manners Bingo

CLASSROOM GUIDANCE NEWS

Dear Parents,

Today in classroom guidance we focused on manners. Manners are important because they affect our social relationships with others—our teachers, friends, and parents. Good manners can affect how we get along with others, which can affect how we feel about ourselves, which can also affect how well we do in school with the effort we put forth. Good manners involve being polite in what we say and do.

In classroom guidance we discussed the following questions regarding good manners:

WHAT? being polite in what we say and do
WHERE? everywhere
WHEN? all the time
WHY? it's the right thing to do and it effects our relationships with others

In class we played the game Great Manners Bingo in which we discussed a variety of manners from "wait until others get off an elevator before you get on" to "do not interrupt while others are talking." It's important for us to encourage our children to keep their good manners on the tip of their brain so that they may be using them. Please continue to encourage your child to be using his/her good manners. With school and home working together we'll encourage them to be doing their best.

Thank you for your continued support. As always, please feel free to contact me if you have questions or concerns about your child, your child's school experience, or our elementary guidance and counseling program.

Sincerely,

G R E A T

6 Do not interrupt someone while they are talking on the phone	**20** Reply "Yes" when answering a question, instead of "Yeh"	**27** Wash your hands before you eat	**37** When meeting grown-ups, shake their hand & say, "It's nice to meet you."	**40** Don't try to talk while you are chewing food
4 Be quiet during the movie	**19** Wait for others to get off the elevator before you get on	**21** Take pride but do not brag when you achieve something special	**36** Give compliments when they are deserved	**45** Do not gossip or talk about other people in a bad way
1 Cover your mouth when you cough or sneeze	**15** Be a good sport about losing a game	**FREE**	**33** Do not open other people's mail	**44** Do not tattle on others
3 Be quiet in the library	**12** Be careful with a borrowed toy	**26** Cut your food into proper bite sized pieces	**29** Always put your trash in the trash can	**41** Greet your guests as they come to your party
9 Hold a door open to help someone	**18** Thank your host or hostess before leaving the party	**25** Pay attention to your teacher	**35** Never use bad language	**42** Use the manner words "Please" & "Thank You"

M A N N E R S

Great Manners Bingo

G R E A T

7 Place your napkin in your lap while eating at the table	**12** Be careful with a borrowed toy	**21** Take pride but do not brag when you achieve something special	**34** Apologize when you are in the wrong	**39** When friends visit you, let them choose what to play
9 Hold a door open to help someone	**11** Ask to be excused before leaving the meal table	**28** Wait patiently for your turn	**30** If you make a mess, clean it up	**42** Use the manner words "Please" & "Thank You"
5 Pick up your toys after you have finished playing with them	**14** Say you are sorry if you call a wrong number	**FREE**	**38** Thank your friend for having you visit	**47** If you do bump into anyone, always say, "I'm sorry."
2 Chew food with your mouth closed	**17** Ask permission before borrowing something	**22** Help as much as possible when a family member is sick	**32** Move to your side of the sidewalk when someone approaches	**48** Chew gum with your mouth closed
8 Do not put your elbows on the table while eating	**16** Return something borrowed in good condition	**23** Talk about only nice things at the dinner table	**29** Always put your trash in the trash can	**46** While shopping, show respect for others— no shouting, no running around

M A N N E R S

Great Manners Bingo

G R E A T

3 Be quiet in the library	**20** Reply "Yes" when answering a question, instead of "Yeh"	**26** Cut your food into proper bite sized pieces	**37** When meeting grown-ups, shake their hand and say, "It's nice to meet you."	**48** Chew gum with your mouth closed
1 Cover your mouth when you cough or sneeze	**13** Wait until everyone is present at a meal before beginning to eat	**25** Pay attention to your teacher	**36** Give compliments when they are deserved	**40** Don't try to talk while chewing food
5 Pick up your toys after you have finished playing with them	**19** Wait for others to get off the elevator before you get on	**FREE**	**33** Do not open other people's mail	**41** Greet your guests as they come to your party
10 Help clear the table after eating	**17** Ask permission before borrowing something	**23** Talk about only nice things at the dinner table	**38** Thank your friend for having you visit	**42** Use the manner words "Please" & "Thank You"
2 Chew food with your mouth closed	**18** Thank your host or hostess before leaving the party	**27** Wash your hands before you eat	**35** Never use bad language	**46** While shopping, show respect for others— no shouting, no running around

M A N N E R S

162

Great Manners Bingo

G R E A T

7	17	24	29	41
Place your napkin in your lap while eating at the table	Ask permission before borrowing something	Be on time	Always put your trash in the trash can	Greet your guests as they come to your party
6 Do not interrupt someone while they are talking on the phone	**14** Say you are sorry if you call a wrong number	**23** Talk about only nice things at the dinner table	**37** When meeting grown-ups, shake their hand and say, "It's nice to meet you."	**39** When friends visit you, let them choose what to play
3 Be quiet in the library	**16** Return something borrowed in good condition	**FREE**	**34** Apologize when you are in the wrong	**40** Don't try to talk while you are chewing food
8 Do not put your elbows on the table while eating	**12** Be careful with a borrowed toy	**22** Help as much as possible when a family member is sick	**32** Move to your side of the sidewalk when someone approaches	**46** While shopping, show respect for others - no shouting, no running around
2 Chew food with your mouth closed	**11** Ask to be excused before leaving the meal table	**21** Take pride but do not brag when you achieve something special	**31** Listen to you parents with respect	**48** Chew gum with your mouth closed

M A N N E R S

Great Manners Bingo

G R E A T

9 Hold a door open to help someone	11 Ask to be excused before leaving the meal table	26 Cut your food into proper bite sized bites	30 If you make a mess, clean it up	43 When someone sends you a gift, write a thank you note
10 Help clear the table after eating	13 Wait until every-one is present at a meal before beginning to eat	28 Wait patiently for your turn	36 Give compliments when they are deserved	42 Use the manner words "Please" & "Thank You"
1 Cover your mouth when you cough or sneeze	19 Wait for others to get off the elevator before you get on	**FREE**	34 Apologize when you are in the wrong	45 Do not gossip or talk about other people in a bad way
3 Be quiet in the library	15 Be a good sport about losing a game	27 Wash your hands before you eat	35 Never use bad language	47 If you do bump into anyone, always say, "I'm sorry."
4 Be quiet during the movie	20 Reply "Yes" when answering a question, instead of "Yeh"	22 Help as much as possible when a family member is sick	38 Thank your friend for having you visit	39 When friends visit you, let them choose what to play

M A N N E R S

164

© YouthLight, Inc. (Handout)

G R E A T

7 Place your napkin in your lap while eating at the table	15 Be a good sport about losing a game	21 Take pride but do not brag when you achieve something special	35 Never use bad language	42 Use the manner words "Please" & "Thank You"
8 Do not put your elbows on the table while eating	14 Say you are sorry if you call a wrong number	28 Wait patiently for your turn	38 Thank your friend for having you visit	47 If you do bump into anyone, always say "I'm sorry."
2 Chew food with your mouth closed	12 Be careful with a borrowed toy	**FREE**	31 Listen to your parents with respect	41 Greet your guests as they come to your party
9 Hold a door open to help someone	17 Ask permission before borrowing something	26 Cut your food into proper bite sized pieces	32 Move to your side of the sidewalk when someone approaches	39 When friends visit you, let them choose what to play
6 Do not interrupt someone while they are talking on the phone	20 Reply "Yes" when answering a question, instead of "Yeh"	27 Wash your hands before you eat	33 Do not open other people's mail	43 When someone sends you a gift, write a thank you note

M A N N E R S

Great Manners Bingo

G R E A T

5 Pick up your toys after you have finished playing with them	**19** Wait for others to get off the elevator before you get on	**22** Help as much as possible when a family member is sick	**37** When meeting grown-ups, shake their hand and say, "It's nice to meet you."	**45** Do not gossip or talk about other people in a bad way
3 Be quiet in the library	**18** Thank your host or hostess before leaving the party	**25** Pay attention to your teacher	**29** Always put your trash in the trash can	**48** Chew gum with your mouth closed
1 Cover your mouth when you cough or sneeze	**14** Say you are sorry if you call a wrong number	**FREE**	**36** Give compliments when they are deserved	**40** Don't try to talk while you are chewing food
4 Be quiet during the movie	**11** Ask to be excused before leaving the meal table	**24** Be on time	**30** If you make a mess, clean it up	**39** When friends visit you, let them choose what to play
10 Help clear the table after eating	**13** Wait until everyone is present at a meal before beginning to eat	**23** Talk about only nice things at the dinner table	**34** Apologize when you are in the wrong	**44** Do not tattle on others

MANNERS

166

**Great Manners Bingo**

G R E A T

10 Help clear the table after eating	**13** Wait until everyone is present at a meal before beginning to eat	**28** Wait patiently for your turn	**31** Listen to your parents with respect	**43** When someone sends you a gift, write a thank you note
4 Be quiet during the movie	**18** Thank your host or hostess before leaving the party	**24** Be on time	**32** Move to your side of the sidewalk when someone approaches	**39** When friends visit you, let them choose what to play
5 Pick up your toys after you have finished playing with them	**16** Return something borrowed in good condition	**FREE**	**33** Do not open other people's mail	**44** Do not tattle on others
2 Chew food with your mouth closed	**12** Be careful with a borrowed toy	**21** Take pride but do not brag when you achieve something special	**29** Always put your trash in the trash can	**46** While shopping, show respect for others- no shouting, no running around
3 Be quiet in the library	**20** Reply "Yes" when answering a question, instead of "Yeh"	**22** Help as much as possible when a family member is sick	**37** When meeting grown-ups, shake their hand and say, "It's nice to meet you."	**47** If you do bump into anyone, always say, "I'm sorry."

M A N N E R S

G R E A T

7	15	27	30	41
Place your napkin in your lap while eating at the table	Be a good sport about losing a game	Wash your hands before you eat	If you make a mess, clean it up	Greet your guests as they come to your party
5	**16**	**21**	**31**	**40**
Pick up your toys after you have finished playing with them	Return something borrowed in good condition	Take pride but do not brag when you have achieved something special	Listen to your parents with respect	Don't try to talk while you are chewing food
9	**19**	FREE	**35**	**45**
Hold a door open to help someone	Wait for others to get off the elevator before you get on		Never use bad language	Do not gossip or talk about other people in a bad way
2	**20**	**28**	**33**	**46**
Chew food with your mouth closed	Reply "Yes" when answering a question, instead of "Yeh"	Wait patiently for your turn	Do not open other people's mail	While shopping, show respect for others- no shouting, no running around
10	**13**	**22**	**29**	**39**
Help clear the table after eating	Wait until everyone is present at a meal before beginning to eat	Help as much as possible when a family member is sick	Always put your trash in the trash can	When friends visit you, let them choose what to play

M A N N E R S

Great Manners Bingo

G R E A T

7 Place your napkin in your lap while eating at the table	**12** Be careful with a borrowed toy	**27** Wash your hands before you eat	**30** If you make a mess, clean it up	**48** Chew gum with your mouth closed
8 Do not put your elbows on the table while eating	**11** Ask to be excused before leaving the meal table	**22** Help as much as possible when a family member is sick	**29** Always put your trash in the trash can	**45** Do not gossip or talk about other people in a bad way
3 Be quiet in the library	**19** Wait for others to get off the elevator before you get on	**FREE**	**38** Thank your friend for having you visit	**43** When someone sends you a gift, write a thank you note
10 Help clear the table after eating	**15** Be a good sport about losing a game	**28** Wait patiently for your turn	**37** When meeting grown-ups, shake their hand and say, "It's nice to meet you."	**47** If you do bump into anyone, always say, "I'm sorry."
9 Hold a door open to help someone	**20** Reply "Yes" when answering a question, instead of "Yeh"	**21** Take pride but do not brag when you achieve something special	**36** Give compliments when they are deserved	**46** While shopping, show respect for others- no shouting, no running around

M A N N E R S

169

G R E A T

8 Do not put your elbows on the table while eating	**11** Ask to be excused before leaving the meal table	**25** Pay attention to your teacher	**29** Always put your trash in the trash can	**48** Chew gum with your mouth closed
6 Do not interrupt someone while they are talking on the phone	**14** Say you are sorry if you call a wrong number	**21** Take pride but do not brag when you achieve something special	**32** Move to your side of the sidewalk when someone approaches	**39** When friends visit you, let them choose what to play
2 Chew food with your mouth closed	**13** Wait until everyone is present at a meal before beginning to eat	**FREE**	**36** Give compliments when they are deserved	**42** Use the manner words "Please" & "Thank You"
1 Cover your mouth when you cough or sneeze	**17** Ask permission before borrowing something	**28** Wait patiently for your turn	**38** Thank your friend for having you visit	**44** Do not tattle on others
4 Be quiet during the movie	**18** Thank your host or hostess before leaving the party	**24** Be on time	**34** Apologize when you are in the wrong	**43** When someone sends you a gift, write a thank you note

M A N N E R S

Great Manners Bingo

G R E A T

5	20	23	38	43
Pick up your toys after you have finished playing with them	Reply "Yes" when answering a question, instead of "Yeh"	Talk about only nice things at the dinner table	Thank your friend for having you visit	When someone sends you a gift, write a thank you note
8	**18**	**24**	**36**	**41**
Do not put your elbows on the table while eating	Thank your host or hostess before leaving the party	Be on time	Give compliments when they are deserved	Greet your guests as they come to your party
10	**19**		**33**	**45**
Help clear the table after eating	Wait for others to get off the elevator before you get on	**FREE**	Do not open other people's mail	Do not gossip or talk about other people in a bad way
9	**17**	**26**	**35**	**48**
Hold a door open to help someone	Ask permission before borrowing something	Cut your food into proper bite sized pieces	Never use bad language	Chew gum with your mouth closed
6	**14**	**27**	**29**	**47**
Do not interrupt someone while they are talking on the phone	Say you are sorry if you call a wrong number	Wash your hands before you eat	Always put your trash in the trash can	If you do bump into anyone, always say, "I'm sorry."

M A N N E R S

G R E A T

6	13	24	36	40
Do not interrupt someone while they are talking on the phone	Wait until everyone is present at a meal before beginning to eat	Be on time	Give compliments when they are deserved	Don't try to talk while you are chewing food
3 Be quiet in the library	**15** Be a good sport about losing a game	**27** Wash your hands before you eat	**29** Always put your trash in the trash can	**39** When friends visit you, let them choose what to play
2 Chew food with your mouth closed	**12** Be careful with a borrowed toy	**FREE**	**31** Listen to your parents with respect	**44** Do not tattle on others
1 Cover your mouth when you cough or sneeze	**16** Return something borrowed in good condition	**23** Talk only about nice things at the dinner table	**30** If you make a mess, clean it up	**43** When someone sends you a gift, write a thank you note
10 Help clear the table after eating	**17** Ask permission before borrowing something	**22** Help as much as possible when a family member is sick	**35** Never use bad language	**41** Greet your guests as they come to your party

M A N N E R S

G R E A T

4 Be quiet during the movie	**11** Ask to be excused before leaving the table	**28** Wait patiently for your turn	**32** Move to your side of the sidewalk when someone approaches	**45** Do not gossip or talk about other people in a bad way
8 Do not put your elbows on the table while eating	**18** Thank your host or hostess before leaving the party	**26** Cut your food into proper bite sized pieces	**33** Do not open other people's mail	**46** While shopping, show respect for others- no shouting, no running around
9 Hold a door open to help someone	**19** Wait for others to get off the elevator before you get on	**FREE**	**36** Give compliments when they are deserved	**47** If you do bump into anyone, always say, "I'm sorry."
5 Pick up your toys after you have finished playing with them	**14** Say you are sorry if you call a wrong number	**23** Talk about only nice things at the dinner table	**38** Thank your friend for having you visit	**48** Chew gum with your mouth closed
7 Place your napkin in your lap while eating at the table	**12** Be careful with a borrowed toy	**25** Pay attention to your teacher	**37** When meeting grown-ups, shake their hand and say, "It's nice to meet you."	**39** When friends visit you, let them choose what to play

M A N N E R S

G R E A T

4 Be quiet during the movie	11 Ask to be excused before leaving the table	23 Talk about only nice things at the dinner table	30 If you make a mess, clean it up	48 Chew gum with your mouth closed
1 Cover your mouth when you cough or sneeze	15 Be a good sport about losing a game	25 Pay attention to your teacher	34 Apologize when you are in the wrong	46 While shopping, show respect for others- No shouting, no running around
7 Place your napkin in your lap while eating at the table	12 Be careful with a borrowed toy	FREE	32 Move to your side of the sidewalk when someone approaches	44 Do not tattle on others
2 Chew your food with your mouth closed	13 Wait until everyone is present at a meal before beginning to eat	22 Help as much as possible when a family member is sick	31 Listen to your parents with respect	39 When friends visit you, let them choose what to play
10 Help clear the table after eating	19 Wait for others to get off the elevator before you get on	28 Wait patiently for your turn	37 When meeting grown-ups, shake their hand and say, "It's nice to meet you."	42 Use the manner words "Please" & "Thank You"

M A N N E R S

Great Manners Bingo

G R E A T

1 Cover your mouth when you cough or sneeze	**16** Return something borrowed in good condition	**22** Help as much as possible when a family member is sick	**35** Never use bad language	**44** Do not tattle on others
6 Do not interrupt someone while they are talking on the phone	**14** Say you are sorry if you call a wrong number	**26** Cut your food into proper bite sized pieces	**30** If you make a mess, clean it up	**43** When someone sends you a gift, write a thank you note
5 Pick up your toys after you have finished playing with them	**17** Ask permission before borrowing something	**FREE**	**33** Do not open other people's mail	**39** When friends visit you, let them choose what to play
7 Place your napkin in your lap while eating at the table	**12** Be careful with a borrowed toy	**25** Pay attention to your teacher	**34** Apologize when you are in the wrong	**48** Chew gum with your mouth closed
4 Be quiet during the movie	**15** Be a good sport about losing a game	**23** Talk about only nice things at the dinner table	**32** Move to your side of the sidewalk when someone approaches	**47** If you do bump into anyone, always say, "I'm sorry."

M A N N E R S

G R E A T

3 Be quiet in the library	**11** Ask to be excused before leaving the meal table	**22** Help as much as possible when a family member is sick	**37** When meeting grown-ups, shake their hand and say, "It's nice to meet you."	**46** While shopping, show respect for others- no shouting, no running around
6 Do not interrupt someone while they are talking on the phone	**13** Wait until every-one is present at a meal before beginning to eat	**24** Be on time	**38** Thank your friend for having you visit	**45** Do not gossip or talk about other people in a bad way
9 Hold a door open to help someone	**20** Reply "Yes" when answering a ques-tion, instead of "Yeh"	**FREE**	**36** Give compliments when they are deserved	**40** Don't try to talk while you are chewing food
8 Do not put your elbows on the table while eating	**18** Thank your host or hostess before leaving the party	**26** Cut your food into proper bite sized pieces	**31** Listen to your parents with respect	**42** Use the manner words "Please" & "Thank You"
10 Help clear the table after eating	**19** Wait for others to get off the ele-vator before you get on	**21** Take pride but do not brag when you achieve something special	**29** Always put your trash in the trash can	**41** Greet your guests as they come to your party

M A N N E R S

G R E A T

3	12	24	31	46
Be quiet in the library	Be careful with a borrowed toy	Be on time	Listen to your parents with respect	While shopping, show respect for others- no shouting, no running around
8 Do not put your elbows on the table while eating	**13** Wait until everyone is present at a meal before beginning to eat	**22** Help as much as possible when a family member is sick	**33** Do not open other people's mail	**47** If you do bump into anyone, always say, "I'm sorry."
10 Help clear the table after eating	**14** Say you are sorry if you call a wrong number	**FREE**	**29** Always put your trash in the trash can	**40** Don't try to talk while you are chewing food
2 Chew food with your mouth closed	**11** Ask to be excused before leaving the meal table	**26** Cut your food into proper bite sized pieces	**38** Thank your friend for having you visit	**45** Do not gossip or talk about other people in a bad way
9 Hold a door open to help someone	**20** Reply "Yes" when answering a question, instead of "Yeh"	**25** Pay attention to your teacher	**34** Apologize when you are in the wrong	**39** When friends visit you, let them choose what to play

M A N N E R S

G R E A T

5 Pick up your toys after you have finished playing with them	**13** Wait until everyone is present at a meal before beginning to eat	**27** Wash your hands before you eat	**31** Listen to your parents with respect	**44** Do not tattle on others
3 Be quiet in the library	**16** Return something borrowed in good condition	**21** Take pride but do not brag when you achieve something special	**29** Always put your trash in the trash can	**40** Don't try to talk while you are chewing food
10 Help clear the table after eating	**20** Reply "Yes" when answering a question, instead of "Yeh"	**FREE**	**34** Apologize when you are in the wrong	**42** Use the manner words "Please" & "Thank You"
2 Chew food with your mouth closed	**12** Be careful with a borrowed toy	**24** Be on time	**38** Thank your friend for having you visit	**43** When someone sends you a gift, write a thank you note
1 Cover your mouth when you cough or sneeze	**17** Ask permission before borrowing something	**22** Help as much as possible when a family member is sick	**30** If you make a mess, clean it up	**47** If you do bump into anyone, always say, "I'm sorry."

MANNERS

G R E A T

7	15	23	32	48
Place your napkin in your lap while eating at the table	Be a good sport about losing a game	Talk about only nice things at the dinner table	Move to your side of the sidewalk when someone approaches	Chew gum with your mouth closed
2 Chew food with your mouth closed	**17** Ask permission before borrowing something	**21** Take pride but do not brag when you achieve something special	**36** Give compliments when they are deserved	**41** Greet your guests as they come to your party
4 Be quiet during the movie	**19** Wait for others to get off the elevator before you get on	**FREE**	**37** When meeting grown-ups, shake their hand and say, "It's nice to meet you."	**40** Don't try to talk while you are chewing food
6 Do not interrupt someone while they are talking on the phone	**16** Return something borrowed in good condition	**25** Pay attention to your teacher	**35** Never use bad language	**44** Do not tattle on others
5 Pick up your toys after you have finished playing with them	**18** Thank your host or hostess before leaving the party	**28** Wait patiently for your turn	**29** Always put your trash in the trash can	**42** Use the manner words "Please" & "Thank You"

M A N N E R S

G R E A T

4 Be quiet during the movie	**17** Ask permission before borrowing something	**26** Cut your food into proper bite sized pieces	**30** If you make a mess, clean it up	**43** When someone sends you a gift, write a thank you note
8 Do not put your elbows on the table while eating	**18** Thank your host or hostess before leaving the party	**23** Talk about only nice things at the dinner table	**29** Always put your trash in the trash can	**45** Do not gossip or talk about other people in a bad way
6 Do not interrupt someone while they are talking on the phone	**19** Wait for others to get off the elevator before you get on	**FREE**	**33** Do not open other people's mail	**46** While shopping, show respect for others- no shouting, no running around
3 Be quiet in the library	**12** Be careful with a borrowed toy	**21** Take pride but do not brag when you achieve something special	**38** Thank your friend for having you visit	**47** If you do bump into anyone, always say, "I'm sorry."
1 Cover your mouth when you cough or sneeze	**20** Reply "Yes" when answering a question, instead of "Yeh"	**25** Pay attention to your teacher	**37** When meeting grown-ups, shake their hand and say, "It's nice to meet you."	**48** Chew gum with your mouth closed

M A N N E R S

Bingo Calling Cards

G-1 Cover your mouth when you cough or sneeze	**R-11** Ask to be excused before leaving the meal table	**E-21** Take pride but do not brag when you achieve something special	**A-29** Always put your trash in the trash can
T-39 When friends visit you, let them choose what to play	**G-2** Chew food with your mouth closed	**R-12** Be careful with a borrowed toy	**E-22** Help as much a possible when a family member is sick
A-30 If you make a mess, clean it up	**T-40** Don't try to talk while you are chewing food	**G-3** Be quiet in the library	**R-13** Wait until everyone is present at a meal before beginning to eat
E-23 Talk about only nice things at the dinner table	**A-31** Listen to your parents with respect	**T-41** Greet your guest as they come to your party	**G-4** Be quiet during the movie
R-14 Say you are sorry if you call a wrong number	**E-24** Be on time	**A-32** Move to your side of the sidewalk when someone approaches	**T-42** Use the manner words "Please" and "Thank you"
G-5 Pick up your toys after you have finished playing with them	**R-15** Be a good sport about losing a game	**E-25** Pay attention to your teacher	**A-33** Do not open other people's mail

T-43 When someone sends you a gift, write a thank you note	**G-6** Do not interrupt someone while they are talking on the phone	**R-16** Return something borrowed in good condition	**E-26** Cut your food into proper bite sized pieces
A-34 Apologize when you are in the wrong	**T-44** Do not tattle on others	**G-7** Place your napkin in your lap while eating at the table	**R-17** Ask permission before borrowing something
E-27 Wash your hands before you eat	**A-35** Never use bad language	**T-45** Do not gossip or talk about other people in a bad way	**G-8** Do not put your elbows on the table while eating
R-18 Thank your host or hostess before leaving the party	**E-28** Wait patiently for your turn	**A-36** Give compliments when they are deserved	**T-46** While shopping, show respect for others – no shouting, no running around
G-9 Hold a door open to help someone	**R-19** Wait for others to get off the elevator before you get on	**A-37** When meeting grown-ups, shake their hand and say, "It's nice to meet you."	**T-47** If you do bump into anyone, always say, "I'm sorry"
G-10 Help clear the table after eating	**R-20** Reply "Yes" when answering a question, instead of "Yeh"	**A-38** Thank your friend for having you visit	**T-48** Chew gum with your mouth closed

Great Manners Bingo

You are a winner with…

6 Do not interrupt someone while they are talking on the phone	20 Reply "Yes" when answering a question, instead of "Yeh"	27 Wash your hands before you eat	37 When meeting grown-ups, shake their hand & say, "It's nice to meet you."	40 Don't try to talk while you are chewing food
4 Be quiet during the movie	19 Wait for others to get off the elevator before you get on	21 Take pride but do not brag when you achieve something special	36 Give compliments when they are deserved	45 Do not gossip or talk about other people in a bad way
1 Cover your mouth when you cough or sneeze	15 Be a good sport about losing a game	**FREE**	33 Do not open other people's mail	44 Do not tattle on others
3 Be quiet in the library	12 Be careful with a borrowed toy	26 Cut your food into proper bite sized pieces	29 Always put your trash in the trash can	41 Greet your guests as they come to your party
9 Hold a door open to help someone	18 Thank your host or hostess before leaving the party	25 Pay attention to your teacher	35 Never use bad language	42 Use the manner words "Please" & "Thank You"

GREAT MANNERS

How Far Would You Go?

GRADE LEVEL(S): 2-4

DESCRIPTION:
This lesson introduces the concept of peer pressure. Students are able to assess how strong their own assertiveness skills are.

OBJECTIVE(S):
- Students will discuss times they have wanted to fit in.
- Students will recognize that their feelings tell them when something is right or wrong.

ESTIMATED TIME: 30 minutes

MATERIAL(S) NEEDED:
- Small stick on dots
- *A Bad Case of Stripes* by David Shannon
- How Far Would You Go to Fit In activity sheet found on page 187

PROCEDURES:
1. Enter the class with colored dots stuck all over your face. The students will begin to inquire about the stickers immediately. Explain that you did this because some of your friends did it but that you feel a little ridiculous.
2. Lead a discussion about things that students have done just because their friends did them.
3. Read *A Bad Case of Stripes.* Discuss how Camilla wanted to "fit in."
4. Explain that your feelings tell you if something is right or wrong. It is important to listen to your feelings when deciding whether or not to go along with your friends.
4. Have the students complete the "How Far Would You Go To Fit In?" activity sheet. Discuss. Emphasize that when you feel uncomfortable doing something, that is probably a sign that it's not a good choice for you and that real friends will like you anyway.

SUMMARY POSTER OR VISUAL REMINDER:
Listen to your Feelings summary poster found on page 188

VARIATIONS/MODIFICATIONS/EXTENSIONS:
- Have the students role play trying to convince a friend to go along with a bad decision and have that friend role play saying "no."
- Have the students draw a body outline of themselves. On the inside of the body shape, have the students write things that are special, different, and unique about themselves.

How Far Would You Go?

JOURNAL ENTRY

Friendships are important. It's fun to play with and spend time with our friends, but we also need to think for ourselves and make good decisions when playing with others. Write about what you may say if a friend suggested that you do something that you feel is wrong for you.

CLASSROOM GUIDANCE NEWS

Dear Parent,

Today's guidance lesson focused on the desire to fit in. A sense of belonging is very important to children. Each child wants to feel that s/he is a part of some social group. Today students heard a story about a young girl who goes to extreme measures to fit in. In *A Bad Case of Stripes,* Camilla Bean tries to hide her real self just to be like others in her class and peer group. Camilla learns, however, that while it is important to have friends, she doesn't have to give up the things she likes in order to fit in. Following a discussion of this story, students completed the "How Far Would You Go To Fit In?" rating scale.

I encourage you to talk to your child about his/her answers. While you don't want to scold him/her for any of the honest answers given, you may want to create other "what if" scenarios to stimulate more conversation about this topic. Give some real-life examples of how you've had to go against the crowd before. Discuss how true friends like you even if you make a choice not to be exactly like them.

The influence of friends is a powerful force in almost everyone's life. Children face this pressure from the first time they play with other children. Although the words "fitting in" may conjure up negative images in your mind, your child's friends can also be very positive influences in the life of your child. By staying involved in your child's life and keeping the lines of communication open, you can more readily alert him/her to pitfalls, teach and discipline, and help him/her solve problems independently.

As always, please feel free to call me with questions or concerns that you may have about your child, your child's school experience, or our elementary guidance and counseling program.

Sincerely,

How Far Would You Go To Fit In?

If your friend did not know the answers on a test, would you tell your friend the answers to help him or her out?

| I would | I probably would | Maybe | I probably would not | I would not |

If all the other kids you were playing with went into the woods, and your parents had a rule that you should not go into the woods, would you go anyway?

| I would | I probably would | Maybe | I probably would not | I would not |

Your feelings tell you when something is right or wrong. Listen to your feelings.

Cooperation

GRADE LEVEL(S): 1-3

DESCRIPTION:
This lesson not only emphasizes the importance of cooperation but also gives students an opportunity to practice cooperating.

OBJECTIVE(S):
- Students will define cooperation.
- Students will recognize the importance of cooperation.
- Students will cooperate with others in a group.

ESTIMATED TIME: 30 minutes

MATERIAL(S) NEEDED:
- Cards with the letters c-o-o-p-e-r-a-t-i-o-n written on the front and small numbers 1-11 on the back
- Set of sequence cards for each group (found on page 192)
- Set of cooperation shapes for each group (found on pages 193-196)

PROCEDURES:
1. Using the cards with the letters in the word "cooperation," choose 11 children to come to the front of the room and instruct them to form a word using all the letters. Do not tell them what the word is. Let chaos break out and then have them look on the back and arrange themselves left to right by number. Have the class read the word cooperation.
2. Explain that cooperation means working with other people. When you cooperate, everyone has an equal part and takes responsibility for what is being done. Ask the students to recall and share times when they have cooperated.
3. Divide the students into groups of three. Give each group an envelope containing the sequence cards. Each student gets two pieces and cannot touch anyone else's piece. There is to be no verbal communication. Time groups to see how long it takes them to cooperate and get their story arranged.
4. Do the same with cooperation shapes. Each group member gets one shape piece. Again students cannot touch anyone else's piece and there can be no verbal communication. Have the students work together to get their shape put together.
5. Ask the students what it was like completing the assignment. Discuss how cooperating can be beneficial.

SUMMARY POSTER OR VISUAL REMINDER:
Cooperation summary poster found on page 197

Cooperation

VARIATIONS/MODIFICATIONS/EXTENSIONS:
• Read aloud *Swimmy* by Leo Lionni. Discuss how working together can have benefits that working alone cannot.
• Encourage teachers to put students in groups often to give them practice in cooperating.

JOURNAL ENTRY

Cooperation means working well with other people. When people are cooperating each person takes responsibility and shares the work. Write about all the different activities in which you are involved where cooperation is important. Write a plan of how you can cooperate more in these activities.

Cooperation

CLASSROOM GUIDANCE NEWS

Dear Parent,

Today in classroom guidance we discussed cooperation. Cooperation was defined for students as "working with other people." Students worked in groups to complete a picture story and to put together a puzzle.

Cooperation is not an easy skill for students to learn. Some students tend to take charge and be the leader leaving others to feel left out. Others may tend to sit back and let the group do all the work. A cooperative group involves each member having equal responsibility and work. You can practice helping your child learn to cooperate by doing family activities that involve the entire family such as washing a car, painting or cooking. While you are involved in the activity, be sure that you notice when your child is acting in a cooperative manner. If your child is having difficulty cooperating, explore possibilities with him/her that may make cooperating easier.

As always, please feel free to call me with questions or concerns that you may have about your child, your child's school experience, or our elementary guidance and counseling program.

Sincerely,

Sequence Cards

Cooperation

Cooperation Shapes

1. Cut out each shape.
2. Cut each shape into three pieces.
3. Place the three pieces into an envelope.

Cooperation Shapes

1. Cut out each shape.
2. Cut each shape into three pieces.
3. Place the three pieces into an envelope.

Cooperation Shapes

1. Cut out each shape.
2. Cut each shape into three pieces.
3. Place the three pieces into an envelope.

Cooperation

Cooperation Shapes

1. Cut out each shape.
2. Cut each shape into three pieces.
3. Place the three pieces into an envelope.

When we work together, everyone wins!

M&M® Belief

GRADE LEVEL(S): K-2

DESCRIPTION:
Just like M&M®s, students learn that the best part of a person is what is inside.

OBJECTIVE(S):
• Students will identify what is most important about a person.
• Students will appreciate individual differences.

ESTIMATED TIME: 30 minutes

MATERIAL(S) NEEDED:
• One beautifully wrapped and decorated box (wrap only the lid of the box so that you can just take the lid off rather than unwrap the whole box) containing something undesirable such as an old shoe, a dust rag, or trash
• One crinkled, dirty paper sack containing a bag of M&M® candy.
• M&M® Belief activity sheet found on page 201

PROCEDURES:
1. Show the students both the box and the bag. Ask the students to pretend that it is their birthday and that they can choose the present they want. Allow each student to tell which he/she would choose and why.
2. Process how and why most students picked the box. Open the box first and listen to the comments. Remind students that most chose this because the outside was pretty. Ask how they feel about the present now. Most will be disappointed. Explain that people are like this. Sometimes people may look very nice on the outside—nice clothes, pretty—but on the inside, they are not quite as nice.
3. Open the bag and listen to the comments. Ask how students feel about the bag now. Explain that people are like this…they may not be so nice looking, but on the inside they can be wonderful!
4. Explain to the students that they are like M & M®s. Ask the students what they want when they eat M&M® candies—they want the chocolate. The color really does not matter. Demonstrate that the color does not matter. Ask a student to come to the front of the room. Blindfold the student and then ask them to reach into the bag of M&M®s, take one, hold it up for the class to see, then eat it. Then ask the student what color the candy was. They will not be able to tell! Repeat with a few other students.
5. Introduce the M&M® Belief—***The Best Part of People is on the INSIDE!*** Explain that when choosing friends, students should not pay attention to the way the person looks, but choose friends because of what they are like inside—the way they act, the way they treat others.
6. Allow the students to color the M & M® Belief sheet.

 **M&M® Belief**

SUMMARY POSTER OR VISUAL REMINDER:
Leave a copy of the M&M® Belief activitysheet

VARIATIONS/MODIFICATIONS/EXTENSIONS:
- Have the students think of other sayings they have heard that express the same concept as the M&M® Belief—"You can't judge a book by its cover," or "Beauty is only skin deep."
- Read aloud a story that makes the point about physical appearance versus inner beauty such as **Beauty and the Beast** or **The Ugly Duckling.**

JOURNAL ENTRY

 Choosing friends means really getting to know the person on the inside. Think about your good qualities and write or draw what you have to offer to others in being a good friend.

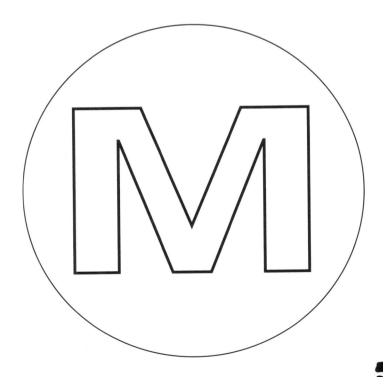

CLASSROOM GUIDANCE NEWS

Dear Parents,

Today's guidance lesson focused on choosing friends. Students were taught the "M&M® Belief"—the best part of a person is on the inside! We've all heard the saying, "You shouldn't judge a book by its cover." This adage was brought to life today with a demonstration of two presents—one beautifully wrapped and decorated that contained an old shoe, the other a wrinkled brown bag that contained M&M® candies. Children were asked which present they would choose based on the looks of the outside. Most chose the beautiful box, but quickly learned that the wrappings had nothing to do with what was inside the box.

People are the same. Often young children will choose friends based on appearances. It takes time to get to know someone on the inside, but as the M&M® Belief reminds us, that's where the really good "stuff" is.

You can help reinforce this concept with your child by pointing out all the positive things about him/her that cannot be seen by merely looking. Place emphasis on the things that are special about your child over which he/she has some control such as favorite activities and things he/she does well. Your modeling this for your child will go a long way in your child doing this for himself/herself as well as friends.

As always, please feel free to call me with questions or concerns that you have about your child, your child's school experience, or our elementary guidance and counseling program.

Sincerely,

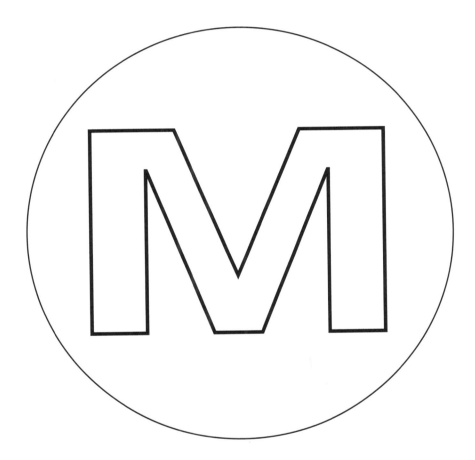

The M&M—Belief...

The best part of people is on the INSIDE!

An Odd Dot

GRADE LEVEL(S): 2-5

DESCRIPTION:
This lesson provides students experience in what it feels like to be left out. It calls upon students to "put themselves in someone else's shoes."

OBJECTIVE(S):
• Students will describe how it feels to be left out.
• Students will understand empathy.

ESTIMATED TIME: 30 minutes

MATERIAL(S) NEEDED:
• Cards with various colored dots on them—there should be four groups of colors and 3 cards that have dots that do not match any of the other colors (example 4 blues, 4 reds, 4 yellows, 4 greens, 1 purple, 1 orange, 1 pink)
• When "I Felt Lonely" activity sheet found on page 205

PROCEDURES:
1. Explain to the students that being able to think about how someone else is feeling is very important if you want to have friends. Describe being able to feel what someone else is feeling by using the example of watching a movie where you have cried or felt really bad for someone. For older students introduce the word "empathy."

2. Explain to the students that they are going to play a game that breaks them into groups. Give each student a card with a colored dot on it. Choose carefully the students you give the "odd" dots (you would not want to choose a child who is already consistently left out by peers.) Be sure that all three odd dots have been distributed. Instruct students to keep their dot covered until you give further directions.

3. Tell the students that when you say "go" they are to find their group—the people with the same colored dot as they have. Students must do this **without talking.** They can show their card and use body language, but they cannot talk. Instruct the students that they are to let no one into their group that has a different colored dot than they have. Give the signal to begin. Watch carefully the body language in this game so that you can use specific examples when you discuss.

4. Stop the game when the four distinct groups have formed. There will be three students with no group. Ask these students how they felt when they discovered there was no group for them. Ask the students in the groups how they felt when they found their group and how they **think** they would feel if they were left out. Explain that if they can understand how it would feel, even if it didn't happen to them, they will be better able to make good friends.

5. Explain that at one time or another we may all do what was done in the game—break off into

groups. Explain that this is not a bad thing unless we exclude someone who wants to be a part just because they are not like us.

6. Have the students complete the top of the When I Felt Lonely activity sheet by writing about a time when they felt left out.

7. Allow for any who wish to share.

8. Brainstorm things that students want others to do when they are feeling left out. Explain that this is how they should treat others. Have the students complete the bottom part of the When I Felt Lonely worksheet.

SUMMARY POSTER OR VISUAL REMINDER:

Everyone Likes To Be Included summary poster found on page 206

VARIATIONS/MODIFICATIONS/EXTENSIONS:

• For older students you can use made up names for the groups instead of colors—the Swips, the Burgs, the Midds, etc.

• Have the class form a welcoming team whose responsibility it is to be sure that new students feel welcome in their class. Have the class think of a list of duties and responsibilities of the welcoming team.

JOURNAL ENTRY

Including others is important.
Write about three things you can do to be a good friend
and include others.

CLASSROOM GUIDANCE NEWS

Dear Parent,

Today's lesson focused on feeling left out and empathy. Empathy is the ability to put oneself in someone else's place and to think about how s/he is feeling. The ability to empathize with others is the quality that is most essential in developing relationships with others. People who are able to empathize will most likely consider how their actions are going to affect others and may choose their actions and words more carefully.

Students played a game that facilitated feeling left out and understanding other people's feelings. Students then wrote about a time that they felt left out and about things they wanted others to do to make them not feel left out.

It's important to acknowledge your child's feelings when s/he feels excluded, but to not try to "fix" everything. When your child shares a hurtful experience, show empathy by reflecting the feeling your child has. You may say something like, "That must have made you feel very sad." This leaves the conversation open for your child to share more and establishes a framework for communicating effectively with your child.

As always, please feel free to call me with questions or concerns that you may have about your child, your child's school experience, or our district's elementary guidance and counseling program.

Sincerely,

An Odd Dot

When I Felt Lonely

I felt lonely when _____

_____

_____

_____

_____

_____

_____

What I want others to do when I feel lonely

1._____

2._____

3._____

Everyone likes to be included.
Reach out to someone who is lonely.

Personal Pan Pizza

GRADE LEVEL(S): 2-4

DESCRIPTION:
This lesson helps students understand about a reputation. Students learn that they are making their reputations by the repeated choices they make about their personal behavior.

OBJECTIVE(S):
- Students will explore the consequences of actions of self and others.
- Students will develop an awareness of the importance of personal responsibility.
- Students will explain how a reputation is developed.

ESTIMATED TIME: 30 minutes

MATERIAL(S) NEEDED:
- A stuffed wolf, wolf puppet, wolf toy, or picture or a wolf—the more menacing-looking, the better
- Reputation pictures and stories on pages 210-217
- Personal Pan Pizza activity sheet on page 218 & 219

PROCEDURES:
1. Show the wolf puppet or picture and ask children to name words that come to their minds when they see or hear about a wolf. Write these on the board. Most likely the words, "big, bad wolf" will be mentioned. Ask the students why they think of the wolf in this way. Inquire about stories that they have read or heard about the wolf being "big, bad."
2. Introduce the word "reputation." Explain that a reputation is what other people think of you. A reputation can be good or bad. Your reputation depends on the actions you choose ***over and over again.***
3. Show the reputation pictures on pages 210-217 and tell the students about each child. Discuss how each got his/her reputation. Each time explain that the reputation was formed by the things the student did "over and over again." Sort these into good and bad reputations.
4. Explain to the students that they get to choose the kind of reputation they have by the way they choose to behave. If they want to have a good reputation, they need to make good choices about their behavior.
5. Make the analogy that forming a reputation is like making a pizza—you can choose what you like and don't like; what you want and don't want. Have students complete a "Personal Pan Pizza" activity sheet on pages 218 & 219 choosing qualities that they would like others to see in them.

Personal Pan Pizza

SUMMARY POSTER OR VISUAL REMINDER:
Choose the Kind of Reputation You Want summary poster on page 220

VARIATIONS/MODIFICATIONS/EXTENSIONS:
- Have the students write "recipes" for a good reputation.
- Read aloud **The Teacher from the Black Lagoon** by Mike Thaler. Discuss how gossip and rumors can be unfair to a person's reputation.

JOURNAL ENTRY

A reputation is what people think of you and is formed from the way you act or behave over and over. Describe the kind of person you would like people to think you are. Write the kinds of behaviors you would need to choose over and over.

CLASSROOM GUIDANCE NEWS

Dear Parents,

Your child had classroom guidance today and we discussed the word "reputation." Today's lesson focused on how reputations are developed and the direct relationship between personal behavior and reputation. When an individual forms certain patterns of behavior, others come to think of him/her in a certain way. Therefore, it is very important to choose behavior carefully. I brought in a wolf puppet and used him to demonstrate how a reputation can "stick" to a person. The children readily identified the wolf as mean, scary, and "big, bad." We discussed that this opinion of the wolf is his reputation and that he earned that from stories like *The Three Little Pigs, Little Red Riding Hood, and The Boy Who Cried Wolf.*

I then asked students how they would like others to think of them, and we thought of decisions and personal behaviors that they could choose that would help them develop this reputation. Your child made a "Personal Pan Pizza" of qualities which he/she would like his/her reputation to consist.

As a parent, you can help your child feel good about his/her reputation by using words that ascribe a positive reputation to him/her. For example, when you see your child doing something without being asked you can say, "You are responsible," or when your child tells you that he/she played with a friend who had no one else to play with, you may say, "You're loyal." Even if a child doesn't know the full meaning of a word, he/she may begin to see himself/herself in a more positive way.

It is a pleasure to work with your child. As always, please feel free to call me with questions or concerns that you may have about your child, your child's school experience, or our elementary guidance and counseling program.

Sincerely,

REPUTATION PICTURES

Pushy Pete:

Pete always has to have his way—or else. When the class lines up, Pete always cuts in front of others. At recess, Pete will call you names or hit or push you if you don't play by his rules. He always shouts out answers in class instead of waiting to be called on. Pete thinks that no one is as smart or fast or funny as he.

REPUTATION PICTURES

Tattling Tammy:

Tattling Tammy can hardly wait to tell on you! When you forget your homework, she's the first one to tell the teacher. When you cut in front of someone in line, she's there to tell. It's always something, "Johnny's looking out the window," or "Tonya's on the wrong page." Tammy pays so much attention to what people are doing wrong, that she doesn't have time to see what people are doing right.

211

REPUTATION PICTURES

Bonnie Bad Sport:

Bonnie likes games—IF she wins. If she doesn't, watch out. Bonnie calls names, kicks sand, turns game boards over, and stomps away if she loses. She'll even say, "You cheated" when you didn't just to make herself feel better. Bonnie's starting to wonder why no one ever wants to play games with her. Do you know why?

REPUTATION PICTURES

Goofy Gordon:

Gordon wants to be funny. He likes making people laugh. But Gordon will do practically anything for a laugh. One day he drew a picture of the principal with horns and showed it to the class when the teacher wasn't looking. One day he stuck straws up his nose during silent reading time and made walrus sounds. Watch out! You could be Gordon's next joke; he may draw an ugly picture of you or make up a mean story about you just to get a laugh!

REPUTATION PICTURES

Helpful Holly:

Holly is someone you can always count on. If you forget your homework assignment, you can call Holly and she'll be glad to give it to you. If you need to borrow a pencil, Holly usually has an extra and will be glad to let you borrow one. When someone gets hurt on the playground, Holly offers to walk him/her to the nurse's office. If you're a new student, Holly will be sure that you know your way around the school.

REPUTATION PICTURES

Cooperative Clyde:

Clyde is a great person to have on a team. He knows the real meaning of teamwork. Clyde listens to other people's ideas and then helps the group agree on what's best for the group. If you are playing with Clyde and suggest a game, Clyde will usually go along with your suggestion (as long as it's safe.) In class, Clyde does what the teacher asks when the teacher asks him.

REPUTATION PICTURES

Listening Louie:

When you've got a problem and need a friend, Louie's there for you. Louie really knows how to listen. When you talk to him, he looks at you. He doesn't interrupt your story to tell his own story. He says things to you like, "That sounds interesting," or "I bet you felt really sad when that happened." The more Louie listens, the more you feel like talking to him. Louie doesn't ever seem to be in a hurry when he's listening.

REPUTATION PICTURES

Generous Georgia:

If Georgia has something that she can share, she will. She's the person people go to when they need to borrow a pencil, some glue, a red crayon, or any of the other many things kids often forget. Not only does Georgia share her things, she shares her time also. Georgia volunteers at a nearby nursing home two days a week. She plays checkers with the people there, reads books to those who can no longer see to read, and just sits and talks with people who are lonely.

PERSONAL PAN PIZZA

Directions:

1. Look at the personal pan pizza toppings.
2. Choose the qualities you want others to think about you.
3. Cut those out and paste on the pizza.

PERSONAL PAN PIZZA TOPPINGS

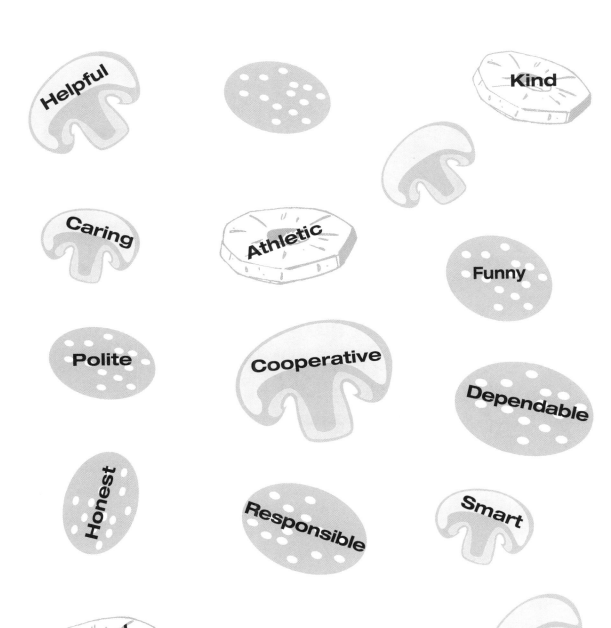

Polite
Kind
Helpful
Generous
Cooperative
Honest
Happy

Choose the kind of reputation you want to have.

Social Entry

GRADE LEVEL(S): 1-3

DESCRIPTION:
This lesson gives students ideas about how to "break the ice" in new social situations.

OBJECTIVE(S):
- Students will understand the importance of facial expression and body language in new social situations.
- Students will recognize how finding common interests can help them make a new friend.

ESTIMATED TIME: 30 minutes

MATERIAL(S) NEEDED:
- 2 large paper clips
- Friend Search activity sheet found on page 224

PROCEDURES:
1. Ask the students to recall and share a time when they were in a situation where they did not know anybody—the new kid at school, a birthday party where they only knew the guest of honor, etc. Ask about the feelings these kinds of experiences evoke.
2. Explain that when we are in these situations it may be hard to know what to say or do in order to be accepted. Tell the students they are going to learn two things they can do when they are in a new social situation.
3. Model for the students how facial expression and body language play a part in making friends. Make an angry grumpy face and ask the students, "If I walked into your room and you didn't know me, do you think you'd want to be my friend?" Discuss and model appropriate facial expressions—smiles, eye contact, etc. Then hold your head down low, slump your shoulders, and don't make eye contact with the students and ask the same question. Discuss and model appropriate body language in new social situations—head held up, back straight.
4. Using the two paper clips, explain to the students that making a new friend is like connecting with someone. Say this, ***"Suppose I walk into a room and I don't know anyone. I just stand by the wall and don't talk to anyone. I wait but no one comes to talk to me. I leave without making any friends."*** As you're telling this story, pass the two paper clips together, but be sure they do not connect. Show the students how the clips have not connected.
5. Using the two paper clips again, and say this, ***"Suppose I walk into a room and I don't know anyone. But I see someone who is wearing a soccer shirt. I like soccer, so I walk over and say, 'Hey. I like your shirt. Do you play soccer?' They say they do and we talk about soccer for a while. Then I see some kids drawing and I go over and say, 'That's a really nice picture. I like to draw also. Mind if I join you?' They let me. I leave with several new friends."*** As you're telling this story, pass the two paper clips together so that they do connect.

6. Explain that the way you "connected" with other kids was by finding a common interest—something that you liked that someone else liked.

7. Distribute the Friend Search sheets found on page 224 and tell students that they are going to have a chance to discover some common interests. Have each child complete the sheet. Then instruct them to find four different people who like the things they like to sign in each box. A person can only sign someone's sheet one time.

8. Have the students reveal what they learned about someone in the class after the activity that they didn't know before.

SUMMARY POSTER OR VISUAL REMINDER:
Connect With Others summary poster on page 225

VARIATIONS/MODIFICATIONS/EXTENSIONS:
• You can also use a break-away-fan found in a magic store instead of paper clips.
• For an awareness of our body language and how we present ourselves, have the students pantomime different feelings and have the class guess which feeling. Discuss the messages we send.
• Have each student create their own list of "chit-chat" questions that can be used to start conversations with others.

JOURNAL ENTRY

Pretend you are a new student in class.
Write about what you would say and do to make friends.

 **Social Entry**

CLASSROOM GUIDANCE NEWS

Dear Parent,

Today's lesson focused on making new friends. Children learned that they are able to determine if they want to make a new friend. We discussed two things that they can look for when deciding if they would like to pursue a new friendship. One is body cues and facial expression like smiles and eye contact. The second component in determining if one wants to enter into a new relationship is to look for common interests. This is sometimes the easiest way to start a conversation with someone new. We played a "Friend Search" game that helped the children find some possible "new" friends in their classroom.

An emphasis was placed upon the idea that, just as we watch others to decide if we would like to pursue a friendship, others are watching us as well. Therefore, it is important to make appropriate choices about personal behavior.

You can help your child to make new friends by pointing out appropriate behavior and explaining how that behavior could encourage a new friend. For example, when your child shares you may comment, "People like to be around others who care enough to share." These types of general statements help children make the connection between their behavior and the effect that it has on others.

As always, please feel free to call me with questions or concerns that you may have about your child, your child's school experience, or our guidance and counseling program.

Sincerely,

Friend Search

A color I like	Something I like to do
A food I like	**A place I like**

decision making

Types of Decisions

GRADE LEVEL(S): 3-5

DESCRIPTION:
Children often think that they do not get to make decisions, that adults are always telling them what to do. This lesson helps children understand that while they do not get to make all the decisions for themselves, they get to make more than they may realize.

OBJECTIVE(S):
- Students will identify three types of decisions.
- Students will categorize decisions into three categories.

ESTIMATED TIME: 30 minutes

MATERIAL(S) NEEDED:
None

PROCEDURES:
1. Define decisions. Ask the students who makes most of the decisions at school and at home.
2. Ask the students to name everything that they have done since waking up this morning. List these on the board. Help them to understand that each time they did something, they were making a decision.
3. Explain that some decisions are made alone, you have all of the say-so in them. Define these as "I" decisions and have the students give examples. The students may struggle with this concept because they may still be convinced that adults make all the decisions. Help them understand that they are making decisions even as you teach—whether they will sit still or wiggle, whether they will listen to you or think about what they are going to do when they get home, etc. Personal behavior is always an "I" decision .
4. Explain that some decisions are made by you and others together, you have some of the say-so but not all. Define these as "WE" decisions. Have the students give examples.
5. Explain that there are times that decisions are made that you have no say-so at all. These types of decisions are called "THEY" decisions. Have the students give examples.
6. Read the following examples of decisions. Have the students stand up if it is an "I" decision, raise their hand if it is a "WE" decision, and stay seated if it is a "THEY" decision (you may wish to draw a ↑ with the word "I", a ↓ with the word "they" and a hand with the word "we" on the board to assist students with knowing what to do.) Point out that the answers will be different for everyone since rules are different in all homes and that there are no right or wrong answers. Ask: "Who decides…"
    - what time you go to bed on a school night
    - what clothes you wear to school
    - who you sit next to at school

Types of Decisions

- what game to play at recess
- what time you eat lunch at school
- when you do your homework
- who your friends are
- what you eat for breakfast
- what chores you do
- what movies you can see

7. Discuss why we need to understand types of choices by explaining that as students get older more choices will become "I" or "WE" but that not every choice will be. Emphasize that everyone has "THEY" decisions in their lives. Most adults do not get to decide the speed limit, what salary they will make, what time they will go to work, etc.

SUMMARY POSTER OR VISUAL REMINDER:
I, We, They Decisions summary poster found on page 231

VARIATIONS/MODIFICATIONS/EXTENSIONS:
- Have the students keep a Decisions Log for a specified time (one hour, three hours, one day) and have them categorize the decisions into I, we, and they decisions.
- Ask the teacher to use the word "decided" or "chose" when speaking to students about positive and negative behaviors, such as "I see you chose to put your papers in your folder without being asked. Thank you," or "You decided to talk when I was teaching." This will help students become aware of the power of personal choice.

JOURNAL ENTRY

As you grow up, there will be changes in who makes decisions for you. Think back two years and compare it to today. Write about what "they" decisions have changed to "we" or "I" decisions.

Types of Decisions

CLASSROOM GUIDANCE NEWS

Dear Parents,

Your child had a classroom guidance lesson today. We discussed three different types of decisions.

Young children often do not feel that they get to make decisions; they feel as though they are constantly told what to do. This is one type of decision—a THEY decision. In a THEY decision, an individual has no part in making that choice—- "THEY" make it. Perhaps a parent, a teacher, or the government makes it. Everyone, including adults, have THEY choices made for them. As adults, we don't get to choose how much money we make or what the speed limit on the highway is going to be. It is important for children to understand that there must be THEY decisions for them in order to keep them safe and protected. It is equally important for children to realize that even as adults, we do not make all the decisions for ourselves and that as they grow older, THEY decisions will still be made for them.

A second type of decision is a WE decision. WE decisions are made with others and an individual has some of the decision making power. Examples of WE decisions for children include what to play when playing with a friend, who to invite to a birthday party, and the extracurricular activities in which they participate.

The third type of decision is an I decision. I decisions are personal decisions made in which the individual has all of the power to make the decision. This is the type of decision that young people feel they do not get to make. However, as we discussed in class today, each individual is constantly making I decisions about the way he/she behaves. Your child is becoming more independent and can begin making more I decisions. Examples include what to wear, when to do homework, and where things can be put in their bedroom.

At home you may wish to discuss these types of decisions with your child as they relate to choices at home. Decide if any current WE or THEY decisions are ready to become I decisions for your child. Discuss why certain choices will remain THEY decisions for a while.

We will continue to focus on the decision making process and the responsibility that goes hand in hand with making decisions. As always, please feel free to call me with concerns or questions that you have about your child, your child's school experience, or our guidance and counseling program.

Sincerely,

Types of Decisions

"I" Decisions

- Your behavior
- How well you do your work
- Your attitude
- What you play when you are by yourself

"We" Decisions

- Who your friends are
- Class projects
- Family Vacations
- What you play with your friends

"They" Decisions

- Your bedtime
- What you are taught in school
- When you go to lunch at school
- Rules and laws

Decision Making Personalities

GRADE LEVEL(S): 3-5

DESCRIPTION:
Using automobiles, this lesson helps students think of their own personality and how it can positively and adversely affect making group decisions.

OBJECTIVE(S):
• Students will identify four types of decision-making personalities.
• Students will identify their own decision-making personality.

ESTIMATED TIME: 30 minutes

MATERIAL(S) NEEDED:
• A pair of toy bumper cars or a picture of bumper cars (pictures provided on page 236)
• A toy race car or a picture of a race car (picture provided on page 237)
• A toy van or a picture of a family van (picture provided on page 238)
• A toy 18-wheeler or a picture of an 18-wheeler (picture provided on page 239)
• Drawing paper for each student
• What's Your Decision Making Personality summary poster (found on page 240)

PROCEDURES:
1. Tell the students that you are going to share with them a problem that a group in another class had in making a decision when the group was given the assignment to choose a famous African American for a research project. The group really struggled and could not agree.
2. Discuss personalities. Define personality as the way a person acts most of the time. Explain that everyone has a decision-making personality—a way they act when it is time to make a decision. Emphasize that everyone has a different personality and that while this is okay, it can sometimes make getting along difficult if we are not sensitive to other people's opinions.
3. Tell the students about each of the people in the group you mentioned earlier.
4. Roberto like's everybody's choice. He has gone along with everyone's idea. He hasn't come up with any suggestions about who to study on his own, and he changes his mind every time a new idea comes along. Tell the students that Roberto is a **bumper car.** Show the bumper cars and discuss bumper car decision making. A person who has a bumper car personality will change his/her mind whenever something new comes along. The problem with a bumper car is that he/she usually never makes up his/her own mind.
5. Tonya decided as soon as she heard the assignment that she wanted the group to study Harriet Tubman. Then she stopped participating in the discussion. She has not really listened to anyone else's suggestions and she does not plan to do so. Compare Tonya to a race car. People with **race car** decision making personalities make up their minds very quickly and then move on. The problem with race car personalities is that they do not always think of

consequences or other people's feelings and opinions.

6. Danny thinks of all the possibilities and has made an extensive list of famous African Americans. He has a list and is still thinking. Anytime he's asked to give one suggestion, Danny just cannot do it. He wants more time. Compare him to a family van. People with **family van** decision making personalities take their time. While they play it safe, the problem is that they are sometimes too slow.

7. Julie made up her mind that she wanted to study Ronald McNair. She disagrees with everyone else and says mean comments about other's suggestions. Anytime someone tries to say something, Julie squints her eyes and makes mean faces and says, "It's going to be Ronald McNair!" Compare Julie to an **eighteen-wheeler.** People with eighteen-wheeler personalities take a stand and stick to it. They do not like to give in. The problem with eighteen-wheeler personalities is that they do not respect other's opinions.

8. Discuss why this group has not yet made a decision. Emphasize that even though people have different personalities, they must still be able to get along with others.

9. Explain that there is no BEST way to be—your personality for making decisions should depend upon the type of decision to be made. Give examples of when it is appropriate to be like each vehicle. Suggestions include:
   - **Bumper car:** when you're trying to decide what game to play with your friends
   - **Race car:** when you're in the lunch line and have to choose between a hot dog and a cheese sandwich
   - **Family van:** when you've been given money for your birthday and are trying to decide how to spend it
   - **Eighteen-wheeler:** when someone is trying to get you to make a choice that's bad for you

10. Give each student a sheet of drawing paper. Ask the students to create a vehicle that best represents their decision making personality. Encourage them to be creative. They may choose to be a bumper van or a race eighteen-wheeler.

11. Allow the students to share their drawings.

SUMMARY POSTER OR VISUAL REMINDER:

Decision Making Personalities summary poster on page 240

VARIATIONS/MODIFICATIONS/EXTENSIONS:

- Have the students pretend that they are a member of the group deciding about which famous African American to research. Have the students write down suggestions of how they might help the group make that decision.
- The class can brainstorm and make a list of situations where it would be appropriate to use the decision making personalities of a bumper car, a race car, a family van, and an eighteen-wheeler.

JOURNAL ENTRY

Think about your day and write about the decisions you have made.
Tell about which decision-making personalities were used.

Decision Making Personalities

CLASSROOM GUIDANCE NEWS

Dear Parent,

Today in classroom guidance we discussed decision making personalities. These personalities were compared to different types of automobiles. The personalities are:

Bumper car: These are people who go in any direction life takes them, risks and all, letting others make decisions for them. These people are typically carefree but may be viewed as irresponsible.

Race car: These are people who make quick decisions without thinking of the consequences beforehand. These people are typically quick but risky.

Family van: These people prefer safe decisions and proceed slowly and cautiously. They tend to choose options with the least risks. These people are typically safe but may be fearful to venture out and can be viewed as indecisive as they take longer to make decisions.

Eighteen wheeler: These people barrel ahead in any direction they want without taking into consideration the opinions of others. They are typically bold but may be seen as bullies.

We discussed which of these personalities is "best." While students tend to think of the family van as the most desirable, we discussed that each of these styles is appropriate depending upon the decision to be made. For example, when going through the lunch line, it is appropriate to be a "race car" as that situation calls for a quick decision. When someone is trying to talk you into doing something that may be a bad decision for you, being an "eighteen wheeler" is most appropriate. If you really don't care what you play with your friend, it's acceptable to be a "bumper car."

Students were asked to think of their own decision making personality and to create a vehicle that represents them. Please ask your child to share his/her picture with you.

It is important to remember that people with different decision making styles often look at the same problem and its possible solutions from very different viewpoints. When solving problems with someone else, it helps to try to think of solutions from as many points of view as possible before selecting a solution.

As always, please feel free to call me with any questions or concerns you may have about your child, your child's school experience, or our elementary guidance and counseling program.

In partnership,

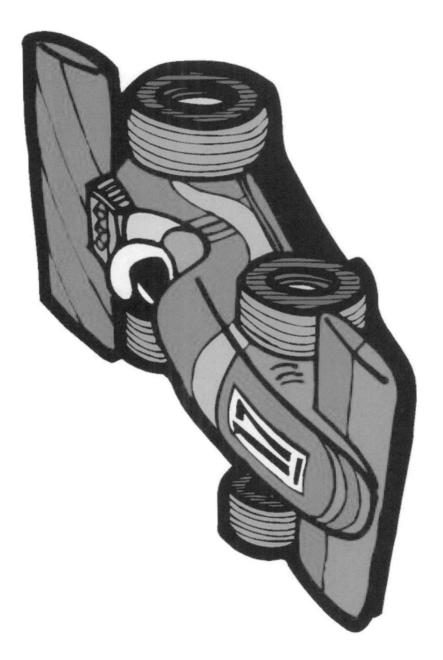

What is Your
Decision Making Personality?

Web of Support

GRADE LEVEL(S): 3-5

DESCRIPTION:
Using the popular children's novel *Charlotte's Web,* this lesson helps students understand that they need other people and that other people are there to support them in making good choices.

OBJECTIVE(S):
- Students will recognize that there are times when all people need to seek help in making choices.
- Students will identify when and where to seek help.

ESTIMATED TIME: 30 minutes

MATERIAL(S) NEEDED:
- Overhead projector
- Transparency of Web of Support found on page 244
- Copy of Web of Support on page 244 for each child

PROCEDURES:
1. Ask the students to recall and share when they have had a hard time making a decision.
2. Explain that sometimes we have tough "I" decisions to make and that it helps to have some support or help from people that we trust.
3. Ask the students to recall the story of *Charlotte's Web* by asking what Charlotte used her web for. Charlotte used her web for the purpose of nutrition. Make an analogy of emotional nutrition in comparison to physical nutrition.
4. Tell the students that they will be making a web of support today. Included in this web of support will be all the people that are there to help you when you need help making tough choices.
5. Demonstrate on the overhead by making a web of support for yourself. Write your name in the center of the web. Starting in the first ring closest to your name, write the names of those individuals that you turn to most often. In the second ring, write names of people you turn to when those people are not available or are unable to help. In the third ring, write names of those individuals you turn to for help with specific problems (a friend with medical expertise, etc.) In the last ring include agencies such as police, doctors, counselors, etc.
6. Give the students the web worksheet and have them make their own web. Be sure to instruct them to include the same agencies as listed above.
7. Reiterate that these are people they can go to when they have tough choices to make or when there are problems that they need to talk about. Ask the students to keep their web of support in a special place so that they can find it when they are struggling with where to go for help.

SUMMARY POSTER OR VISUAL REMINDER:

Web of Support summary poster on page 245

VARIATIONS/MODIFICATIONS/EXTENSIONS:

- Keep blank copies of the Web of Support in your office for individual counseling. These are great in working with children who have little family support. Assist these students in thinking of people who are willing to listen and help.
- If possible, plan this lesson around Halloween time. Make a display outside your office with spider web netting and use a caption such as "Who is in your web to help you?"

JOURNAL ENTRY

Write about your web of support describing how others help you in making tough "I" decisions.

CLASSROOM GUIDANCE NEWS

Dear Parents,

Your child had classroom guidance today. Students learned about people in their "web of support."

Oftentimes we must make difficult choices. Even children have difficult choices to make such as what to do when a friend is being unkind, whether to do what their peers are doing or do what they think is right, or what to do when they feel worried or stressed about something. When choices are difficult, it is important for children to recognize that they have people around them who are there to help.

We used the popular children's novel **Charlotte's Web** as the context for discussing personal support networks. We discussed how Charlotte used her web to attract insects to her for nutrition. We as people also need to "attract" others to us to help keep us healthy emotionally. Having supportive people to talk to when we are having a difficult time making a choice is crucial in our own emotional well-being.

Your child completed his/her "web of support." Please be sure you see it. Discuss the people your child included. Use caution in not saying things like, "Why didn't you put Grandma on there?" It is important to see whom your child views as being in supportive roles. Discuss with your child who s/he would go to in various situations by asking things like, "Who would you talk to if your best friend started teasing you?" or "Who would you talk to if someone were threatening to hurt you or someone you loved?" This is also an excellent opportunity to review some personal body safety with your child and to give him/her the reassurance that it's always okay to tell you anything, even if someone threatens to hurt him/her if s/he tells.

It is a pleasure working with your child. As always, please feel free to call me with any questions or concerns that you may have about your child, your child's school experience, or our elementary guidance and counseling program.

Sincerely,

WEB OF SUPPORT

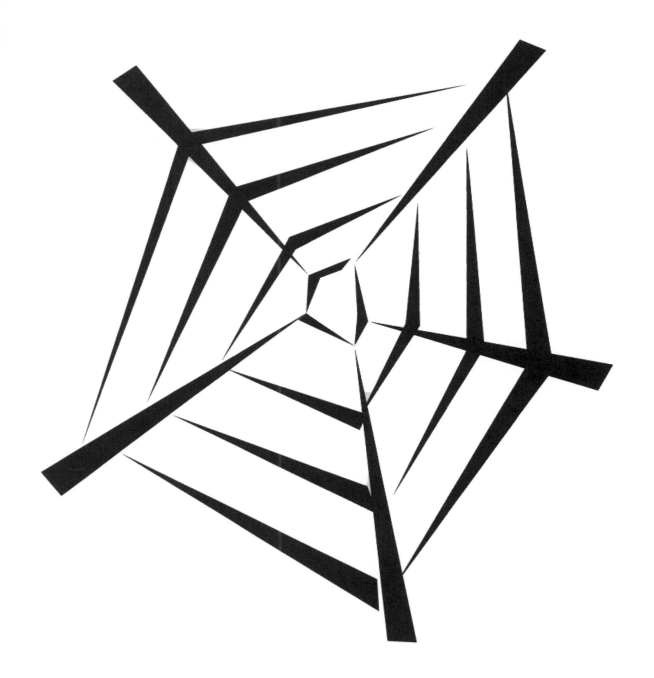

Web of Support

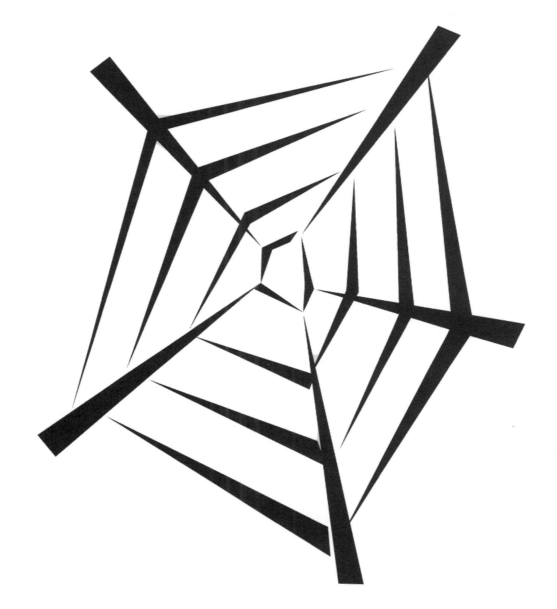

Who is in your Web of Support?

Understanding Consequences

GRADE LEVEL(S): 3-5

DESCRIPTION:
Understanding consequences is a prerequisite to making good choices. This lesson provides experiences in understanding the cause and effect relationship of consequences.

OBJECTIVE(S):
• Students will define the word consequence.
• Students will understand that there are positive and negative consequences.
• Students will demonstrate an understanding of consequences.

ESTIMATED TIME: 30 minutes

MATERIAL(S) NEEDED:
• Egg
• Glass bowl
• Whistle
• Drawing paper for each student
• One decision strip for each student (found on page 249)

PROCEDURES:
1. Show the students the whistle and ask what they think will happen if you blow into the mouthpiece of the whistle. Blow and ask the students how they knew what would happen— they've done it before. Repeat this same process by cracking the egg in the bowl.
2. Explain that the whistle making a loud noise and the egg breaking were "consequences" of a decision you made.
3. Write the word "consequences" on the board and define as things that happen as a result of a decision. Explain that decisions made have good consequences or bad consequences. Allow the students to give examples of decisions they have made that have had good consequences and those with bad consequences.
4. Work through with the students and write on the board the good and bad consequences of staying up late to watch a TV show or going to bed on time. Do not ask the students to decide, but point out that it is important to think through consequences BEFORE making decisions.
5. Give each student one of the decision strips and a blank piece of drawing paper. Ask that they draw a consequence of the decision they are given. Staple the decision to the top of the paper.
6. Share.
7. Summarize the importance of thinking through consequences **before** making a decision. Point out that waiting until the decision is made to consider consequences could cause them harm or trouble.

SUMMARY POSTER OR VISUAL REMINDER:
Consequences summary poster found on page 250

VARIATIONS/MODIFICATIONS/EXTENSIONS:
- Have the students write about a time they suffered a negative consequence for a decision they made. Ask them to include the lesson they learned.
- Ask the teacher to use the word consequence often in both positive and negative situations.
- For a funny look at consequences read aloud *If You Give a Mouse a Cookie* , *If You Give a Moose a Muffin,* and/or *If You Give a Pig a Pancake* by Laura Joffe Numeroff. Discuss all the consequences in the story.

JOURNAL ENTRY

Think about a poor decision you recently made. Pretend to turn back time and write about what you could have done differently to have a positive consequence rather than a negative consequence.

CLASSROOM GUIDANCE NEWS

Dear Parents,

One goal of every parent is to help his/her child learn to make responsible decisions. There is no magic age at which children become responsible—it is a life long learning and teaching process. Today's classroom guidance lesson focused on helping students learn that there are consequences for the decisions we make.

People often fail to think of the consequences of a decision before acting. Young children, especially, react impulsively to situations. However, your child is making more and more decisions on his/her own now in school and with friends. Therefore, learning to consider consequences before acting is essential to social and academic growth.

Today we discussed consequences in terms of cause and effect. Every choice your child makes has an effect on him/her or others. If your child cleans his/her room without being asked, the effect is that mom or dad is pleased and may reward the child with hugs, smiles, praise, etc. If a child forgets to do his/her homework, the effect is that he/she may have to miss recess, grades may suffer, parents and teachers may get frustrated, etc.

Your child did a drawing of a cause/effect situation that was given to him/her by me. Please ask your child to see the drawing and discuss it. This would be a great opportunity for you to emphasize the importance of thinking of consequences and outcomes before acting. Role play some of these situations with your child. This provides them experience with the process of considering consequences. You may even choose to share times that you failed to think of the consequences of a decision with your child.

As always, please feel free to call me with questions or concerns that you have about your child, your child's school experience, or our elementary guidance and counseling program.

Sincerely,

DECISION STRIPS

Someone is mean to you.

You disobey the teacher.

Someone shares with you.

You say something nice to a classmate.

You eat too much candy.

You go to bed too late.

Someone writes on your desk with markers.

You play with matches.

You help set the table.

You clean up your room without being told.

You forget to feed your pet.

You go outside in cold weather without a coat.

You get up late.

You forget to do your homework.

You don't wear your watch
and get home late from a friend's house.

You forget your lunchbox.

You don't do your chores.

You don't pay attention when the teacher is giving
directions.

You make faces at your classmates.

You talk back to your parents.

Consequences happen when you make decisions. Remember to think of the consequences FIRST.

CeCe Dee

The Decision Making Process

GRADE LEVEL(S): 3-5

DESCRIPTION:
This lesson gives students a three-step decision making process. Students are introduced to a monkey named CeCe Dee who learned some important lessons in the jungle.

OBJECTIVE(S):
• Students will develop decision-making skills.
• Students will learn three steps to making good decisions.
• Students will apply the three step decision making process.

ESTIMATED TIME: 30 minutes

MATERIAL(S) NEEDED:
• Copy of the story of CeCe Dee found on pages 253-254
• Stuffed monkey or monkey puppet
• Ruthie Needs Help! activity sheet found on page 255

PROCEDURES:
1. Introduce the monkey named CeCe Dee. Explain that CeCe Dee's name used to be Watch Out. Tell or read the story on pages 253-254.
2. Using the following scenario, work through the three steps to making a good decision—choices, consequences, decision—with the students.
    Dennis has homework to do. He is expected to have it finished by the time his mother gets home from work. His friend, Sam, calls and asks him to go to the park. He says that they will be back in one hour so Dennis will have time to finish his work.
3. Have the students complete the activity sheet entitled Ruthie Needs Help found on page 255.

SUMMARY POSTER OR VISUAL REMINDER:
CeCe Dee summary poster found on page 256

VARIATIONS/MODIFICATIONS/EXTENSIONS:
• To increase interest in the story, use a monkey puppet and have the monkey tell the story. Do not worry if your lips move—the students will not be looking at you!
• Have the students think of a tough decision they need to make. Have them write the three steps and work through the decision.

JOURNAL ENTRY

Write about a time you had a very tough decision to make. Use the three-step decision-making process and tell how you could have decided.

CLASSROOM GUIDANCE NEWS

Dear Parent,

Today your child learned three steps to making responsible decisions. He/she was introduced to a character named CeCe Dee. CeCe Dee is named after the three decision-making steps:

Choices
Consequences
Decision

Students learned that when faced with a tough decision, they should avoid making quick decisions and think carefully through these three steps. First, they should consider ALL the possible choices. Next, think through the consequences, both positive and negative, of each of the choices. Finally, after thoroughly thinking through these choices and consequences, make the best decision possible.

CeCe Dee will be a memorable character for the students and will assist in the retention of this three-step decision making process. Together with CeCe Dee, we role-played some tough decisions.

You have the opportunity to help your child use this decision-making process frequently. When your child comes to you asking, "What should I do?," instead of giving him/her the choice you feel is best, work through these three steps with your child. You may even choose to write down your choices and consequences in order to help make the best decision.

It is a pleasure working with your child. As always, please feel free to call me with any concerns or questions that you may have about your child, your child's school experience, or our guidance and counseling program.

Sincerely,

CeCe Dee

The Story of CeCe Dee
By Gwen M. Sitsch

Once upon a time in a jungle far away from here, a little monkey was born. He was cute and cuddly and his mother looked at him with love in her eyes. Now the custom in the jungle was to observe a baby monkey for several days before naming him. After watching the way the baby played with others and acted, the monkey's parents were to choose a name that best fit the baby. His mother, whose name was Gentle, watched her baby very closely as she was supposed to do.

One thing became clear to her very soon. This monkey did whatever he felt like doing. He loved bananas and whenever he saw a banana, he would go for it! The trouble was he wasn't careful. Once he almost got stampeded by a herd of zebras. He saw a banana tree and ran toward it without looking both ways before he crossed the clearing in the jungle. Gentle saved him by yelling, "Watch out!"

Another time he saw some bananas in a tree and began to climb it. He didn't notice that a family of bees had built their hive in this tree because he didn't stop to look before climbing. Again, Gentle saved him by yelling, "Watch out!"

Once when he saw some bananas on the ground, he ran toward them without noticing that a boa constrictor had her eyes on him. He just ran toward those bananas without observing what was around him. But once again Gentle saw what was about to happen and yelled, "Watch out!"

And so, the little monkey was named Watch Out. At first he did not mind the name. He thought it was cute, and he used it as an excuse for making mistakes. Whenever he got into trouble, he always just said, "But remember, my name is Watch Out. I was named that because I don't think before I do things. I really can't help it."

As Watch Out grew older and began to play with monkeys his own age, his name started to bother him. It also started to bother him that he always seemed to be making the wrong decisions about things and getting into trouble. So one day, he decided to go see the wise old elephant that lived nearby.

He told the elephant his story and the elephant listened. Then she offered Watch Out some advice. She explained to Watch Out that he must use his brain before doing something. He must always think first about his **CHOICES.** "This means thinking about all the things you could do," she explained. Then she told him he must then think of the **CONSEQUENCES** of each of these choices. Watch Out did not understand what "consequences" were so the elephant explained. "Consequences are the good and bad things that could happen to you if you do something. Every action has a consequence." Finally she told Watch Out that after thinking of the choices and consequences he could then make a **DECISION.** "But," she explained, "you must do these things in this order, **CHOICES, CONSEQUENCES,** then **DECISION.** If you do these things out of order, you'll probably still be called 'Watch Out' all your life."

Watch Out left thinking about what the elephant told him. As he was thinking and walking

home, he spotted a banana tree across the river. This tree had the biggest, greenest bananas he had seen in weeks—just the way Watch Out liked them. Just as he started to dash toward the river, he thought of the elephant's words, "Choices, Consequences, Decision." He knew that he was going to have to get across that river somehow, so he thought of all his choices. "I could swim. I could swing on a vine. I could go the long way around the river, or I could just leave them and go home and get bananas there."

Then he thought of the consequences of each of those choices. "Swimming is not a good idea because I'm alone and mom always tells me to never swim alone. Swinging on a vine might work, but I only see one vine and it doesn't look too strong. If it breaks, I'll be in the river alone. There are crocodiles in that river that love monkey meat! Going around the river would work, but it would make me late getting home, and mom will be worried. Leaving those bananas would be safe, but I'd miss getting some really delicious snacks."

Watch Out then had to make a decision. "I think the best choice for me is to keep walking and leave those bananas alone. Maybe mom will have some green, crispy ones at home for me."

When he got home, Watch Out told his mom about his talk with the elephant and about his decision about the bananas across the river. His mom was very proud of him. Watch Out felt proud too.

As the days passed, Watch Out kept thinking about the elephant's words: "Choices, Consequences, Decision." Each time he got ready to do something without thinking, those words came into his mind. When he had to make a tough decision about whether to do his chores at home or go to his friend's house, he thought of those words: choices, consequences, decision.

Before long his mom was saying "Watch Out" less and less. Weeks passed without anyone having to remind him to "watch out." The animals kept hearing Watch Out say these words, "Choices, consequences, decision." One day his mom said, "You say those words so much, why not make a shorter way to remember it like C-C-D?" And so he did. And whenever he had to make a decision, he said those letters, C-C-D.

Before long, he came to be known as CeCe Dee. Everyone forgot that he had been named Watch Out. He kept this new name and lived safely ever after.

CeCe Dee

Ruthie needs help!

Here's Ruthie's problem:
Her best friend is having a sleepover and Ruthie has been planning to go for weeks. The night before the sleepover, Ruthie's grandma calls and says that she is planning to come to spend the night with Ruthie's family the next night. She will only have one night to stay and is looking forward to seeing Ruthie. Ruthie loves her grandma very much. She also really wants to go to the sleepover.

Choice One:	Consequences (+ and -)

Choice Two:	Consequences (+ and -)

Choice Three:	Consequences (+ and -)

My decision would be: _____

_____

_____

Hi! Remember me, CeCe Dee, when making decisions.

**Choices
Consequences
Decision**

Advice Column

GRADE LEVEL(S): 3-5

DESCRIPTION:
This lesson not only provides students practice in using the three-step decision making process but also gives students an opportunity to seek the advice of a peer. You may find it beneficial to teach the lesson entitled CeCe Dee beginning on page 251 before this lesson in order to teach the three steps to decision making.

OBJECTIVE(S):
- Students will practice seeking help for a problem.
- Students will use the three-step decision making process.

ESTIMATED TIME: 30-45 minutes

MATERIAL(S) NEEDED:
- Advice column from the newspaper or a child's magazine (*Highlights* and *American Girls* magazines contain a child's advice column)
- Sample "Dear Beacon" letters found on page 260
- "Dear Beacon" activity sheet found on page 261

PROCEDURES:
1. Read a few sample letters and responses from the advice column.
2. Discuss the purpose of advice columns. Review that in CeCe Dee lesson, they learned three steps for making tough decisions. Point out that an advice columnist uses a model similar to these three steps in order to help the people who write to the column.
3. Explain that they are going to identify a problem they are having and get practice in making decisions. Explain what a beacon is—shines light in the dark—and tell the students that they will be writing a letter to a pretend advice columnist named Beacon.
4. Read some sample letters (found on page 260) and have the students work through the three-step decision making process.
5. Distribute the activity sheets and have the students write their own "Dear Beacon" letter. Remind students that they should NOT sign their real name, but should make up a name that goes along with their problem.
6. Collect letters and exchange. Have the students pretend that they are "Beacon." Explain that they are to think through the choices, consequences, and then make a decision that they think is best to share with the troubled person who wrote them. Have them write a response as "Beacon."
7. As time allows, read some and discuss the advice given.

Advice Column

SUMMARY POSTER OR VISUAL REMINDER:

Lighthouse summary poster found on page 262

VARIATIONS/MODIFICATIONS/EXTENSIONS:

- Instead of having the students write asking for help, prepare several letters ahead of time and give these to students. Have the students write the response.
- Monitor the writing carefully. You may find student needs of which you were unaware.

JOURNAL ENTRY

When you need to make a decision about how to handle a problem, the three-step decision-making process can help:

Think of all the possible **CHOICES.**
Think of the **CONSEQUENCES** of each choice.
Make the best possible **DECISION.**

Make a list of typical problems for students your age. Choose one problem and write about it using the three-step decision-making process.

1
2
3

Advice Column

CLASSROOM GUIDANCE NEWS

Dear Parent

In a previous guidance lesson, students learned a three-step process for making tough decisions. These steps are:

Think of all the possible **CHOICES.**
Think of the **CONSEQUENCES** of each choice.
Make the best possible **DECISION.**

In today's lesson, students practiced this decision-making process by becoming advice columnists. We discussed a number of hypothetical problems that are typical to students—rushing through work, test anxiety, difficulties with friends. During the hypothetical problem discussion, we worked through the decision making process. Students were then asked to come up with a problem they sometimes have and to write a fictitious columnist named Beacon. They were to come up with a name that went along with their problem when signing their letter such as "Tested Beyond My Limits." We then exchanged problems and had the students respond as the advice columnist. Following this, the letters were collected and some were read and discussed. This activity provided students not only the opportunity to practice the decision-making process, but also the opportunity to get ideas about how to manage problems of their own.

When your child is having trouble making a decision, consider using the model above for helping. Remember that your child has to ultimately make the decision, but you can serve as a facilitator in making these decisions. You may even want to allow your child to see you use the decision-making process when you have a tough decision to make.

As always, please feel free to call me with questions or concerns that you may have about your child, your child's school experience, or our elementary guidance and counseling program.

Sincerely,

Advice Column

SAMPLE "DEAR BEACON" LETTERS

Dear Beacon,

I used to try hard on tests, but I didn't do very well. It seems like the harder I work and study, the worse I do. Now I hate all tests and studying for tests. I'm ready to give up on school. What can I do?

Signed,
Tested Beyond My Limits

Dear Beacon,

Every time I get ready to study at home or am right in the middle of studying, I get interrupted by some member of my family playing the TV real loud, or screaming and stuff like that. And no matter where I go in the house, I can still hear the TV and the screaming. I'm afraid my grades are going to go down if this keeps on happening. What should I do?

Signed,
Loud House

Dear Beacon,

My parents are always blaming me for stuff my brother does. When my brother and I get into an argument, my parents just tell me to go to my room or put me on restriction. I try to explain to them when it happens, but they won't listen. What can I do?

Signed,
Not Guilty

Dear Beacon,

My best friend has been acting so bossy lately. If I won't play what he wants to play, he goes off mad and won't play with me at all. He always finds other people to play with, but sometimes I can't and so I'm left with no one to play with. I feel left out. What can I do?

Signed,
Lonely at Playtime

Advice Column

Your Letter to Beacon:

_____

_____

_____

_____

_____

_____

_____

Beacon's Response:

_____

_____

_____

_____

_____

_____

_____

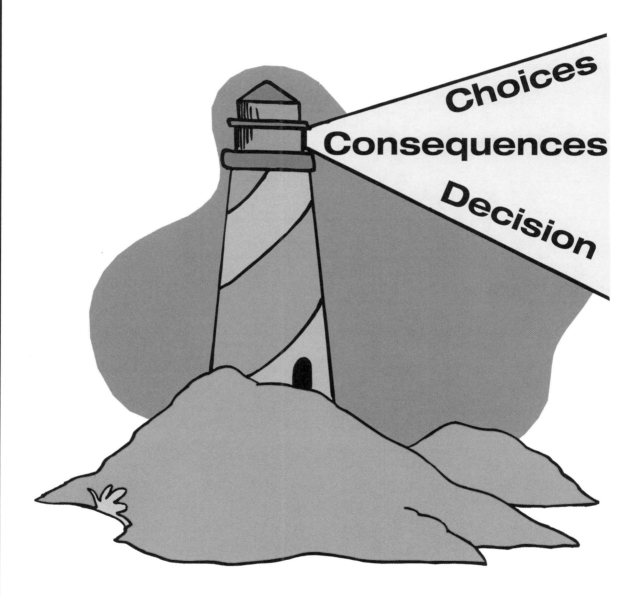

Making "We" Decisions

GRADE LEVEL(S): 3-5

DESCRIPTION:
This lesson provides experience in making "we" decisions.

OBJECTIVE(S):
• Students will cooperate with others in a small group.
• Students will use problem-solving and decision-making skills.

ESTIMATED TIME: 30 minutes

MATERIAL(S) NEEDED:
None

PROCEDURES:
1. Review or explain "we" decisions as those we make with others. Explain that when we make "we" decisions it can be difficult agreeing. Ask the students about times they have had to make "we" decisions.
2. Tell the students they will be making "we" decisions in guidance today. Explain that students may not always get their own way and that the group can use "chance" such as eeny, meeny, miney, mo to help them work out their decisions if needed.
3. Divide the students into groups of not more than 5 students (4 works best). Explain these rules:
   • All members must agree on each answer to each question.
   • When all agree, all group members raise their hand.
   • The group will be recognized by you and given a number. This number is the order that the group will be called upon at the end of the given time period. After the group is given a number, they may not talk to each other.
   • At the end of the time period, groups who have not reached a decision will be put on freeze. Other groups will be called upon to answer and then given the next task. Groups who are on freeze must go back to the prior decision and continue working until the next time period is called.
   • When called upon, the group answers together. If anyone in the group does not answer, it will be assumed that they don't agree and the group must get back together.
4. Give the students the following tasks one at a time. After each task have the students share their answers and discuss how conflicts were managed if they occurred.
   • TASK 1: You have won an all-expense paid vacation. Decide where you will go. You have 4 minutes to decide.
   • TASK 2: Decide how you will travel there. You have 3 minutes.
   • TASK 3: You may take one adult chaperon. Who will it be? You have 4 minutes.

- TASK 4: You may bring back one souvenir. It must fit in a suitcase. It must be something you could actually bring back. What will it be? You have 3 minutes.

5. You may have groups who, because of conflicts, do not move past task one. Discuss the problems that occur in these groups with the entire class and develop some problem-solving strategies.

SUMMARY POSTER OR VISUAL REMINDER:

We Decisions All Around Us summary poster found on page 266

VARIATIONS/MODIFICATIONS/EXTENSIONS:

- If the teacher does not currently have the students working in groups, encourage the teacher to try some group activities.
- Give a small group of students a simple puzzle. Give each child an equal number of pieces. Have them put the puzzle together with these two rules:
  1) you may not touch anyone else's pieces, and 2) you may not talk.
- Discuss how personalities affect our ability to work in groups.

JOURNAL ENTRY

Write about some "we" decisions in your life and tell what skills you need to use to work it out if you have trouble agreeing.

CLASSROOM GUIDANCE NEWS

Dear Parent,

We continued our study of decision-making skills today by practicing making "we" decisions. A "we" decision is one that is made with others—a group decision. In the real world, "we" decisions are made very often. An example may be when we work on committees and make decisions together. A common problem in making "we" decisions is that those making the decision may not agree. This happens because we are different and have different viewpoints, opinions, and ways of accomplishing a goal. When those working together on a decision do not agree, they must work together to decide what will be done and may need to use some conflict management techniques and strategies.

Today in classroom guidance, students were divided into groups to plan a group vacation. They had to decide where they were going, how they would get to their destination, which adult they would take with them, and the one souvenir they would bring back as a group (it had to fit in a suitcase). Students were encouraged to use the steps decision making that they learned: Choices, Consequences, Decision. Our discussion of this activity centered around how they worked problems out in the group and about what caused the most difficulty.

Please ask your child what occurred in his/her group when trying to work together to make decisions. Learning to work in a group is very important. You have the perfect opportunity to help your child learn to make group decisions by practicing this as a family. You may work together to decide dinner menus, make chore lists, plan trips, or schedule and prioritize activities.

As always, please feel free to call me with any questions or concerns that you may have about your child, your child's school experience, or our elementary guidance and counseling program.

Sincerely,

"We" Decisions All Around us

Self-Control

Responding to "They" Decisions

GRADE LEVEL(S): 3-5

DESCRIPTION:
This object lesson provides concrete examples of the importance of self-control when dealing with authority.

OBJECTIVE(S):
* Students will identify "they" decisions.
• Students will recall times when they have been upset by a "they" decision.
• Students will understand the importance of self-control.
• Students will tell specific ways to control themselves when they get frustrated by a "they" decision.

ESTIMATED TIME: 30 minutes

MATERIAL(S) NEEDED:
• Can of shaving cream
• Paper plate
• Wooden board
• Nails
• Hammer
• A copy of A Self Control Lesson found on page 270

PROCEDURES:
1. Remind or explain to the students about "they" decisions. "They" decisions are decisions that other people make for them. You have no decision-making power—"they" do. Have them name some THEY decisions that they do not like or agree with (bedtimes, homework, rules, etc.)
2. Discuss who makes THEY decisions and bring out that this person is usually someone with authority. Emphasize that it is, therefore, very important to use self-control when thinking about a THEY decision with which they don't agree.
3. Define self-control as being able to restrain or control a feeling to do something. Discuss how difficult this can be by using examples like:
   • your friend is making goofy faces at you during class.
   • you stub your toe while your baby sister is taking a nap.
4. Tell the students you're going to demonstrate the importance of self-control with two examples. First, ask a student to come up to the front with you and give him/her the tube of shaving cream. Ask the student to squeeze out as much shaving cream as he/she would like onto the paper plate (the student will have a blast with this!) After he/she is done, ask the student to place all the shaving cream back in the can *just like it was before.* Even though the stu-

dent may try, he/she will be unable to do so. Make this point about self-control: Just like the shaving cream, once you say or do something, you cannot take it back.

5. Use the nails and the board to tell A Self-Control lesson on page 270. As you tell it, nail a few nails in the board and then take them out at the appropriate time in the story. At the end of the story, show the students the nail holes.

6. Give the students suggestions of things they can do when they don't agree with or like a THEY decision. These include talking to someone about it (but be careful what you say and how you say it), get busy doing something you like, or change the way you're thinking about it.

SUMMARY POSTER OR VISUAL REMINDER:
Leave the board with the nail holes in it for the class.

VARIATIONS/MODIFICATIONS/EXTENSIONS:
• Instead of shaving cream, you can use toothpaste.
• Play a self-control game with the students. Ask the students to sit perfectly still and quiet. Each time someone moves or makes a noise, he/she is out. The last person in is the winner.

JOURNAL ENTRY

Think about a "they" decision recently with which you did not agree. Write about it and tell what you would need to say to yourself or do using self-control to cope with that "they" decision.

CLASSROOM GUIDANCE NEWS

Dear Parent,

We have previously discussed three types of choices: I, We, and They. Today's lesson focused on coping with THEY decisions and the importance of using self-control.
Children have many THEY decisions in their lives and this can lead to feelings such as anger, disappointment, and frustration. Therefore, it is important that students learn appropriate ways to deal with decisions made by those in authority with which they may not agree.

We discussed the importance of self-control. Self-control means being able to restrain one's own behavior. We explored some consequences of not having self-control. These include getting into trouble, losing friends, and developing a negative reputation. Be sure to ask your child what s/he learned from the can of shaving cream and from the nails in the board!

Coping strategies that we discussed included talking it out, getting busy doing something else, and choosing to change the way you may think about a decision with which you don't agree.

Everyone, children as well as adults, has others make decisions for them. As adults, we don't choose the speed limit or what time we report to work (although it would be nice!) For that reason, it is important to teach children that, even though we don't always agree with decisions made for us, we must use self-control and cope with these decisions.

As always, please feel free to call me with any questions or concerns that you may have about your child, your child's school experience, or our elementary guidance and counseling program.

Sincerely,

A Self-Control Lesson

There once was a boy who had a problem with self-control. He said and did whatever popped into his head. He especially had trouble when someone said or did something he didn't like.

The boy's father worried about him, so one night he said to his son, "I have a project for you. Every time you lose your self-control and say or do something you shouldn't do, I want you to go out back to the fence and hammer a nail into the fence." The boy thought this was a ridiculous idea and said so. "Son," said the father, "you can start now." So the boy nailed a nail in the fence.

Later that night his mother called him to supper. When he saw that they were having his least favorite meal, meatloaf, the boy said, "Oh, man! I hate meatloaf." Another nail. When it was bedtime, the boy argued with his parents that he should get to stay up later—he did; long enough to hammer another nail in the fence.

The next day at school the boy pushed down a classmate who was in his way, made a face at the teacher, and talked back to the bus driver. By the end of the next day, the boy had nailed 25 nails into the fence. He was getting tired of this nail thing. So he started trying to stop himself BEFORE he said or did something that would cause him to have to hammer another nail in the fence.

When his teacher told him he'd have to miss recess for forgetting his homework, he almost slammed his book on his desk, but remembered the nails, and went back quietly to his desk. When someone accidentally pushed him down in a basketball game, he almost called them a name. But again, he thought of the nails, and kept it to himself.

Finally the day came when he didn't have to hammer one nail into the fence. He was so proud and he told his father. His father said, "Son, I'm proud of you. But I have another project for you. Now every time you control yourself, I want you to go take a nail out of the fence." The boy thought this was another dumb idea, and he almost said so, but didn't. That was one nail out of the fence. When his mother served meatloaf that week, he put lots of ketchup on his and ate it—another nail out. After several weeks, the day came that the boy removed the last nail. Again he was proud and went to tell his father.

His father was proud too. He asked his son to follow him out to the fence. "Son, look at the fence. What do you see?" "Nothing except some old nail holes," said the son. "That's right," said his father. "You see, when you say or do things and try to take them back, you may take it back some but the scar will always be there. It's better not to say a hurtful word at all because even when you take it back, a little bit of the hurt will never go away."

—-Author Unknown

Problem Solving Lagoon

GRADE LEVEL(S): 1-3

DESCRIPTION:
Students will be introduced to Freddie the Frog and his problem solving lagoon. This lesson creatively presents the problem solving model and provides a framework for the application of solving their own problems.

OBJECTIVE(S):
- Students will learn three steps of problem solving.
- Students will be able to name five problem solving strategies.
- Students will recognize the importance of managing madness in order to deal with a problem effectively.

ESTIMATED TIME: 30-45 minutes

MATERIAL(S) NEEDED:
- Copy of the following: stepping stones, life preserver, alligator, sign, lily pads (see patterns on pages 275-277)
- Problem Solving activity sheet – one for each student (see page 282)
- Problem Situation Frog Cards – copied and cut (see pages 280 & 281)
- Frog (stuffed animal, puppet or picture that you can introduce as Freddie)

PRODEDURES:
1. Share with the class that you have brought a friend of yours along today. Show the frog and proceed to tell the following story.

Meet Freddie the Frog – he lives in a lagoon. Now if you're not a frog you may be wondering what in the world a lagoon is. Well, a lagoon is a small body of water. Freddie lives there with his other frog friends. They play together and go to school together but sometimes they had problems getting along. They would fight about who would jump first when they played hop scotch, or sometimes they fought about whose turn it was to ride on the lily pad. Freddie got tired of all of the fussing, fighting and unhappiness going on so he came up with a plan for he and his friends to use to handle problems getting along. He called his plan the "Problem Solving Lagoon." He first added one stepping stone in the water of the Problem Lagoon. On the stone he wrote one of the three steps needed to solving problems. (Place the first stepping stone on the class board or wall space. As you place the stepping stone, read the step: **What's the Problem?** *Specify the background as water of the lagoon.)*

Freddie told his friends, "The first thing we need to do whenever we have a problem is to actually talk about what the problem is to make sure we are clear about the problem. After we both agree what the problem is then we can move on to step 2 (place the second stepping stone on the board or wall space). Step 2 says to **Think About What To Do.** *"Step 2 is important so that we stop and use our head to think about all the good ways we could handle the problem. After we stop and think and come up with some possible ways to handle the problem then we can hop over to step 3 which is to **Try An Idea.***" (Place the third stepping stone on the board or wall).

Now Freddie knew how smart and creative his friends were to come up with good ideas so Freddie knew he needed to share just a few ideas to get them thinking. He added some lily pads of ideas and added some blank ones so his friends could come up with some good ideas of their own.

Freddie shared, *"There can be many good lily pad ideas to try to solve our problems. Sometimes we need to share or take turns, sometimes we may need to compromise, talk it out, or perhaps send an "I" message. Or sometimes we can put our heads together and come up with a really creative way to solve the problem."* (Add the blank lily pads to the three lily pads with Freddie's steps on them to the board for new ideas that could be used.) *"We need to think ahead about what might happen if we tried that idea in order to choose our best idea to try. Once we know the idea to try then we need to hop on to that lily pad. If that lily pad doesn't take care of the problem then we need to try another. With the help of the stepping stones and the lily pads we can cross our problem solving lagoon and get to safety."*

The frog friends shouted, *" Hooray! What a wonderful plan to get across Problem Solving Lagoon."*

All shouted *"Hooray,"* that is except one, Jeremiah – Jeremiah the bull frog. Jeremiah was trying to tell about a problem that he saw with the plan but we had trouble understanding what Jeremiah was saying until we all quieted down and listened. He said, *"What happens if we get mad with the other person about the problem? We could end up fighting and pushing each other into the water."*

Freddie replied, *"Yes, our madness out of control can be a problem. If we end up in the water in the Problem Solving Lagoon we run the risk of getting eaten up by the alligator in the water."* (Place the alligator on the board/wall).

"Why don't we post a sign in the lagoon that would help us remember the rules for controlling our madness," suggested Kermit. They could count on Kermit to come up with a good suggestion.

"That sounds like a good idea," they all croaked.

So they added a *"Beware of the Alligator"* sign that listed the madness management rules. The rules are: 1: Do not hurt yourself; 2: Do not hurt others; and 3: Do not hurt property. The frogs were learning to handle their madness in a way that followed the rules and didn't hurt themselves, others or property – that way they could still stay under control and could think of good ways to work things out. (Add the *"Beware of the Alligator"* sign to the board/wall).

"I know," said Freddie, *"we can also add a lifesaver of ways to calm down when we are mad."*

They all liked the idea and worked together to come up with suggestions of ways to handle their madness and to be able to calm down. They added these to the lifesaver. (Ask the class for suggestions of good ways to handle their anger/madness. Write their suggestions on the lifesaver and add to the board or wall. They may include such suggestions as: hum a tune, take several deep breaths, count to 10 and calm down, and get busy doing something active.)

They looked at their problem solving plan to get across the lagoon – they had their 3 steps, the lily pad ideas, their reminder sign about their madness, and their lifesavers so they could calm down if they got mad. They liked their new plan and began using their plan to handle the problems that came up – like when they fussed about who would go first, or whose turn it was. Following the steps were not always easy at first, it was easier just to get mad and complain, but the more they practiced the plan the easier it became, and they realized that it worked. From that day on the steps were always used in the Problem Solving Lagoon and Freddie and his frog friends lived happily ever after.

2. Explain to the students that you know some of the problems the frogs had to handle to get safely across the Problem Solving Lagoon. Share a Problem Situation frog card with the class and together work through each step.

(Optional)
3. Pair the students and hand a Problem Situation frog card and a Problem Solving activity sheet to each pair. Have the students work together to help the frogs solve their problems and complete the Problem Solving activity sheet. When the class has completed the activity, have each pair share their problem and their steps to safety with the rest of the class. Discuss.

SUMMARY POSTER OR VISUAL REMINDER:
Leave the board/wall display used in the story or leave the summary poster on page 283

VARIATIONS/MODIFICATIONS/EXTENSIONS:
- Give each student a frog outline and have each write a problem he/she may have had with a friend. Place these in a box and draw them out during the day and discuss using the problem solving steps.
- Relate the problem solving steps to a traffic light. The first step **What's the Problem?** is the color red to remind us to stop when there is a problem. The second step is yellow to caution us to think about what to do. And the last step is green – go and try the idea. Have the students draw the stepping stones and color each the corresponding color of a traffic light.

JOURNAL ENTRY

Think about a problem that you may have had in getting along with others recently. Write about handling this problem using the three stepping stones.

Problem Solving Lagoon

CLASSROOM GUIDANCE NEWS

Dear Parent,

I enjoyed visiting in your child's class. Our lesson today introduced Freddie and his Problem Solving Lagoon. In a diverse world, problems with getting along occur. Even as adults there may be many times we struggle with our problems. Therefore, we need to teach our children a variety of skills and a framework so they can best learn how to handle their problems. Our lesson taught three steps to give us that framework in handling problems. They are:

1. **What's the Problem?** It's important to clarify the problem to know exactly what the problem is.
2. **Think About What to Do.** We need to stop and think about all the possible ways to solve the problem and then think about what would happen if we made that choice. Some of the choices we talked about were to share, compromise, take turns, talk-it-out, or send an "I" message.
3. **Try An Idea.** Follow through with the choice you made to see if it solves the problem. If not, go back and try something else.

These steps were presented as stepping stones in the Problem Solving Lagoon. Freddie the frog cautioned us about not getting mad – he didn't want us to fall off into the water where the alligator lived. The rules of madness management (do not hurt ourselves, others or property) were posted in the Lagoon along with the lifesavers with ideas listed to help us calm down when we are mad.

Talk with your child about using this model to deal with problems that arise. Pretend to walk on each stepping stones as they talk through a problem. Tell them to be careful to control their madness so they don't fall off in the water!

Thank you for reinforcing this lesson with your child. Working together we can help our children be their best. Please feel free to call me with any questions or concerns that you may have about your child, your child's school experience, or our elementary guidance and counseling program.

Sincerely,

Step Three:
Try An
Idea

Step Two:
Think About
What To Do

Step One:
What's the
Problem?

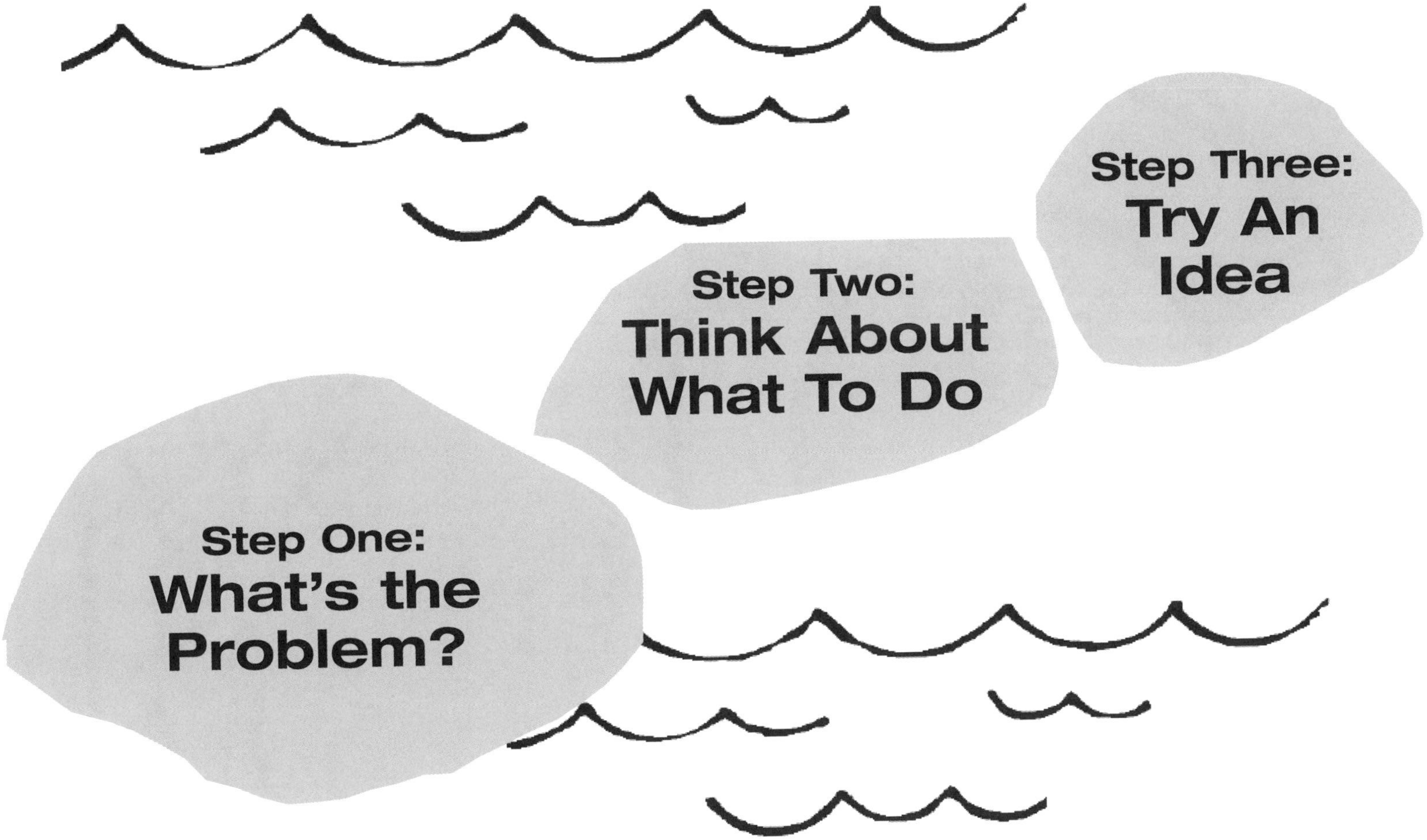

Ways to Calm Our Madness

Beware of the Alligator

Follow the
Madness Mangement Rules

1. Do not hurt yourself.
2. Do not hurt others.
3. Do not hurt property.

Share

Compromise

Take Turns

Talk It Out

Send an "I" Message

PROBLEM SITUATION FROG CARDS

My friend and I always argue over who gets to jump first when playing hopscotch. What can I do?

My sister and I argue over who gets to sit on the front part of the lily pad when crossing the river. What can I do?

I am trying to do my math homework in the afternoons but my brother is croaking so loud that I can't think. What can I do?

I borrowed a book from the library but my little sister got it and accidently dropped it into the pond and got it all wet. What can I do?

PROBLEM SITUATION FROG CARDS

When my friends come over to play with me they always leave my room a mess. What can I do?

When we get in line to hop to lunch, Billy always cuts in front of me. What can I do?

Problem Solving Lagoon

Problem Solving Steps

Step 1:

Step 2:

Step 3:

Think about what to do? (Think about all of your choices - list your choices below.?)

Try an idea? (Choose your best idea and try it. List the idea you chose below.)

_____

_____

What is the problem?

Choice 1:

_____

_____

_____

_____

Choice 2:

_____

_____

_____

_____

Choice 3:

_____

_____

_____

Choice 4:

_____

Did you follow the madness management rules? YES or NO

Remember to calm down and use self-control if you get mad.

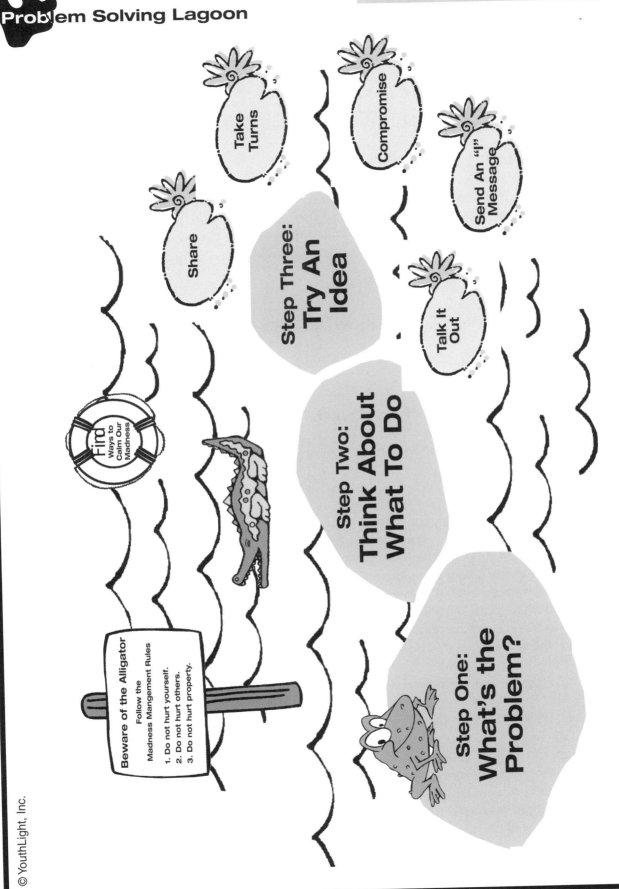

Problem Solving Lagoon

Take Turns

Compromise

Send An "I" Message

Share

Step Three:
Try An Idea

Talk It Out

Find
Ways to Calm Our Madness

Step Two:
Think About What To Do

Beware of the Alligator
Follow the
Madness Mangement Rules
1. Do not hurt yourself.
2. Do not hurt others.
3. Do not hurt property.

Step One:
What's the Problem?

Think, Say, Do

LEVELS: Grades 2-4

DESCRIPTION:

We cannot always control situations or other people, but we can control ourselves and what we think, say, and do. This lesson helps the student take a problem or difficult situation and find a good way to think about it, or think of something they can say or something they can do that is appropriate in order to help them feel okay about the problem. The words Think, Say and Do are put on a special signal to remind them to search for good ways to handle the problem.

OBJECTIVES:
- Students will identify problems.
- Students will identify three ways to deal with problems or situations.

ESTIMATED TIME: 30 minutes

MATERIALS NEEDED:
- Storybook, ***Alexander and the Terrible, Horrible, No Good, Very Bad Day*** by Judith Viorst
- "Think, Say and Do" Signal poster (see page 287)
- A bag large enough to put your hand in

PROCEDURE:

1. Ask the students if they have ever had one of those days that everything seems to go wrong. Encourage them to share some of those times.
2. Introduce the story ***Alexander and the Terrible, Horrible, No Good, Very Bad Day***. Explain that it is about a boy, Alexander, who is having one of those really bad days. Ask them, as they listen to the story, to try to remember some of his problems. Tell the students that you have invented a special signal to help with difficult problems and that you'll be needing their help to make that special signal work.
3. Read the story and briefly discuss some of Alexander's problems.
4. Share with them that it seems Alexander could use that special problem-solving signal you brought. Put your hand down in the bag and pull your hand out with your hand in the shape of an OKAY signal (pointer finger and thumb forming a circle with the other three fingers pointing up). Say, "Oh, these are not just any ordinary fingers but they have some powerful imaginary words written on them. Let me show you the three words." Hold up the poster of the okay signal with the three words "Think," "Say" and "Do" written on them. Talk with the students about the importance of finding a good way or an okay way to **"Think"** about the problem. Or maybe something they could **"Say."** Or maybe something they can **"Do"** that would help the problem be okay or at least for them to feel okay about it.
5. Have the students hold up their hand with the okay signal and to point to each of the three fingers saying the three words – "Think," "Say," "Do."

284

6. Tell the students that we need to use that signal to go back and help Alexander. Open the book and choose a problem from the story and ask the students to hold up their signal and share a way that Alexander might "Think," "Say," or "Do" about the problem that would help. Continue eliciting answers until you have an example of each. The following is an example of some possible answers for the situation in the book in which each of Alexander's brothers found a toy in their breakfast cereal but all he found was breakfast cereal:

Think: No big deal. I have plenty of toys already to play with.

Maybe next time, with a different cereal I'll get a toy.

I'm just glad that I have cereal to eat – there are some people in this world who have nothing and are starving.

Say: Ask the brother if he could play with the toy with him or play with it when he was finished. Ask his mother next time to buy him a different cereal.

Do: Get busy eating his cereal so he won't be late for school.

Get a toy from his toy shelf to play with while his bothers play with theirs.

Continue going back through the book and choosing several other problems to discuss using the signal.

7. Tell the students that this signal cannot only help Alexander, but it also can help each of us with problems or difficult situations that come up. Share that we cannot always control the situations or others, but we can control ourselves and how we "Think," "Say" and "Do" about the problem. Recall some of the problems the students shared at the beginning of the lesson. Use the signal in talking through some of those problems.

8. Challenge the students to use their signal during their day to help. Ask the students to share and explain the signal to their parents and teacher so they can also use the signal to help themselves.

SUMMARY POSTER:

OKAY Signal summary poster found on page 287

VARIATIONS/MODIFICATIONS/EXTENTIONS:

- As problems come up during the school day, stop and use the "Think," "Say," and "Do" signal to process.
- Do a creative writing activity in which students can pair up and rewrite a page in the book **Alexander and the Terrible, Horrible, No Good, Very Bad Day** to a good thought using the OKAY signal. Put the book together and you have written a new book – **Alexander and the Wonderful, Fantastic, Super, Not So Very Bad Day.**

JOURNAL ENTRY

Write about a problem that you have had recently.
Write about an okay way to THINK, SAY, and DO about the problem in order to handle it in an okay way.

 **Think, Say, Do**

CLASSROOM GUIDANCE NEWS

Dear Parents,

In our classroom guidance lesson today, we read the story *Alexander and the Terrible, Horrible, No Good, Very Bad Day* by Judith Viorst. In the story Alexander has one problem after another. We looked at several of the problems from the story and the students discussed a better way that Alexander could THINK, or something he could SAY. or something he could DO that would help him handle his problem in an appropriate way.

In real life when problems come up for our children we want to encourage them to stop and think— to come up with a good way to THINK, SAY or DO about the problem. So often we cannot control the situation or others, but we can control how we choose to handle the problem. A signal was shared that students can send themselves to remind them to find a good way to handle the problem. The signal is the "okay" sign made with your hand. Then you simply say the words , THINK, SAY and DO as you touch each of the fingers in the sign. By choosing to find a good way to THINK, SAY, or DO about the problem, we are finding an "okay" way to handle the problem.

As problems come up for your child you may choose to send the "okay" sign and ask him/her to find a good way to THINK, SAY, or DO about the problem. Compliment your child as he/she shares good suggestions on ways to handle. To provide an opportunity for your child to practice, make up some "what if" problems and have your child tell you a good way he/she might choose to handle the problem. Examples of "what if" problems are:

- What if your best friend said he/she didn't want to play with you at recess. What could you THINK, SAY, or DO about it that would help?

- What if you are trying to do your reading homework but you are having trouble sounding out the words. What could you THINK, SAY, or DO about it that would help?

Thank you for taking the time to reinforce this lesson as we work together to help our children be their best. Please feel free to call with questions or concerns you may have about your child, your child's school experience, or our elementary guidance and counseling program.

Sincerely,

Find an OKAY way to handle the problem by what you THINK, SAY, and DO so that you can feel OKAY about the problem.

Coping

Introduction to Coping

GRADE LEVEL(S): 3-5

DESCRIPTION:
There are many unchangeable life events that have occurred and will occur in a child's life. This lesson introduces the concept of coping which is defined for students as "dealing with difficult things in an OK way."

OBJECTIVE(S):
- Students will define coping.
- Students will become aware of coping as a way to positively manage stress.
- Students will distinguish between problems which they can change or control and those with which they must learn to cope.

ESTIMATED TIME: 30 minutes

MATERIAL(S) NEEDED:
- Small lump of clay for each student
- Rock for each student
- Clay or Rock? activity sheet found on page 293
- Summary poster found on page 294

PROCEDURES:
1. Discuss with students the role of the counselor in helping people with problems. Students may be confused in that they think that a counselor MAKES everything OK. Clarify that one of the roles of a counselor is to help students understand that some problems can't be "fixed" and to find the best way to "attack" a problem.
2. Tell the students that they will learn the three "C's" of attacking a problem.
3. Give each child a lump of clay. Ask each child to make something out of the clay. Allow 3 minutes.
4. Allow the students a few minutes to share what they made. Ask them if the clay told them what to make. Bring out that the students CONTROLLED the clay. Write the word "Control" on the board as a way to attack a problem. Tell the students that when they have a problem, the first question they should ask themselves is, "Can I control this problem?" Explain that the other two "C's" will deal with probelms you can control and problems you cannot control. Give examples of problems such as homework, divorce, friends not getting along. Have the students identify with the sample problems given, whether the problem is controllable or not controllable.
5. Ask each child to make something different with the clay. Allow 3 minutes.
6. Again allow students a few minutes to discuss what they made. Discuss what they just did— they CHANGED the clay. Write the word "change" on the board as a way to attack a prob-

lem that can be controlled. Discuss how sometimes things can be changed to fix a problem. If you can't see, you get glasses. If you don't like the way your handwriting is, you change it. Elicit other examples.

7. Take up the clay and distribute a rock to each student. Ask the students to make something out of the rock. Ham it up. When they say they can't, explain that some problems are "clay problems"—they can be controlled by making a change. But some problems are "rock problems"—they cannot be controlled. With "rock problems," we must learn to COPE. Write the word "cope" on the board as the third way to attack a problem. Show the summary poster with the definition of coping..."Dealing with difficult things in an OK way." Have the students name some problems with which they may have to cope - problems that cannot be controlled.

8. Have each student complete the Clay or Rock? activity sheet found on page 293. Share as time allows.

SUMMARY POSTER OR VISUAL REMINDER:

Coping summary poster found on page 294.

VARIATIONS/MODIFICATIONS/EXTENSIONS:

- This lesson provides the counselor an opportunity to identify student needs for small group or individual counseling. Pay special attention to what students identify on their worksheets as "rock problems."
- Have the students search for agencies that help people cope with a variety of issues such as weight, divorce, alcoholism, grief, etc. Have them write these agencies and numbers in a class directory for reference. One idea is a minature phone book similar to the yellow pages with information and phone numbers listed.

JOURNAL ENTRY

Write questions you can ask yourself about a problem to determine if it is a clay problem or a rock problem.

CLASSROOM GUIDANCE NEWS

Dear Parent,

I visited in your child's class today. The topic of classroom guidance was COPING. Coping has been simply defined for students as "dealing with difficult things in an OK way." Today's lesson was an introduction to coping. Students learned today about the 3 C's of attacking a problem. They learned that there are "clay problems" which can be controlled by making a change. Students enjoyed controlling and changing lumps of clay as a concrete way to understand "clay problems." These problems may include a problem with attitude, a problem with a certain behavior, or a problem with a bad habit. Students also learned about "rock problems." Rock problems are those that cannot be controlled. These are the problems with which we must learn to cope. Examples may include the loss of a friend, family member or pet, or problems with how another person is treating us or acting.

Your child completed a writing activity about "clay problems" and "rock problems." Ask your child to show you his/her activity sheet. You may wish to read through what your child wrote and discuss it with him/her.

The next time your child is shares a problem with you, you may wish to use the 3 C's. Ask your child if it's something he/she can control. If so, ask your child what changes he/she can make to control the problem. If not, help your child think of ways to cope with the problem. Work to "attack" the problem using the most effective tool.

Thank you for your support and reinforcement of our guidance lessons. Please feel free to call me if you have questions or concerns about your child, your child's school experience, or our elementary guidance and counseling program.

In partnership,

Clay or Rock ?

Some problems are like **Clay** . . .

These are problems that you can:

CONTROL by making a **CHANGE**

A clay problem that I can **CHANGE** is _____

_____

_____

Other problems are like a **Rock** . . .

These problems cannot be controlled.
With these problems you must learn to:

COPE
Coping means dealing with difficult things in an OK way.

A rock problem that I must **COPE** with is _____

_____

_____

Coping...
dealing with difficult things in an OK way.

Coping with Peer Pressure
Part One

GRADE LEVEL(S): 3-5

DESCRIPTION:
This lesson is an introduction to peer pressure and is designed to help students identify both positive and negative peer pressure.

OBJECTIVE(S):
- Students will define peer pressure.
- Students will identify appropriate times for saying "no."
- Students will recognize how peers and the media affect choices.

ESTIMATED TIME: 30 minutes

MATERIAL(S) NEEDED:
- Magazine ads with both positive and negative products (tobacco, alcohol, milk, toothpaste, etc.)
- Chart tablet
- Marionette puppet

PROCEDURES:
1. Ask the students to recall and share times when their friends or a peer have tried to talk them into doing something. Explain that this is called **PEER PRESSURE.** Define peer pressure as when someone about your age tries to influence you do to something.
2. Simulate peer pressure by having the students make some forced choices. Tell the students you want them to choose between two things. Have one group stand on one side of the room and the other group on the other side facing each other to show which they would choose. Examples of choices include:
   - McDonald's® or Burger King®
   - Basketball or football
   - Broccoli or Spinach
   - Good grades or good at sports
   - Smart or popular

   As the students move about, watch for the students who seem to follow or lead their circle of friends. When you notice this happening, point it out and discuss that this is an example of peer pressure.
3. Discuss how no matter what the issue, most of us look around and see what others are doing and saying. It's natural to do this, but sometimes it can get us into difficult situations. Have the students cite examples of when they have had others trying to influence them to do something they were not sure about. List these on the board (include examples such as making fun of someone).
4. Discuss how peer pressure is not always negative. Classify the examples on the board as neg-

ative or positive peer pressure and write these on the chart tablet under the appropriate heading. If there are no examples of positive peer pressure named, suggest some. Examples may include: your friend keeps telling you to study harder, your friend encourages you to exercise, a friend wants you to come to his/her scouting group with him/her.

5. Explain that friends are not always the ones pressuring us. Show ads from a magazine and discuss how the media attempts to influence us.

6. Show the marionette puppet and explain that we can act like the puppet and allow others to "pull our strings" or that we can decide what's right for us and act accordingly. Acknowledge that while it is difficult to do, we can resist negative peer pressure. Explain that in the next lesson the students will learn about some ways to do just that.

SUMMARY POSTER OR VISUAL REMINDER:
Leave the chart tablet of positive and negative peer pressure examples in the classroom.

VARIATIONS/MODIFICATIONS/EXTENSIONS:
- Read and discuss the book *A Bad Case of Stripes* by David Shannon. This funny story illustrates an extreme case of a girl who wants to fit in.
- Ask the students to keep a Peer Pressure Log to document times during the next week that they feel peer pressure, either negative or positive. Have them record their responses in their log as well.

JOURNAL ENTRY

Create a list of questions you could ask yourself to check if a decision you are making is being influenced by others or the media.
What are some questions you could ask yourself to determine if it was positive peer pressure or negative peer pressure?

CLASSROOM GUIDANCE NEWS

Dear Parents,

I visited in your child's class today and we began a two-part lesson on coping with peer pressure. The goal of today's lesson was to help students understand and recognize negative and positive peer pressures and social influences and to promote independent and responsible decision making. Peer pressure was defined for students as pressure from people your age to do things that you may not normally do on your own. It's important to recognize that, although peer pressure usually carries a negative connotation, some peer pressure can be positive.

To grasp and understand peer pressure, we first played a forced choices game where students actually got to experience peer pressure. We then discussed some times that students may have felt peer pressure and categorized these as either positive or negative. A discussion about other influences led us to looking at and talking about ads and commercials and how these attempt to influence us. In order to better help students understand how others influence us, I used a marionette puppet and made the connection of how peers and other influences may try to "pull our strings."

The desire to fit in is evident in all people. We all want to find a place to belong. As a parent, help your child to understand how his/her choices affect others. Let your child know that the lines of communication are open so that when he/she is faced with negative peer pressure, he/she will come to you to discuss the issues.

In our next lesson, students will actually learn several ways to deal with someone who is pressuring them in a negative way. Students will learn appropriate ways to respond to pressure techniques such as **The Broken Record, The Pity Party, The Humiliator,** and others.

I am enjoying teaching and getting to know your child even better. As always, please feel free to call me at with any concerns that you may have about your child, your child's school experience, or our elementary guidance and counseling program.

Sincerely,

Coping with Peer Pressure
Part Two

GRADE LEVEL(S): 3-5

DESCRIPTION:
This lesson expands the previous lesson to include specific ways to deal with negative peer pressure.

OBJECTIVE(S):
• Students will become aware of coping skills to positively manage negative peer pressure.
• Students will recognize seven tactics that are common to negative peer pressure.

ESTIMATED TIME: 30 minutes

MATERIAL(S) NEEDED:
• Stopping a Peer Pressurer summary poster found on page 301.

PROCEDURES:
1. Remind the students about the definition of peer pressure—when someone about your age tries to influence you to do something. Help them recall examples of positive and negative peer pressure.
2. Explain that today's lesson will focus on specific ways that someone may try to pressure you negatively.
3. Share with the students the different types of peer pressure techniques (summary information of these techniques is provided in the parent letter found on page 300.) Role play how to manage each of the following types of pressure. Discuss how to deal with each and write each on the board. The more you ham this up, the more effective it is with students. You play the role of the peer pressurer by using the following scenarios:

   • **The Yeah, But-ter:** Try to convince a friend at the bus stop to skip school with you for the day. ANSWER: Just keep saying "No"
   • **The Chicken Caller:** You found the science test before the big test day and are trying to convince your friend to cheat with you. ANSWER: Say, "So?" or use humor ("You should've seen the egg I laid this morning!")
   • **The Broken Record:** "Let's put this toilet paper in the toilet and overflow it at school." Keep repeating :Come on, it'll be funny." ANSWER: Be a broken record yourself and keep sending your "no" message.
   • **The Pity Party:** Your parents had a fight last night and your dad left home so you did not get to study for the science test. You're going to get in trouble if you fail so you're trying to convince your best friend to let you cheat off his/her paper. Say, "If you were my friend, you would." ANSWER: Say, "If you were my friend, you wouldn't ask me to do something I don't feel right about doing."

- **The Smooth Talker:** You want to sneak into a rated R movie when you're supposed to be going to a PG movie. Keep reassuring that you've got it all worked out, that no one wil find out. Say, "Don't worry." ANSWER: Just keep saying, "No, that's not for me. But thanks for asking."
- **The Humiliator:** You stole something from the school store and you're trying to convince your friend to do it too…just for the thrill. When your friend refuses, put him/her down by saying something like, "You never do anything fun. You're always so perfect." ANSWER: "So?" or "Your point is…?"
- **The Bully:** You want money from your peer and you're not going to take "no" for an answer! ANSWER: Get help. Tell someone who can help you. Keep telling until you get help.

4. Emphasize that while it's easy to resist when you're role-playing, it's harder to do in real life.
5. Give examples of each type of pressure and see if the students can identify the tactic and tell how to resist.
6. Be sure to send a copy of these tactics found on the summary poster page home with each child.

SUMMARY POSTER OR VISUAL REMINDER:
Stopping a Peer Pressurer summary poster found on page 301.

VARIATIONS/MODIFICATIONS/EXTENSIONS:
- Have the students write some scenarios like the ones above. Then have them switch and pair up with another student to continue to role play.
- There are many videos available about peer pressure. Make these available to teachers.

JOURNAL ENTRY

Write about a time when you handled a negative peer pressure situation well. What did you say or do?

CLASSROOM GUIDANCE NEWS

Dear Parents,

Today in classroom guidance we continued our lesson on coping with peer pressure. You may recall that in the last guidance lesson students learned that peer pressure is pressure from people your age to do things that you may not normally do on your own. We discussed that peer pressure can be positive or negative.

The focus of this week's lesson was on coping with negative peer pressure. When peers try to talk one another into doing something negative, they may use a variety of techniques and methods. Today we discussed some of these methods and practiced some specific assertive behaviors geared to those methods. Please review the seven styles and coping methods we learned about today:

- **THE BROKEN RECORD:** This person repeats the same thing over and over trying to wear down your resistance. The challenge is to outlast the person, stating your refusal just as persistently.

- **THE YEAH, BUT-TER:** This person likes to debate. He/she starts by challenging you with the question "Why not?" and when you state your reason, tries to talk you out of it. Instead of endlessly arguing with such a person, just continue to say "no" without giving any reasons why you are refusing.

- **THE CHICKEN CALLER:** This person tries to trick you into proving that you're not afraid by calling you a "chicken." Don't fall for it! There's nothing wrong with being reluctant to do something that's bad for you. Say, "So?" or use humor. Besides, a real "chicken" is a person who is afraid to do the right thing.

- **THE BULLY:** This person makes physical threats. S/he may even hurt you in some way. Ask an adult to intervene. If no adult is nearby, leave the situation immediately and find someone to help you.

- **THE PITY PARTY:** A person who tries to make you feel sorry for them often uses bribes or threats related to your relationship or friendship. These people are usually bluffing. Since a real friend does not try to control you, stand up for yourself. Show that you have a mind of your own.

- **THE HUMILIATOR:** This person puts others down in an effort to get his/her way. Like the chicken caller, the humilator hopes that you'll go along in order to prove that you're an okay person. You are okay, and you don't have to prove a thing!

- **THE SMOOTH TALKER:** This person pretends to take all the responsibility, calming your fears and reassuring you that everything will be all right. Keep in mind that no one can guarantee a good outcome when what you are doing is wrong or dangerous. You have to look out for yourself.

We practiced each of these ways by role-playing situations that may actually occur. As a parent, you may want to do the same thing. Play "what if" games with your child..."What would you do if someone was trying to get you to steal something on a dare and kept calling you a "chicken?" "What would you do if your best friend tried to talk you into sneaking out of the house in the middle of the night and kept telling you that it would be okay because she had done it hundreds of times?" Just like any other skill, the more a child practices resisting negative peer pressure, the better s/he becomes. As always, please feel free to call me with any questions or concerns that you have about your child, your child's school experience, or our elementary guidance and counseling program.

Sincerely,

STOPPING A PEER PRESSURER

The "Yeah, but-ter..."
Way to stop him/her: Just simply say "No, thanks."

The Chicken Caller
Ways to stop him/her: Say, "So?" or use humor.

The Broken Record
Way to stop him/her: Be a broken record yourself.

The Pity Party
Way to stop him/her: Say, "If you were my friend, you wouldn't ask me to do something I don't feel right about doing."

The Smooth Talker
Way to stop him/her: Say "No, that's not for me. But thanks for asking."

The Humiliator
Way to stop him/her: Say, "So?" or "Your point is...?"

The Bully
Way to stop him/her: TELL someone who can help you. Keep telling until you get help.

Coping with Difficult Tasks

GRADE LEVEL(S): 3-5

DESCRIPTION:
This lesson helps students understand that while circumstances may seem overwhelming, determination and hard work are key factors in coping. The concrete example of a hurdle gives students a visual picture of beating difficult odds.

OBJECTIVE(S):
- Students will identify things that are difficult for them.
- Students will identify ways to cope with difficult tasks.
- Students will recognize the relationship between determination and achievement.

ESTIMATED TIME: 30 minutes

MATERIAL(S) NEEDED:
- Pieces of paper and scissors
- Coping with Difficult Tasks activity sheet found on page 305

PROCEDURES:
1. Describe something that you have difficulty doing—something that seems almost impossible for you. Ask the students to think of something that is difficult for them, but do not allow them to share at this time.
2. Explain that many times things seem almost impossible. Show the piece of paper and ask the students if they think you can cut a hole in the paper that's large enough to pass your whole body through. If the students think they can do it, allow a few to try (don't worry, they won't be able to do it.) Discuss how this seems almost impossible and then demonstrate how you can do it using the following steps.
   - Fold paper in half (square or rectangle).
   - Cut in a straight line from fold to open edges—but not all the way—at both ends.
   - Continue to cut strips all the way across, alternating open edges to fold—fold to open edges—but DO NOT cut all the way down.
   - Cut along the fold—EXCEPT 2 outer strips.
   - Open and step through the hole.

   Discuss how sometimes things we think are impossible are really possible, we just have to find a different way to do them.
3. Tell the students about Tom Dempsey:

   Tom Dempsey set a National Football League record in 1970 while playing as a place-kicker for the New Orleans Saints. He kicked a 63-yard field goal. The previous record was 56 yards and had been set 17 years prior. While this may just seem like any ordinary story of a record-breaker, Dempsey's story is anything but ordinary. Tom was born without a right hand and with only half of his right foot—his kicking foot. Tom beat the odds. He did not want people to think of him as "handicapped" so he never let his physical condition become an excuse to not try hard. He knew it would be harder for him to become a successful NFL player, so he TRIED harder.

4. Explain what a hurdle is and discuss Tom Dempsey's "hurdle". Discuss what helped him overcome his hurdle—DETERMINATION. Ask:
   - What does it take to show determination? (staying focused, not giving up, try-try-then try a different way)
   - What would have happened if Tom Dempsey did not have determination?
5. Have the students think of several "hurdles" they need to get over. Using the worksheet, have the students draw hurdles, label them, and draw themselves jumping over them. Have them write three specific things that they plan to do to get over the "hurdle" they identified.
6. Share as time allows.

SUMMARY POSTER OR VISUAL REMINDER:
Hurdle summary poster found on page 306.

VARIATIONS/MODIFICATIONS/EXTENSIONS:
- Set up hurdles on a track outside or in the gym and allow the students to practice jumping the hurdles.
- Have the students make a list of things that they used to find difficult but can now do.

JOURNAL ENTRY

Pretend that you are a parent helping your child deal with a difficult task. Write about the difficult task and what you would say or do to help your child have determination to overcome that "hurdle."

CLASSROOM GUIDANCE NEWS

Dear Parent,

Today in classroom guidance students learned about coping with difficult tasks. As a parent you have no doubt heard this before: "I can't do it. It's too hard." Perhaps you've even said or thought this yourself. Students learned about the power of hard work and determination. Ask your child to tell you the story of Tom Dempsey, the New Orleans Saints place-kicker who was born without a right hand and only half of a right foot. His story makes a powerful testament to the importance of determination and hard work.

There may be difficult tasks in students' lives—multiplication facts, spelling tests, baseball, etc. Students learned that these tasks present hurdles but that hurdles were made for jumping. Students then drew a hurdle in their lives and made a plan for getting over that hurdle. Be sure to ask your child to see his/her drawing. Discuss the hurdle and the plan for getting over the hurdle.

It is a pleasure to work with your child. As always, please feel free to call me if you have any questions or concerns about your child, your child's school experience, or our elementary guidance and counseling program.

Sincerely,

COPING WITH DIFFICULT TASKS

All it takes is determination and hard work. Below draw a hurdle and label it with a difficult task for you. Then draw yourself jumping over the hurdle. Write a plan for helping yourself get over this hurdle. Include at least three specific ideas in your plan.

My plan for getting over this hurdle...

1. _____

   _____

   _____

2. _____

   _____

   _____

3. _____

   _____

   _____

Sometimes things are difficult, but HARD WORK and DETERMINATION can get you over the hurdle.

Coping
A Matter of Attitude

GRADE LEVEL(S): 3-5

DESCRIPTION:
This lesson helps students understand that their attitude is a matter of choice. Using attitude glasses, students are able to understand how they can see things differently.

OBJECTIVE(S):
- Students will identify three ways to look at situations.
- Students will recognize the relationship between thoughts and attitude.

ESTIMATED TIME: 30 minutes

MATERIAL(S) NEEDED:
- Glass filled halfway with water
- 3 pairs of sunglasses: one with red lenses, one with blue lenses, and one with yellow lenses (these can be made with colored plastic wrap or are available in most dollar discount stores)

PROCEDURES:
1. Show the glass half filled with water and ask the students if the glass is half full or half empty. Allow both sides to explain their point. Try to pin the students down to the "right" answer. Listen carefully until a student says that both are right; it just depends on how you "look" at it.
2. Discuss how sometimes things happen to us that we don't like—our friend is mean, we fail a test, we have to go visit relatives when we had planned to spend the weekend with friends.
3. Ask the students to define attitude. Simply stated, your attitude is how you act. Tell the students that our thoughts lead to our attitudes and that, just like with the glass of water, our attitude depends on how we "see" a situation.
4. Show the students the glasses one pair at a time. Explain that when wearing the red glasses, you see things with a "fiery red attitude." A red attitude blames everyone else; nothing is ever your fault. The blue attitude is the "poor little me" attitude. People with a blue attitude always make things out to be worse than they actually are. The yellow attitude allows you to look for a positive in a negative situation. People with yellow attitudes do not always have good things happen to them; they just do not allow negative events to ruin their attitude.
5. Use this example: I'm driving to school and I'm running late. I have just enough time to make it when a car pulls out in front of me and is driving 35 miles an hour in a 55 mile an hour zone. Place the glasses on as you respond with each of the following attitudes:
   - Red: "Hey! What do you think you're doing? You're going to cause me to be late. I can't believe they give a driver's license to someone like you!"
   - Blue: "Oh, man. This always happens to me. Now I'm going to be late for work and my boss is going to be mad and I might even lose my job. Oh, why do I even try? This day is ruined before it ever even starts."

- Yellow: "Oh, no. I can't believe this happened just when I thought I was going to be on time. Well, I'll only be a few minutes late and I'm sure my boss will understand. Tomorrow I'm going to set my clock ten minutes earlier so I'll be sure I won't have to rush."

6. Allow the students to practice. Read a situation like those below and call three students to model each of the attitudes.
   - You strike out at bat.
   - Your parents let your brother go to the movie with his friends but won't let you go.
   - Your teacher chooses someone who is not as good an actor as you for the lead in the class play.
   - You are not invited to a popular classmate's birthday party.
   - You study hard but still fail a science test.

7. Discuss which glasses help you to truly feel the best. Reiterate that you choose the attitude you are going to have. By taking control of your thoughts, you take control of your attitude.

SUMMARY POSTER OR VISUAL REMINDER:

Half full or Half Empty summary poster found on page 310.

EXTENSION:

Have the students work in small groups to list real life situations in which a person might have a "fiery" attitude and a "blue" attitude. Collect and mix the situations up. Then redistribute. This time have each group write a "yellow" attitude way to look at the situation.

JOURNAL ENTRY

Pretend you are a traveling salesperson and you are promoting your new product, "The Positive Attitude Glasses." They only come in one color...sunny yellow. Write a promotional for the product and include the answer to the questions: who? what? when? where? and how?

Coping

A Matter of Attitude

CLASSROOM GUIDANCE NEWS

Dear Parent,

Attitude is everything.
ATTITUDE determines ALTITUDE.

You may have heard these popular sayings about attitude. Attitude is defined as a way of thinking, acting, or feeling. Certainly attitude influences the way that we choose to react or respond to a situation. A positive attitude can make a tiresome activity less dreadful while a negative attitude can make a fun activity dreadful.

Attitude also plays a part in how we perceive situations. Today's lesson focused on another coping strategy—that of seeing difficult or troublesome situations differently. We have all heard the example of the glass being half full or half empty. This depends on how we choose to focus. Our attitude depends upon what we choose to focus on when a situation happens.

We discussed three different attitudes that we can "put on" when frustrations and disappointments occur. One is the "yellow" attitude, which means looking for the positive. A second is the "blue" attitude which can also be referred to as the "poor little me" syndrome. The third is the "red" attitude, which is the angry response. We had fun putting on "attitude glasses" and role-playing different situations where attitude can make a big difference. Students were encouraged to think of their attitude when frustrations occur and to try to wear the "yellow glasses" to see the positive in the situation.

I enjoy working with your child in classroom guidance. As always, please feel free to call me with questions or concerns that you have about your child, your child's school experience, or our elementary guidance and counseling program.

Sincerely,

Half full or half empty?
Your attitude depends on how you see things.

Red attitude: blames others; angry

Blue attitude: "poor little me"; makes things out to be worse than they are

Yellow attitude: may not like the situation but tries to make the best of things

WHICH ARE YOU?

The Ripple Effect of Attitude

GRADE LEVEL(S): 3-5

DESCRIPTION:
One person's attitude can affect another person's attitude. This lesson helps students understand what others' attitudes can do to them and what their attitude can do to others.

OBJECTIVE(S):
- Students will identify the ripple effect of attitude.
- Students will distinguish between negative ripples and positive ripples.
- Students will identify what to do when someone sends them a negative ripple.

ESTIMATED TIME: 30 minutes

MATERIAL(S) NEEDED:
- A round pan with water
- The book **Andrew's Angry Words** by Dorothea Lachner or **The Quarreling Book** by Charlotte Zolotow or **Snail Started It!** by Katja Reider and Angela von Roehl
- The Ripple Effect at Work activity sheet found on page 314

PROCEDURES:
1. Explain that today's lesson is about how your attitude affects others. Ask the students if a situation like the following has ever happened to them: You go home in a good mood but mom (dad, brother, sister, grandma) comes home in a bad mood and pretty soon everyone is in a bad mood. Allow the students to share.
2. Read one of the stories above which depict how one person's actions/attitude spill over to others. Discuss the story.
3. Illustrate how attitude affects others with a pan of water. Place a small drop of water in the pan of water. Tell the students that this represents their attitude. Let them watch the ripples. If the phrase RIPPLE EFFECT is not brought out, give it this terminology. Explain that attitude does the same thing as this drop of water.
4. Explain that positive and negative attitudes have the ripple effect. Have the students think of a positive and a negative ripple they have begun. Have them complete the activity sheet The Ripple Effect at Work found on page 314. At the center of each ripple, students write what action they did (either positive or negative.) Then they write how their action affected another person either positively or negatively, and then how that person's action affected someone else, etc.
5. Share as time allows.
6. Explain to the tudents that when someone sends them a negative ripple, they can choose to return a positive one. Challenge them to do this (I offer the example of when a check-out clerk is being rude or not talking, to say something like, "You must have to be on your feet a long time which I'm sure is not easy.")

 **The Ripple Effect of Attitude**

SUMMARY POSTER OR VISUAL REMINDER:
Ripple Effect summary poster found on page 315

VARIATIONS/MODIFICATIONS/EXTENSIONS:
- Prior to this lesson, speak to the students' science teacher. The ripple effect is a concept covered in many science curricula and it may be possible to time this lesson with the science study.
- As a class, brainstorm and list general positive statements or ripples that can be used to counteract someone who says or does something that is not nice. What positive statements could you say if;
  - someone brags about how well they can kick the ball
  - someone changes the TV channel without saying anything
  - someone says "Where did you get those awful looking shoes?"
  - someone angrily pushes their books off their desk onto yours

JOURNAL ENTRY

Create a start to a positive ripple and write a story about what positive things might happen in your positive ripple. Then put your positive ripple into action.

The Ripple Effect of Attitude

CLASSROOM GUIDANCE NEWS

Dear Parent,

Today in classroom guidance, we explored the effects of personal attitudes on others. A person's attitude, positive or negative, has far-reaching effects on other people. We termed this the "ripple effect." We've all experienced something similar to this: a family member comes home after a bad day at school or work and says or does something negative to another family member who in turn does something negative to another family member, etc. Before long, everyone in the household is upset, frustrated, or angry. This is the ripple effect! On the other hand, if someone in the household has a positive attitude and begins to share compliments, smiles, or words of encouragement with other family members, this can also have a ripple effect.

I read students a book which depicts a scenario similar to the negative one mentioned above. Students were then asked to think about two situations from their own lives—one positive and one negative—where they recalled the ripple effect at work. We discussed we can handle negative ripples by returning a positive ripple.

Attitude is everything! As a parent, you model behavior that your child will imitate. Thus, it is important to watch the ripples you send to your child. One way to do this is to talk to your child when you are having a bad day and show him/her how you are going about getting yourself into a better frame of mind so that the ripples you send out are positive ones.

As always, please feel free to call me with any questions or concerns that you have about your child, your child's school experience, or our elementary guidance and counseling program.

Sincerely,

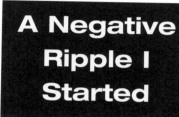

A Negative Ripple I Started

A Positive Ripple I Started

The Ripple Effect of Attitude

Your attitude affects others.
Send positive ripples.
Stop a negative ripple with a caring comment.

Positive Disks

GRADE LEVEL(S): 3-5

DESCRIPTION:
This lesson uses the analogy of a tape recorder and a computer disk to emphasize the importance of playing positive messages in your mind when difficult or negative situations occur.

OBJECTIVE(S):
- Students will distinguish between positive and negative thoughts.
- Students will understand the correlation between our thoughts and our feelings.
- Students will make positive statements about themselves.

ESTIMATED TIME: 30 minutes

MATERIAL(S) NEEDED:
- A tape recorder
- A computer disk
- Saving Positive Messages activity sheet found on page 319

PROCEDURES:
1. Ask the students if they have ever had someone tell them that they couldn't do something because they were not smart enough, strong enough, or good enough. Allow the students to share.
2. Discuss how we sometimes get negative messages in our heads and how these messages play over and over like a tape in our heads. Using a tape recorder, tape a negative message like "You're not fast enough to be on the track team." Rewind and allow students to hear the message several times.
3. Explain that these negative messages sometimes keep us from doing things that we really want to do. In order to keep this from happening, we can re-write those messages and say positive things about negative situations. Tape over the message that you just recorded with a reframed message like, "I may not be as fast as some people, but I run every day and I'm getting faster every day. If I keep trying, I can make my goal."
4. Write this on the board:

Thought ➞ Feeling ➞ Action
Discuss how the way we think about something greatly influences our feelings. In turn, our feelings influence our actions. Say, "If I think I'm not fast enough for the track team, I will feel negatively about myself. Then when it's time to run, I probably will not perform as well as I could."
5. Explain that we must have many positive messages saved to replay in our minds when the negative ones come. If these messages are not saved, we will find ourselves going back to the same old negative ones.

Positive Disks

6. Compare the tape from the recorder to a computer disk. Show a computer disk and discuss how we can save messages on it.

7. Distribute copies of the Saving Positive Messages activity sheet. Have each student write some positive messages that they can "SAVE" to replay in their minds when tough situations happen.

SUMMARY POSTER OR VISUAL REMINDER:

Computer Disk summary poster found on page 320

VARIATIONS/MODIFICATIONS/EXTENSIONS:

- Read the book **The Eagles Who Thought They Were Chickens** by Mychal Wynn.
- Have the students type positive message about themselves on the computer and save them to a disk. Ask the teacher to continue to allow the students to add positive messages throughout the year.

JOURNAL ENTRY

A computer sets up different files. Think of several places where you need to think positive messages (school, sports, chores, etc.) These are your "files." List several "files" and then write some positive messages under each.

Positive Disks

CLASSROOM GUIDANCE NEWS

Dear Parent,

Today in classroom guidance we discussed how negative thoughts can keep us from doing and being our best. At some point we have all been told or made to think, "You can't do that." Maybe you believed you were not strong enough or smart enough or creative enough. Your child may have also already encountered a similar situation.

Students learned a formula for how important our thoughts are:

Thought ➝ Feeling ➝ Action

We discussed how if you think you are not good enough, you will feel badly about yourself. Then when it is time to act (to actually do the task), you most likely will not do as well as you could do.

In order to think more positively, it is important to have positive messages saved so that when we need them, they are there. We used the analogies of a tape recorder which plays messages and a computer disk where we save messages. Students wrote some positive thoughts and messages. Ask your child to see his/her activity sheet. Discuss other messages that you could give your child to add to his/her "disk."

At home when your child becomes discouraged, encourage him/her to change a thought so that his/her feelings may change. Avoid saying, "You shouldn't think like that." Instead say, "How could you think differently about that?"

Thank you for your continued support. As always, please feel free to call me with any questions or concerns that you may have about your child, your child's school experience, or our elementary guidance and counseling program.

In partnership,

SAVING POSITIVE MESSAGES

Below write three positive messages that you can send yourself when negative thoughts come into your mind. These can be positive experiences you have, things you're good at, or sayings that you've heard.

1. _____

_____

_____

2. _____

_____

_____

3. _____

_____

_____

Whenever negative thoughts pop up, pull up these positive thoughts and say them over and over to yourself.

Thought ➞ Feeling ➞ Action

**You control your thoughts!
Save positive messages!
Use these positive thoughts
when tough times come!**

The Roller Coaster

GRADE LEVEL(S): 3-5

DESCRIPTION:
This lesson helps students understand that setbacks are a part of life. The analogy "life is like a roller coaster" gives students a mental image of the highs and lows of life.

OBJECTIVE(S):
- Students will understand that all people experience changes.
- Students will identify specific ways to cope with difficult circumstances.
- Students will identify the highs and lows in their lives.

ESTIMATED TIME: 30 minutes

MATERIAL(S) NEEDED:
- Roller Coaster activity sheet found on page 324

PROCEDURES:

1. Ask the students to recall and share times they have felt disappointed.
2. Distinguish that in most cases disappointments occur about things over which we have no control. Explain to the students that they have control over their actions.
3. Ask the students how many of them like roller coasters. Draw two roller coasters on the board—one with highs and lows and one that is fairly even and flat. Ask which would be the most exciting and why. Explain that the first is filled with highs and lows, ups and downs.
4. Tell them that "Life is like a roller coaster" and explain this by saying that there are high times and low times. Give examples of feelings that we experience when we are at or building to a high and those that we experience when we are at or going to a low.
5. Give each student the Roller Coaster activity sheet. Call out some life events and have them point on the roller coaster at the top of the page to indicate where their feelings would be.
   - You try out for a part in a play and get it.
   - Someone teases you because your clothes are not "cool."
   - Your friends are going to a movie that your parents will not let you see.
   - You overhear your parents bragging about something you did.
   - You forget your homework.
   - You win a science prize.
   - You get to spend the night with a friend.
   - A loved one dies.
6. Have the students fill in the three lines above the high points to name three of their happiest times and the two lines below the lows to indicate two of their saddest times.

The Roller Coaster

7. Refer back to the roller coaster on the board and explain that when the coaster is at a low, it must work hard to get back up to the high. Many students who have ridden a roller coaster will be able to describe how the coaster feels as it is pulling itself up the first hill. The same is true for us—when we are low, we must work hard to get back "up." Refer to the bottom of the activity sheet. Show that there are some suggestions for getting back up. Read the suggestions that may help and have the students add four of their own.

8. Caution about doing harmful or negative things to get back up (drugs, gangs, etc.) Discuss how these "quick fixes" only take you lower because after the "high" you have two problems with which to deal: the original problem and the problem of using drugs (or alcohol, or breaking the law, etc.)

SUMMARY POSTER OR VISUAL REMINDER:
Life Is Like a Roller Coaster poster found on page 325

VARIATIONS/MODIFICATIONS/EXTENSIONS:
• Have the students develop other analogies that illustrate coping with difficult circumstances.
• Monitor the students carefully as they write their two lows. This is helpful in assessing student needs in terms of group or individual counseling.

JOURNAL ENTRY

Life is like a roller coaster with its ups and downs. Write the positive suggestions to help you get out of the downs and head back up on your roller coaster of life.

CLASSROOM GUIDANCE NEWS

Dear Parent,

It has been said that life is like a roller coaster. Events over which we have little or no control take us to high points in our lives and bring us to low points as well. In order to deal with these ups and downs, we must learn to cope. We define coping as "dealing with difficult things in an OK way." Today's lesson focused on coping with tough circumstances.

It is important for children to begin to understand things over which they have control and things over which they have little or no control. People always have control over their own behavior and actions. However, bad things do happen that leave us feeling sad, angry and/or helpless. Therefore, it is important to be able to take responsibility for the negative feelings associated with these events and engage in appropriate activities that relieve stress and build positive energy rather than continuing to dwell on the actual event—**THAT'S COPING.**

In our lesson today, students thought of some of the "highs" of their "roller coaster ride through life" and some of the "lows." Ask your child to see his/her activity sheet. Please discuss these with your child and talk to him/her about the feelings as well as how he/she coped with the lows. You will also find some suggestions and your child's own thoughts on activities that could help him/her regain positive energy following a negative event.

It is a pleasure working with your child. As always, please feel free to call me with any questions or concerns that you have about your child, your child's school experience, or our elementary guidance and counseling program.

Sincerely,

We all have HIGHS and LOWS.
Write two of each of yours below:

<u>Highs</u>   <u>Lows</u>

1. _____   1. _____

   _____   _____

2. _____   2. _____

   _____   _____

Directions: When you are at a low point, you will need to do something to help you feel better. Here are some ideas. The four blank lines are for you to write four ideas of your own.

Talk to someone you trust
Write a letter to yourself stating all the great things about you
Go visit a neighbor who needs cheering up
Dance
Play with your pet
Exercise

_____

_____

_____

_____

The Roller Coaster

WAYS TO HELP YOURSELF GET BACK "UP" AFTER A "DOWN"

- Talk to someone you trust.
- Ride a bike, walk, jog, skateboard.
- Write about your feelings in a journal or diary.
- Read a book.
- Play with a friend or with your pet.
- Draw, paint, or make something from Legos®.
- Dance.
- Listen to music or play a musical instrument.
- Go visit a neighbor who needs cheering up.
- Write a letter to a friend or relative who lives far away.

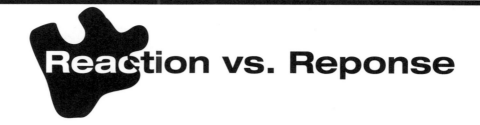

Reaction vs. Reponse

GRADE LEVEL(S): 3-5

DESCRIPTION:
This lesson is especially for students who say, "It wasn't my fault," or "I couldn't help it." The idea of responsibility for actions is emphasized along with thinking through appropriate ways to handle feelings.

OBJECTIVE(S):
- Students will identify ways to appropriately express feelings.
- Students will develop an awareness of the importance of personal responsibility.
- Students will explore the consequences of actions of self and others.

ESTIMATED TIME: 30 minutes

MATERIAL(S) NEEDED:
- Magnets and/or balloons
- One strip of drawing paper (6" x 18") for each student

PROCEDURES:
1. Share a story about a child tearing up her homework last night because he/she got very frustrated. Explain that this hurt only him/her but at the time she/he felt "out of control."
2. Demonstrate natural reactions by using some of the following: magnets attracting and pushing, blowing into a balloon or party favor.
3. Discuss why the reactions occurred—they are natural and give no thought to the outcome. Write the word "reaction" on the board. Say that the child you mentioned earlier gave a reaction to being frustrated by his/her homework but that it was not a natural reaction. However, it occurred without thought to the outcome.
4. Have the students share other natural reactions. Then have students share times they have reacted to a situation—-acted without thinking of the outcome.
5. Write the word "response" on the board and indicate that this is often confused with reaction. Explain that a response to a situation is when you think first of the outcome. Give the example of the child with the homework problem asking for help with him/her homework, and ask why this is a response rather than a reaction.
6. Read several situations and have the students indicate if it is a reaction or a response:
   You are suddenly frightened and you scream.
   You are called a name and you call a name back.
   You drop an egg and it breaks.
   You are being tickled and you laugh.
   You see somebody who needs help and you help him/her.
7. Write the word "responsibility" on the board and print the two words "response" and "abil-

ity" underneath the components of the word. Explain that responsibility means acknowledging one's own power to choose how to act. Contrast a responsible attitude with one of blaming others by giving the following examples:

- You fail a math test and admit it's because you did not study.
- You fail a math test and tell your parents it's because the test was not fair.

8. Provide each student with a 6" x 18" strip of drawing paper. Have the students fold the paper into four squares.

9. Have the students illustrate the following scene in square 1: A friend laughs at you when you accidentally trip on a book left on the floor. In square 2, have the student illustrate a reaction they could make. In squares 3 and 4 have them illustrate two responses they might make instead that demonstrate taking control of the situation and acting in a thoughtful way to try to bring about a positive resolution.

10. Share illustrations upon completion and reinforce the idea that responsible behavior means thinking and taking control.

11. Review by asking:
   - What does it mean to be responsible?
   - What are the advantages of taking responsibility?
   - What can happen if you consistently react rather than respond?

SUMMARY POSTER OR VISUAL REMINDER:

Responsibility summary poster on page 329

VARIATIONS/MODIFICATIONS/EXTENSIONS:

- Make a class list of common classroom problems such as cutting in line, making irritating noises, interrupting, etc. Then have the class think of appropriate responses to each of the problems. Keep the list posted so that students have options for handling each of these situations. As new problems arise, add these and appropriate responses to the list.
- Have the students think of their own problem and do the activity listed in step number eight above.

JOURNAL ENTRY

Write about a situation that typically bothers you. Rather than react to the situation, write about a response that shows acting in a thoughtful, responsible way to bring about a positive resolution.

CLASSROOM GUIDANCE NEWS

Dear Parents,

What is the difference in a reaction and a response? This was the subject of today's classroom guidance lesson. We focused on examining the outcomes of personal choices which occur as a result of a natural reaction versus those made in response to a situation or circumstance.

Children are basically in a powerless position in our society and thus they often lack a sense of their own power and fail to perceive their own responsibility when making choices about interactions with others. You've probably heard this, "I couldn't help it, " or "I just couldn't control myself." However, developing a sense of internal control is essential to getting along with others as well as being successful in school and in careers later in life.

Today we studied the two words reaction and response. A reaction was defined as something that naturally happens or occurs without thought to the outcome. For example, if you touch a hot stove you will pull your hand away. This occurs as a natural reaction. Or if someone pulls out in front of you while you are driving you may blow your horn. This is an example of a reaction without thought to the outcome. However, a response occurs when you think of how you will choose to deal with a circumstance. Children learned that the word response is part of the word responsibility which means acknowledging one's own power to choose how to act.

Your child illustrated the difference in a reaction and a response by drawing a scenario of accidentally tripping on a book that was left on the floor. Ask your child to share his/her drawing with you and discuss with him/her the consequences of reacting versus responding. You may share times in your own life when you have chosen to respond rather than react to situations that were difficult for you.

I enjoy working with your child. As always, please feel free to call me with questions or concerns that you may have about your child, your child's school experience, or our elementary guidance and counseling program.

Sincerely,

Reaction vs. Reponse

RESPONSIBILITY

Response   **Ability**

Umbrella of Self-Confidence

GRADE LEVEL(S:) 3-5

Description:

An umbrella, which is used for protection against the rain or sun, is correlated to our self-confidence, which is used to protect us from getting "all washed up" from our negative experiences.

Objectives:

- Students will define self-confidence and will explore its importance in dealing with negative experiences.
- Students will develop strategies for strengthening their self-confidence.

Estimated Time: 30 minutes

Materials Needed:

- Large poster/paper cut-out of an umbrella with the word "Self-Confidence" (pattern on page 333)
- Poster/paper cut-out of raindrops (pattern on page 334)
- Umbrella
- Umbrella activity sheet (page 335) copied for each student

Procedures:

1. Open up the umbrella in the classroom. (If need, add a few made-up magic words so when a student says you are going to have bad luck you can reply that your magic words took care of that.) Ask the students what an umbrella is used for. Draw from students that the purpose of an umbrella is to protect you from the rain or in some cases from the sun. If it were raining outside and we went outside without an umbrella we would get soaked – all washed up! Share with the students that today we are going to talk about a different kind of umbrella.

2. Display the poster umbrella with the word "Self-Confidence." Ask the students what self-confidence means. Elicit responses similar to: belief in yourself and your ability that you can do it; that you're special.

3. Relate that self-confidence can be thought of as our protection. It protects us from negative things that happen to us by not letting it get to us but continuing to know that we are capable and special.

4. Display the poster/paper cut-out of raindrops found on page 334 above the poster umbrella of self-confidence. Discuss some of these negative things that can happen to all of us— getting laughed at or being left out or having trouble learning something new, etc. Have the students add additional raindrops (write their suggestions on the blank raindrops) of negative things that can happen to us.

5. Relate for students that when these negative things happen in our lives it is our self-confidence, or belief in ourselves that we are good, that can protect us from being "all washed up."

6. Ask the students whose responsibility it is to get their umbrella or raincoat when going outside when it is raining. Elicit the response that it is their responsibility. Relate that the same is true of their self-confidence. However, there may be help from others – parents, teachers, friends in building our self-confidence just as there are times when others may remind us to take out our umbrella when it's raining.

7. Share with the students that our self-confidence can be strengthened from the way we choose to think about or look at a situation or ourselves. Review each of the negative situation raindrops and discuss a way we could choose to think about or look at the situation so that we continue to feel capable and worthwhile.

8. Express to the students that building a strong self-confidence takes effort and thought. The students can begin strengthening their self-confidence by completing the Umbrella activity sheet. The sheet focuses on each person appreciating what they do well, their positive qualities and things they do about which they feel proud.

Summary Poster or Visual:

Umbrella of Self-Confidence summary poster found on page 336

Variations / Modifications / Extensions:

- If a student asks you what to do with their completed Umbrella Activity Sheet, a reply may be: "It's not as important what you do with that sheet of paper, but it is important for you to put that information from the sheet in your head and to always remember your strengths and what you are proud of about yourself. " After that initial statement you may encourage them to display their paper at home or in their notebook to remind them about their strengths.

- Have the students write a creative story of a time their main character used self-confidence to handle a negative situation.

- Have the students write self-confidence statements and display these on a poster umbrella with the negative situation raindrops.

JOURNAL ENTRY

Write about a time you chose to use your self-confidence to deal with a negative experience in your life.

CLASSROOM GUIDANCE NEWS

Dear Parents,

In our lesson today, Umbrella of Self-Confidence, we talked about the importance of having confidence in ourselves. So often we see our children get discouraged and down on themselves when they encounter a negative experience in their lives such as trouble learning something new, getting laughed at, or being left out. As our children are growing up we cannot protect them from these negative experiences of the real world that are inevitable. However, we can equip our children with the skills to handle these negative experiences. Today's focus was on building up our own confidence in ourselves - that we are capable and then choosing good ways to think about these negative situations.

The idea of self-confidence was related to the concept of an umbrella – just as an umbrella protects us from the rain (or sun) our self-confidence can protect us against these negative experiences, so we don't feel "all washed up". We talked about building up and strengthening our self-confidence by appreciating the things we are good at, acknowledging our positive qualities and characteristics, and being proud of the things we do well. When a negative situation occurs we need to remind ourselves that we are a capable and confident person, and then we need to think about or look at the situation to deal with it positively. If we have made a mistake, we need to forgive ourselves and to learn from that mistake. If we are having trouble learning something new, then we can remind ourselves to stick with it because that is the only way to learn (we may recall earlier events that were hard to first learn but that are easy now, such as when we were first learning to ride a bike).

To help your child build up their Umbrella of Self-Confidence to protect themselves, ask him/her to point out in his/her day the things done well and encourage him/her to be proud of those things. Somehow we seem to focus on the negative, but help your child develop the skill to focus on the positive. When negative experiences happen, ask your child if he/she has the confidence umbrella up to protect him/her from getting "all washed up." Ask him/her to share a good way to think about the problem.

I appreciate your help in working together so that our students feel good about who they are. This enables their learning to be their best. If you have any questions or concerns about your child, your child's school experience, or our elementary guidance and counseling program, please feel free to call me.

Sincerely,

Umbrella of Self-Confidence

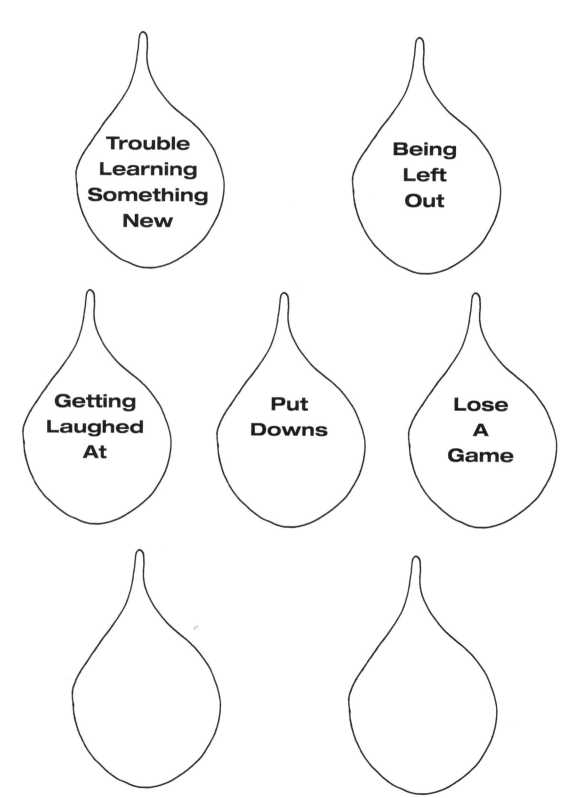

Trouble
Learning
Something
New

Being
Left
Out

Getting
Laughed
At

Put
Downs

Lose
A
Game

Self-Confidence

3 things I do well...

_____

_____

_____

3 positive qualities or characteristics I have...

_____

_____

_____

Something I have done recently that I am proud of...

_____

_____

_____

335

Umbrella of Self-Confidence

Umbrella of Self Confidence

**Remember the things you do well,
your positive qualities or characteristics,
and the things of which you are proud.**

Tune Into WPOS

GRADE LEVEL(S): 3-5

DESCRIPTION:
This lesson focuses on taking control of your own behavior by taking charge of your thoughts. It explains the use of positive self-talk to deal with negative thoughts.

OBJECTIVE(S):
- Students will demonstrate the ability to use positive self-talk to deal with negative thoughts and feelings.
- Students will recognize and identify unique personal characteristics and strengths.
- Students will demonstrate a positive attitude about themselves.

ESTIMATED TIME: 30 minutes

MATERIAL(S) NEEDED:
- A radio
- A glass half-filled with water
- Tuning into WPOS activity sheet found on page 340

PROCEDURES:
1. Tell a story about a child who did not make a baseball team. Explain that the child is saying things about himself/herself like, "I stink at sports. All my friends are on the team and now they probably won't want to play with me anymore. I'm left out when they go to practices and games. And I know my parents are disappointed. They really wanted me to play baseball this season."
2. Acknowledge that this child has had a disappointing experience and that at times we all have "bad" things to happen. If the students would like to share some, allow this.
3. Show a radio. Demonstrate how a radio works and that if you don't like what's on one station how you can change stations to get rid of what was on before. Compare this to the "voicebox" inside our heads—the little voice we hear when we are trying to make decisions or when we experience something good or bad.
4. Explain that our "voiceboxes" have two stations—WNEG—the negative channel which gives us self put-downs. The other is WPOS—the positive channel. It gives us positive messages. Explain that we can CHOOSE which we will tune into just like on a radio.
5. Show the glass half filled. Ask if the glass is half-full or half-empty. Discuss. Compare this to how we think about ourselves when we are disappointed.
6. Use some of the following examples and have the students tell what WNEG and WPOS would say in each circumstance:
   - You strike out in a game.
   - You don't get invited to a sleep-over.

- You didn't get a part in the school play.
- You work hard on your science project but don't win a prize and your friend who didn't work as hard does.

7. Explain that in order to have positive messages "stick" we must have saved them inside our heads—similar to a computer. Acknowledge how difficult it is to tune into WPOS when we're disappointed. Emphasize that staying tuned there can help because it keeps you in practice. Use the analogy of playing a sport you have not played in a long time. If you have not practiced, it's hard to be good when you start again. However, if you practice routinely, when you want to play, you will do better.

8. Using the Tuning Into WPOS worksheet, have the students write three positive statements about themselves beginning with "I am..."

9. Summarize by telling the students to give themselves an inside hug each night before they go to sleep. This is done by telling yourself at least one thing you are proud of about yourself.

SUMMARY POSTER OR VISUAL REMINDER:

What Station Are You Listening To? summary poster found on page 341

VARIATIONS/MODIFICATIONS/EXTENSIONS:

- Have the students write positive statements about others in the class. Have each child choose a name from a hat and write at least one positive characteristic about that person. Ask the students to write something that has nothing to do with a physical characteristic. Then distribute the statements to the students. It's fun to keep the writer a secret—that way the students may work harder to always display that characteristic to ALL people since they will not know who thinks that about them.

- Have the students write about a negative circumstance that may be currently happening in their lives or may have happened in the past. Encourage them to write some positive thoughts about how they did or can handle this circumstance.

JOURNAL ENTRY

Create a list of positive self-talk statements about you and the good things you can do. Program them into your brain so that you can retrieve this positive information when you need it.

Tune Into WPOS

CLASSROOM GUIDANCE NEWS

Dear Parents,

I enjoyed being in your child's class today. Our lesson today focused on taking charge of one's thoughts and using positive self-talk to deal with self put-downs. We've all done this before: something goes wrong and we think things like, "I'm so dumb. I should've known better. It seems I never do anything right." Children certainly do this. A child may struggle with math in school and begin to think of himself/herself as stupid or lazy. A child may not be invited to a birthday party and think that it is because no one likes him/her.

Negative self-talk can be dealt with, however, by simply replacing those thoughts with more positive thinking. Positive self-talk can be a powerful strategy for coping with self put-downs. Today in class, we role-played situations that may lend themselves to self put-downs. The analogy was made to think of a voicebox inside your head and when situations occur that may make you feel badly about yourself, remember the positive things about yourself and say them inside your head. It is important to have "saved" positive messages in your mind so that they can be brought out when needed. In class students wrote three positive statements about themselves.

It is a pleasure working with your child. As always, please feel free to call me with questions or concerns that you have about your child, your child's school experience, or the school's guidance and counseling program.

Sincerely,

© YouthLight, Inc. (Handout)

339

TUNING INTO WPOS

The way to be able to think positive thoughts about yourself is to practice thinking these thoughts. Below write three positive statements about yourself.

1. I am _____

2. I can _____

3. I almost always _____

Which station are you tuning into?
For good feelings, stayed tuned to WPOS.

school
to
work

Baking Up School Success

GRADE LEVEL(S): 3-5

DESCRIPTION:
A recipe for school success is shared with the students in which the ingredients/skills for academic success are discussed. The areas discussed are: listening and participating in class, using time wisely, controlling inappropriate behavior and talking, completing all assignments, and understanding the material.

OBJECTIVIES:
- Students will identify the five skills that increase academic success.
- Students will identify the strategies they plan to implement for academic success.

ESTIMATED TIME: 30-45 minutes

MATERIALS/SPECIAL PREPARATION:
- large baking pot with a top
- long spoon for stirring
- inflated balloon with smiley face drawn on the front with permanent marker - place the balloon in the bottom of the pot, hidden from students
- copy of Recipe for School Success (found on page 351) taped inside a folder labeled as Recipe for School Success
- 5 boxes, round tins, or plastic containers labeled as follows and containing the following items:

  Listening and Participating in Class
  - pair of sunglasses with cut out open eyes from a magazine taped to them
  - child's drawing of a hand
  - pair of earmuffs
  - radio head phone set

  Use Time Wisely
  - stop watch

  Control Inappropriate Behavior and Talking
  - 7 plastic ice cubes with ice cube messages taped to them (see page 349).

  Complete All Assignments
  - pencil
  - a stop light shape made from poster board and label "Stop," "Think" and "Go"
  - chair and desk/table - either a picture or a toy set from a doll house
  - X-Spot (see page 350)

  Understand The Material
  - large question mark
  - 5 index cards, any size

Baking Up School Success

PROCEDURES:

1. Enter the class with the baking pot and the ingredient boxes and inform the students that you have found a recipe for School Success and thought it might come in handy this year.

2. Share with the students that you are going to do some baking today - baking up school success that is. Pull out the recipe. Begin reading and as you read "add ingredient from the ..." go to that ingredient box and pull out each ingredient. Talk about how that ingredient would help someone be successful in school. Put each ingredient into the baking pot, stirring occasionally.

The following gives a suggestion for discussion of how each item can help the student be successful:

- **Pair of "eye" glasses:** Students need to look at the teacher when he/she is teaching, listen and be tuned in, when the eyes wander our brain wanders.
- **Hand:** Raise your hand to share an answer and be a part of the class discussions. It helps us to stay tuned into the lesson when we are participating.
- **Pair of earmuffs:** When you have work to do, a way to block out distractions is to pretend to put on a pair of earmuffs to block out extra noises and class distractions. Role play for the students an attempt to complete a math sheet with distractions. Work to #2 on the sheet and then dialogue someone knocking a book off their desk, then someone getting up to get a drink of water, then someone asking the teacher a question at the desk and you trying to eavesdrop. Each time these distractions happen your head is up watching what is going on. When back to the math sheet, you are still on #2. Share with the class the importance of pretending to put on your earmuffs to block out the distractions and stay focused on your work to get the work done.
- **Radio head phone set:** The radio only has one channel – the teacher channel. Encourage the students to stay tuned into the teacher while he/she is teaching and not be distracted by perhaps a neighbor whispering or someone walking down the hallway.
- **Stop watch:** Reminds us of how valuable time is and how we need to use time wisely. Discuss ways to use time wisely such as studying spelling words throughout the week at extra times during the day and saving time by staying organized and keeping a clean desk so that you do not waste time searching for something. (May choose to dramatize with your students digging to the bottom of your desk to find a sheet – and proclaiming that " I am sure none of you ever have a messy desk and have to go through this!")
- **Ice cube messages:** Toss these to selected students and have them read the messages, discuss as a class, and return the ice cubes to the baking pot.
- **Pencil:** One of our most valuable treasures! Share that this pencil can help us take notes to study, write down our homework in order to practice what we are learning, and help us write down our answers on a test to prove we have learned the information. Encourage the students to treasure their pencil.

- **Stop sign:** Joke with the students that you are sure this problem has never happened to any one of them in the class, but you have known one or two students before that have gotten home at the end of the school day, started to do their homework and realized that they had left the book they need at school. Discuss with the student how important it is to "STOP" and take time at the end of the day to "THINK" about what homework they have and to decide what books they need to pack in their book bag to take home. Then they may "GO" and begin packing. Display the stop sign and encourage them to take time at the end of the day to go through this process of "STOP," "THINK," then "GO."

- **Chair and desk:** Discuss with the students study tips for completing homework such as the importance of a quiet place to study at home - either a desk or table. Also it helps to study your hardest subject first and take short stretch breaks between subjects. Include the caution to beware of the TV monster that grabs you and keeps you at the TV all afternoon continually watching just one more show before doing homework.

- **X-Spot:** X marks the spot in your home where your book bag holding your completed work needs to be placed so it can easily be picked up the next morning. Encourage the students to have a set place whether it be on a specific table, shelf or by the door where their materials for school are packed and ready to go so that in the rush of the school morning nothing is left behind.

- **Question mark:** Share with the students that it is important to ask questions about any material they do not understand. Caution that before asking a question it is important to first make sure that they have listened to the teacher and have tried hard to understand, so that the teacher does not confuse them with a student who was daydreaming and not listening. Share with them the following way to ask the question – don't say "I don't understand" instead say, "I understand this part… but I'm having trouble with this…" or "I know how to do this… but I got lost when you said…" This lets your teacher know you are trying and also gives the teacher more specific information about what you need.

- **Index cards:** Share that the index cards are a wonderful study tool not only as math flash cards but also to learn vocabulary words (word on one side and the definition on the other), and to study important facts in science, social studies, etc. Take notes on your index cards by putting them in a question/answer format – front and back - and use them to study by. Make the cards out each night as you study new material and then they are ready to review for the test.

3. After all the ingredients have been added to the pot, read the last paragraph in the recipe and as you are reading, "...so that you can be a happy, successful student!" pull out the balloon that was hidden in the bottom of the pot.

4. Reinforce the lesson by asking the students which of the ingredients in the recipe would be most helpful to them in being successful in school. Challenge them to use these ingredients.

SUMMARY POSTER/VISUAL:
Display the balloon and a copy of the recipe in the classroom as a reminder of the skills/ingredients needed to be successful in school.

VARIATIONS/MODIFICATIONS/EXTENSIONS:
After the lesson, have the students draw pictures of as many "ingredients" (strategies) for academic success as they can recall – creating a "success collage." Have them circle the pictures of the strategies that they feel would be most helpful to them.

JOURNAL ENTRY

Write about which ingredients in the "Baking Up School Success" recipe can best help you be successful in school. Tell how and why these ingredients can be of help.

CLASSROOM GUIDANCE NEWS

Dear Parent,

Today's lesson, **Baking Up School Success,** focused on encouraging students to utilize the skills needed to be successful with learning. As children are getting older and are working more independently, we need to make sure they have knowledge of the skills necessary to be successful in school as well as be encouraged to use these skills. In the lesson today, we used the **Recipe for School Success** and added the different ingredients to our baking pot to cook up success. Below is a copy of the recipe. Ask your child what he/she remembers of the different ingredients needed to be successful at school. Follow-up with your child to see how s/he is using these skills. If I can be of help, please feel free to call.

Sincerely,

RECIPE FOR SCHOOL SUCCESS

Add the ingredients from the **LISTENING AND PARTICIPATING IN CLASS** box:
> 1 pair of eyes – Always look at the teacher and stay involved in the lesson.
> 1 raised hand – Be involved in the class by answering questions and sharing.
> 1 pair of earmuffs – Shut out extra distractions when completing seatwork.
> 1 radio head phone set - tune into the "Teacher Channel."

Add the ingredients from the **USE TIME WISELY** box:
> 1 stop watch – Each minute counts. Use your extra time to study, review or read. Stay organized (folders, clean desk); it will save you time!

Add the ice cubes from the **CONTROL INAPPROPRIATE BEHAVIOR AND TALKING** box – COOL IT!
> • Remind yourself of the consequences if you misbehave.
> • Ask your friends to help you by encouraging and reminding.
> • Keep your mouth closed if talking is getting you into trouble.
> • Remind yourself about the class rules.
> • Ask your friends to help by not trying to talk to you during class time.
> • Turn your brain on before talking.
> • Tell yourself not to talk now but to talk at recess or other OK times.

Add the ingredients from the **COMPLETE ALL ASSIGNMENTS** box:
> 1 pencil – Write down your homework assignments.
> 1 "STOP," "THINK," and "GO" sign – At the end of the day, need to stop and think about the books and materials you need to take home, then go pack up your books.
> 1 chair and desk/table – Have a quiet place at home to study.
> 1 X-Spot – X marks the spot where books and material should be placed to bring to school the next morning.

Add the ingredients from the **UNDERSTAND THE MATERIAL** box:
> 1 question mark – Ask questions if you do not understand.
> Flash cards – Make flash cards each night reviewing information covered in class that day. These can be used for social studies, health, vocabulary, etc. These are great for studying at test time!

KEEP THESE INGREDIENTS MIXED TOGETHER AND USE THEM FOR THE ALL THE SCHOOL DAYS OF THE YEAR SO THAT YOU CAN BE A HAPPY, SUCCESSFUL STUDENT!

Ice Cube Messages for
"Control Inappropriate Behavior and Talking"

Remind yourself of the consequences if you misbehave.

Ask your friends to help you by encouraging and reminding.

Keep your mouth closed if talking is getting you into trouble.

Remind yourself about the class rules.

Ask your friends to help you by not trying to talk to you during class time.

Turn your brain on before talking.

Tell yourself not to talk now but to talk at recess or other OK times.

X-SPOT

Baking Up School Success

RECIPE FOR SCHOOL SUCCESS

Add the ingredients from the **LISTENING AND PARTICIPATING IN CLASS** box:

1 pair of eyes – Always look at the teacher and stay involved in the lesson.
1 raised hand – Be involved in the class by answering questions and sharing.
1 pair of earmuffs – Shut out extra distractions when completing seatwork.
1 radio head phone set - tune into the "Teacher Channel."

Add the ingredients from the **USE TIME WISELY** box:

1 stop watch – Each minute counts. Use your extra time to study, review or read. Stay organized (folders, clean desk); it will save you time!

Add the ice cubes from the **CONTROL INAPPROPRIATE BEHAVIOR AND TALKING** box – COOL IT!

- Remind yourself of the consequences if you misbehave.
- Ask your friends to help you by encouraging and reminding.
- Keep your mouth closed if talking is getting you into trouble.
- Remind yourself about the class rules.
- Ask your friends to help by not trying to talk to you during class time.
- Turn your brain on before talking.
- Tell yourself not to talk now but to talk at recess or other OK times.

Add the ingredients from the **COMPLETE ALL ASSIGNMENTS** box:

1 pencil – Write down your homework assignments.
1 "STOP," "THINK," and "GO" sign – At the end of the day, need to stop and think about the books and materials you need to take home, then go pack up your books.
1 chair and desk/table – Have a quiet place at home to study.
1 X-Spot – X marks the spot where books and material should be placed to bring to school the next morning.

Add the ingredients from the **UNDERSTAND THE MATERIAL** box:

1 question mark – Ask questions if you do not understand.
Flash cards – Make flash cards each night reviewing information covered in class that day. These can be used for social studies, health, vocabulary, etc. These are great for studying at test time!

KEEP THESE INGREDIENTS MIXED TOGETHER AND USE THEM FOR ALL THE SCHOOL DAYS OF THE YEAR SO THAT YOU CAN BE A HAPPY SUCCESSFUL STUDENT!

Test Stress First Aid

GRADE LEVEL(S): (can be adapted for any grade level)

DESCRIPTION:
Test anxiety is common. This lesson uses a first aid kit to offer students some practical ideas they can use to help ease test stress.

OBJECTIVE(S):
Students will learn test stress relievers.

ESTIMATED TIME: 20 minutes

MATERIAL(S) NEEDED:
- First Aid Kit with the words "Test Stress" printed above First-Aid
- A bagel wrapper or single serving cereal box
- Alarm clock
- Pencil
- Pair of glasses
- Large rubber ear
- Speed limit sign (found on page 355) with tongue depressor attached
- Eye patch
- Instructions found on page 356
- Ice pack

PROCEDURES:
1. Ask the students to tell you words that come to their minds when they hear the word "test." Discuss that there are different types of tests in school. If standardized testing is coming up, discuss that this test may be different than the ones they are accustomed to taking in their class.
2. Explain that some students get nervous when it is time to take a test. They feel stress. Define stress as the uptight, nervous feeling you get before you do something you are unsure about. Discuss how this feeling sometimes seems to get the best of us, like a big "stress monster" coming after you.
3. Show the students the Test Stress First Aid Kit. Explain that this kit has some things in it that will remind them of things they can do to prepare themselves for a test and reduce stress. Explain each item.
   - **Bagel wrapper or cereal box:** Eat a good breakfast the morning of a test. Discuss the importance of good nutrition.
   - **Alarm clock:** Be sure you're on time the day of a test. Rushing can get your day off to a bad start.
   - **Pencil:** Be prepared. Come with all the supplies you'll need for the test.

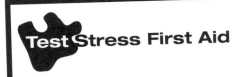
- **Glasses and rubber ear:** Look at the teacher and listen to the directions for the test.
- **Speed Limit Sign:** Do not work too quickly or too slowly. Pace yourself at a medium speed.
- **Instruction cards:** Use these hints if you get stuck on a multiple-choice item.
- **Eye patch:** If you get nervous, close your eyes for a few seconds, take a few deep breaths, and relax.
- **Ice pack:** Chill Out! You're going to do your best and that's what counts!

4. Have the students draw cartoons of themselves overcoming the test stress monster.

SUMMARY POSTER OR VISUAL REMINDER:
Control the Test Stress Monster summary poster on page 357

VARIATIONS/MODIFICATIONS/EXTENSIONS:
- Read aloud *Hurray for Diffendoofer Day* by Dr. Seuss.
- Have the students make a placemat for their desk the day of a test. On the placemat they are to write positive statements to themselves such as "You can do it!" or "You're awesome!"

JOURNAL ENTRY

Choose the items from the "Test Stress First Aid Kit" that may best help you in taking a test. Write about the items you choose.

CLASSROOM GUIDANCE NEWS

Dear Parent,

Test anxiety is common to students. While a little anxiety can help spur a child on to do his/her best, too much anxiety can interfere with test performance. Today students saw a Test Stress First Aid Kit. Students learned some important points about relieving test stress. These include:

- Eat a nutritious breakfast.
- Be on time for school. Be early if possible.
- Be prepared with the supplies you need for the test.
- Look at the teacher and listen to directions.
- Don't work too quickly or too slowly. Pace yourself at a medium speed.
- If you get nervous, close your eyes for a few seconds and take a few deep breaths.
- If you don't know an answer on a multiple choice item:
  - Re-read the question and all answers.
  - Skip it and come back to it.
  - Re-read the question and all answers.
  - Eliminate the absolute wrongs.
  - Give it your best shot.

While tests are important, be cautious of the emphasis you put on tests. Let your child know that you feel the test is important and that you have confidence in him/her that he/she will do the best possible. Avoid asking your child about specific test items after a test and then making statements like, "You knew that one. Why didn't you get it right?"

As always, please feel free to call me with questions or concerns that you may have about your child, your child's school experience, or our elementary guidance and counseling program.

Sincerely,

SPEED LIMIT

MEDIUM

INSTRUCTION CARDS

Cut apart, mount on heavy paper, and laminate for durability.

Re-read the question and all the answers.

1

Skip it and come back to it.

2

Re-read the question and all the answers.

3

Eliminate the absolute wrongs.

4

Give it your best shot.

5

Test Stress First Aid

Control the Test Stress Monster

✔ Eat a nutritious breakfast.

✔ Be on time for school. Be early if possible.

✔ Be prepared with the supplies you need for the test.

✔ Look at the teacher and listen to directions.

✔ Don't work too quickly or too slowly. Pace yourself at a medium speed.

✔ If you get nervous, close your eyes for a few seconds and take a few deep breaths.

✔ If you don't know an answer on a multiple choice item:
  • Re-read the question and all answers.
  • Skip it and come back to it.
  • Re-read the question and all answers.
  • Eliminate the absolute wrongs.
  • Give it your best shot.

Keys to Success

GRADE LEVEL(S): 4-5

DESCRIPTION:
Students will love being tricked as they take a few "tests" to discover the three keys to success.

OBJECTIVE(S):
• Students will identify three keys to school and future success.
• Students will explore careers.

ESTIMATED TIME: 30 minutes

MATERIAL(S) NEEDED:
• Two copies of Job Test One worksheet found on page 362 for each student
• Transparency of Job Test Two -Type and put on transparency the following sentence: FINISHED FILES ARE THE RESULT OF YEARS OF SCIENTIFIC STUDY COMBINED WITH THE EXPERIENCE OF YEARS.
• Two copies of Job Test Three activity sheet on page ___ for each student
• Copy of Three Keys summary poster found on pages___

PROCEDURES:
1. Have the students name as many jobs as they can in 3 minutes. List these on the board.
2. Tell the following story and have the students see if they can guess about Todd's job:
   Todd has a job that he reports to Monday through Friday. He works a seven hour day. Part of Todd's job he does independently and part is supervised by his boss. Basically he just has to do what his boss tells him to do. But Todd is having problems. First, he is supposed to be at work at 7:30 but he usually arrives sometime around 7:45. By that time, his boss has already given out the duties for the day so he has to take time to go over Todd's with him again. Second, he usually arrives without his tools that he needs to do his job. He tries to borrow from his co-workers but they sometimes don't have extras to lend him. Also, Todd is not being effective in his job. Many times while he's supposed to be working, he starts thinking about what he would rather be doing. Todd has a difficult time doing what his boss says to do. Sometimes this is because Todd wasn't listening when his boss told him what to do and sometimes it's because Todd thinks he has a better way of doing the job. Most of the time, he ends up having to do things again. Sometimes Todd will talk nasty to his boss or his co-workers when he gets upset about having to do things over. Todd really doesn't seem to care, but his boss and his co-workers are getting tired of his ways.
3. Discuss some of the problems Todd is having:
   • Late for work
   • No supplies
   • Not concentrating
   • Not following directions
   • Disrespect of boss and co-workers

4. Have the students guess about what Todd's job is and then explain that Todd is a student. His JOB is SCHOOL. Discuss why Todd is not being successful. Discuss the kind of reputation Todd is developing at his job.

5. Tell the students that today they will learn three KEYS to being successful at their current job, school, and at any other job they would like to have in the future. Explain that in order to get your point across, they will be taking some job "tests."

6. Distribute copies of the Job Test One but have the students keep the test face down on their desks. When all are distributed say this, "When I tell you to start, please read the directions carefully and follow them exactly. There is to be no talking to other students. Okay, turn it over and begin."

7. After the students finish or catch on, discuss what happened. Ask how they felt when they discovered they had been tricked. Ask if they've ever done the same thing in a real situation. Discuss the point in this activity and show the first key—FOLLOW DIRECTIONS.

8. Discuss how following directions can help them now and in any future job. Go back to the list of jobs given at the beginning of class and discuss how following directions would be important in each.

9. The second test is put on the overhead projector. Put up a transparency with this sentence: FINISHED FILES ARE THE RESULT OF YEARS OF SCIENTIFIC STUDY COMBINED WITH THE EXPERIENCE OF YEARS. Instruct the students to count the F's in that sentence ONLY ONCE. Turn the projector off after about 30 seconds.

10. There are 6 F's in that sentence. Many people overlook the "of"s because the human brain tends to see them as V's and not F's. Introduce the second key: CONCENTRATE. Concentrating means focusing on what you are doing and putting all your energy into it. Discuss times in school when it's very important to concentrate. Look back at the list of jobs created in the beginning and discuss how lack of concentration could affect them on their job.

11. Distribute Job Test Three. Place it face down and then say, "You have the final test in front of you. You are to write your answer for each question as quickly as possible. Since this is a timed test, you will only have 3 minutes to complete the test. No talking during the test. Begin."

12. After three minutes, read the correct answers and have the students discuss why they got wrong answers. The correct answers are:
    - #1: Neither. Roosters don't lay eggs.
    - #2: 1812
    - #3: Electric trains don't blow smoke.
    - #4: All of them.
    - #5: Yes, they have a fourth of July, a fifth of July, etc.
    - #6: Halfway because after that he's walking out of the woods.
    - #7: Every person has just one birthday. When is yours?
    - #8: The outside.

13. Stress the idea that errors often result from lack of thinking, such as focusing on a single word

rather than the entire question, jumping to conclusions, and acting on assumptions or expectations rather than what is actually written. Display the third key: THINK. Thinking involves stopping yourself from making impulsive decisions. Discuss how these can help in their current job, school, and then go back to the list and discuss how other jobs require workers to think.

14. Review the three KEYS with the students. Emphasize that it's up to them whether they use the keys to unlock a successful future.

SUMMARY POSTER OR VISUAL REMINDER:
Leave the three keys in the class as a reminder.

VARIATIONS/MODIFICATIONS/EXTENSIONS:
• Assign each student a career prior to taking the three tests. Then after each test, discuss if they keep or lose their job based on their performance on the test. For example, a doctor who fails the following directions test may lose his job because he/she removes the wrong organ during an operation. Or a firefighter who fails to concentrate could let a home burn to the ground.

• Have the students write about times in school when it is most important to follow directions, concentrate, and think.

JOURNAL ENTRY

Choose a future job/career that interests you and tell how the three keys—following directions, concentrating, and thinking—would be important in that career.

Keys to Success

CLASSROOM GUIDANCE NEWS

Dear Parent,

Today in classroom guidance students learned the relationship between success in school and future success in a career. Students had a great time taking some job "tests."

We began the lesson by having students name any type of job. This led the students to the realization that they do currently have a job—school. We then talked about behavior and about how repeated patterns of behavior can become habits. Once a behavior becomes a habit, it can be difficult to break. Habits tend to influence our reputation. I used examples of habits that students could have right now that would greatly affect them later in life in a career or occupation—being late, failing to complete a task, speaking disrespectfully to authority, or not getting along with peers.

Students then learned about three keys to being successful at any job. The first is **following directions.** Be sure you ask your child if you can see his/her following directions test. The second key is **concentrating.** The third key is to **think** before any choice. Your child will most likely try to trick you with their extra copy of a "Job Test Number Three." The point of this test is that you cannot always go with your first impulse when answering a question or performing a task. Most times decisions require thought and concentration.

These ideas that we discussed in class can help students not only in future careers but also in their current schoolwork. School is the practice field for most of life's experiences, and your child is at an age where realizing that everything s/he is learning is relevant and applicable to everyday life is crucial.

As always, please feel free to call me with any questions or concerns that you may have about your child, your child's school experience, or our elementary guidance and counseling program.

Sincerely,

JOB TEST ONE

DIRECTIONS: Read all the questions on the page and then go back to number 1 and begin answering them.

1. Write your full name. _____

2. When is your birthday? _____

3. What did you have for supper last night? _____

4. Look at the person sitting beside you and write down the color of their eyes. _____

5. Say your teacher's name out loud three times. Go ahead, do it—it's part of the test.

6. Stand up beside your desk, reach up in the air, then bend down and touch your toes.

7. If you could be a famous person who would you be?_____

8. Put one of your thumbs in each ear, spread your fingers, and say out loud, "Look at me. I'm Bullwinkle Moose."

9. Say the Pledge of Allegiance out loud.

10. Ignore all of the above directions. Sign your name at the bottom and be quiet so no one else catches on.

JOB TEST THREE

Note: You have only 3 minutes to complete this test.

1. If a rooster lays an egg on the peak of a roof, which way will the egg roll off? _____

2. When was the War of 1812? _____

3. If an electric train is traveling west at 65 mph, which way will its smoke blow? _____

4. Some months have 31 days; some have 30 days. How many have 28? _____
   _____   _____

5. Do they have a Fourth of July in Italy? _____

6. How far can a bear walk into the woods? _____

7. How many birthdays does the average person have? _____

8. On which side of a chicken are the most feathers? _____

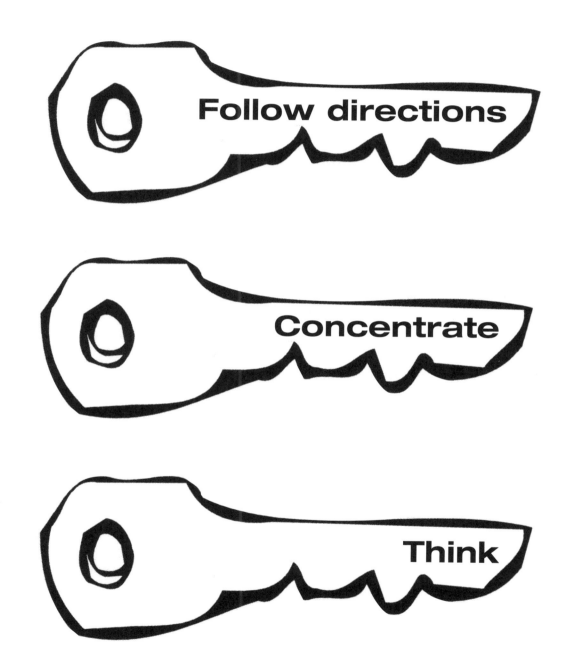

Follow directions

Concentrate

Think

Organizational Ladders

GRADE LEVEL(S): 3-5

DESCRIPTION:
In this lesson students build ladders to help break down a large task into organized, manageable steps.

OBJECTIVE(S):
- Students will describe feeling overwhelmed.
- Students will break down a large task into smaller pieces.
- Students will prioritize small tasks in order to accomplish a larger task.

ESTIMATED TIME: 30 minutes

MATERIAL(S) NEEDED:
- One task strip for each student (found on page 368). It is acceptable for students to have duplicate task strips
- Four additional strips of paper for each student
- Clear tape

PROCEDURES:
1. Discuss the meaning of the word "overwhelmed." Use the analogy of having to eat 12 pizzas and how you would do it—one slice at a time. Describe "overwhelming" as having so much to do and not knowing how to get started. Have the students name things that overwhelm them.
2. Describe the bedroom of a pretend child. Explain that the bedroom is a mess—clothes all over the floor, bed unmade, paper scraps from an art project everywhere, dust on all the furniture, toys, etc. Have the students brainstorm small details of things that this child needs to do in order to have a clean room. List these on the board or overhead. Be very specific—vacuum, dust, put away toys, etc.
3. After the students have named these things, have them prioritize. Put numbers beside them for first, second, etc.
4. Explain that this is the process for doing things that seem overwhelming:
   1) list all the details that need to be done (be very specific)
   2) prioritize them, and
   3) do it.
   Use the analogy of a ladder—climbing up one step at a time.
5. Give each student a task strip (found on page 368.) Also give each student four strips of blank paper. Instruct the students to write four steps to reach their goal—one on each strip. Then have them arrange the steps like a ladder with the goal at the top and the first step at the bottom. Have them tape the strips together.

6. Several students will have the same task. Discuss the various approaches taken.
7. Explain how students can utilize this process with schoolwork, homework, chores, etc.
8. Read the following object lesson:

   An old farmer had plowed around a large rock in one of his fields for years. He had broken several plowshares and a cultivator on it. After breaking another plowshare one day, and remembering all the trouble the rock had caused him through the years, he finally decided to do something about it. When he put the crowbar under the rock, he was surprised to discover that it was only about six inches thick and that he could easily break it up with a sledgehammer. As he was carting the pieces away, he had to smile remembering all the trouble the rock had caused him over the years and how easy it would have been to get rid of it sooner.

   Challenge students to break up and get rid of any "rocks" that are in their path.

SUMMARY POSTER OR VISUAL REMINDER:
Organization summary poster on page 369

VARIATIONS/MODIFICATIONS/EXTENSIONS:
- Use tongue depressors instead of strips of paper for the four steps to give the visual image of a ladder.
- Give the students tasks to accomplishing a project such as baking a cake in mixed up order. Have them arrange the steps in the most logical order.
- Brainstorm tasks where logical order is essential.

JOURNAL ENTRY

Think back and choose a task that has been overwhelming to you. Break this task into smaller steps that are needed to get the job done. Draw these steps on the steps of a ladder with the completed task at the top.

Organizational Ladders

CLASSROOM GUIDANCE NEWS

Dear Parent,

Today students learned how to deal with seemingly overwhelming tasks. Reaching a goal is like climbing the steps of a ladder. In order to reach a goal, steps must be taken one at a time. Therefore, the first step is to list all of the little steps involved in reaching the goal. The second step is to organize these steps into a logical matter. The third step is to do the steps in order. Students completed a "problem ladder" today. Please be sure that you ask your child to see his/her problem ladder.

At home you can reinforce this concept. When your child comes home with a project for school or says, "I don't know what to do," have him/her list all the steps involved in the project. Then have your child organize these steps. Assist as needed. Finally, praise your child as s/he completes a step towards accomplishing the project or goal.

I read the students this story which teaches a lesson about seemingly overwhelming tasks:

> *An old farmer had plowed around a large rock in one of his fields for years. He had broken several plowshares and a cultivator on it. After breaking another plowshare one day, and remembering all the trouble the rock had caused him through the years, he finally decided to do something about it. When he put the crowbar under the rock, he was surprised to find that it was only about six inches thick and that he could break it up easily with a sledge-hammer. As he was carting the pieces away, he had to smile remembering all the trouble that the rock had caused him over the years and how easy it would have been to get rid of it sooner.*

What "rocks" are standing in the way of your child doing his/her best? Help him/her identify the rocks and break them up into small pieces so that they can be easily carted away.

As always, please feel free to call me with concerns that you may have about your child, your child's school experience, or our elementary guidance and counseling program.

In partnership,

Task Strips

You have a science project to do.

Your notebook is a mess and
you can't find your homework.

You have a book report to do.

You have three days to write a report on the Civil War.

You need to learn your 12 times tables
before a test in 4 days.

Organizational Ladders

Getting organized is like climbing a ladder.

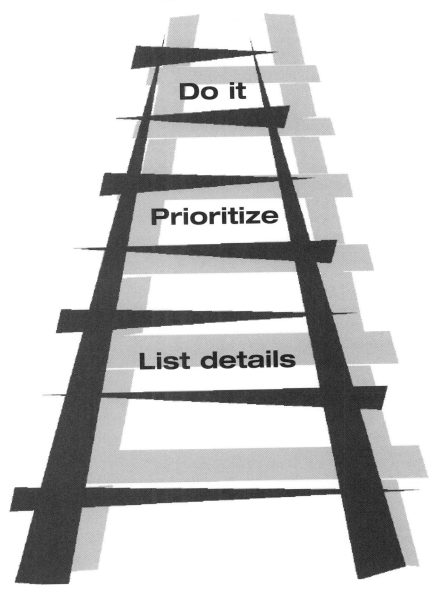

GOAL

Do it

Prioritize

List details

369

Who Uses This Stuff?

GRADE LEVEL(S): 3-5

DESCRIPTION:
This hands-on lesson helps students see the relevance of schoolwork.

OBJECTIVE(S):
• Students will explore a variety of careers.
• Students will recognize the importance of responsibility and good work habits.
• Students will understand how schoolwork relates to jobs in society.
• Students will explore their own individual interests.
• Students will cooperate in groups.

ESTIMATED TIME: 30 minutes

MATERIAL(S) NEEDED:
• Career props such as a stethoscope (a toy one is fine), a pair of toy binoculars, a camera, a computer mouse, a telephone, a calculator, a wrench, a measuring cup, a stopwatch. Be sure you have one prop for every 4-5 students in the class. Place the props in paper bags.
• Who Uses this Stuff? activity sheet on page 373

PROCEDURES:
1. Ask the students if they have ever said or wondered when studying, "Why do I need to learn this?" Emphasize that many times it's hard to see the usefulness of schoolwork.
2. Ask the students what they think they would like to be when they grow up.
3. Divide students into groups of 4 and give each group a career prop bag. Instruct the students to work in groups to complete the "Who Uses This Stuff?" activity sheet.
4. Once the students are finished, have each group share and allow others to contribute ideas as well. Emphasize the things that students are currently learning.
5. Contribute that there are things that students are learning that are not related to "academics" that will help them in their future as well. Ask for ideas such as responsibility, attitude, cooperation, etc.

SUMMARY POSTER OR VISUAL REMINDER:
Who Uses This Stuff summary poster on page 374

VARIATIONS/MODIFICATIONS/EXTENSIONS:
• Plan a career dress up day.
• Give the students several words to read written in Chinese or Japanese. Explain that their frustration in not knowing how to read them will be similar to frustrations they may feel in the future if they do not work hard at schoolwork.

• Have the students interview high school seniors or college freshmen and inquire about things the seniors or freshmen wish they had given more attention to in elementary school.

JOURNAL ENTRY

Pretend that you are a parent talking to your child about how important it is to get a good education in elementary school in order to have a successful career when you are older. Write about what you would say to your child.

Who Uses This Stuff?

CLASSROOM GUIDANCE NEWS

Dear Parent,

Have you ever heard this question from your child: "Why do I have to learn this?" An immediate answer may be something like, "Because you're going to need it someday." While that answer is accurate, school-age students live in the present. It is our job as adults to help make work as meaningful and relevant for children as possible.

Today in classroom guidance, students learned how various occupations use skills that students are currently learning such as writing skills, multiplication, and reading comprehension. Students had fun working in groups to complete a sheet entitled, "Who Uses This Stuff?" We discussed how all of the skills that students learn in school, both academic and interpersonal, are relevant and how not learning them may later affect a career choice.

While it is frustrating when you feel that your child is not taking schoolwork seriously, remember that he/she is still a child. Talk to your child about jobs that he/she would like to have in the future and then try to brainstorm ways that he/she may need that particular skill. Make it funny by saying something like, "Can you imagine a basketball player who doesn't know how to count money? Boy, could someone take him to the cleaners!"

As always, please feel free to call me with any questions or concerns that you may have about your child, your child's school experience, or our elementary guidance and counseling program.

Sincerely,

WHO USES THIS STUFF?

1. What is your "tool?" _____

_____

_____

2. Name one career where this "tool" would be used._____

_____

_____

3. How would a person with this career use reading? _____

_____

_____

4. How would a person with this career use writing?_____

_____

_____

5. How would a person with this career use math? _____

_____

_____

6. What is something you are learning right now in school that this person may use daily?

_____

_____

7. Who in your group would be interested in finding out more about this career?

_____

_____

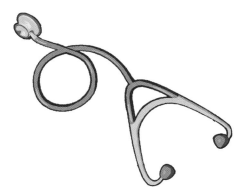

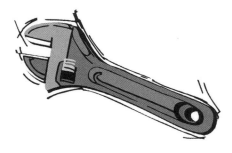

Who uses the stuff you're learning in school now?
YOU WILL!

But WHY Do I Need To Learn To...?

GRADE LEVEL(S): K-2

DESCRIPTION:
Young children have a difficult time relating schoolwork to anything outside of the walls of the building. This lesson helps students understand how people they see everyday are putting into practice the things that the students are learning.

OBJECTIVE(S):
- Students will recognize the importance of responsibility and good work habits.
- Students will understand how school prepares them for future jobs.
- Students will explore their own individual interests.

ESTIMATED TIME: 30 minutes

MATERIAL(S) NEEDED:
Occupation pictures found on pages 378-387. Copy the pictures onto cardstock and place all of the pictures in one bag.

PROCEDURES:
1. Ask students if they've ever wondered why they have to learn to do something. Allow the students to share.
2. Explain to the students that they will somehow use everything they are learning in school which is why it is important to do your best. Have the students name some things they are learning in their class—-reading, math, and writing. List these on the board for use in step three. Tell the students that today they will be learning about some different types of jobs and about how each uses skills the students are currently learning.
3. Have one student reach in the bag of occupation pictures and pull one out. Have the student act out the occupation. The rest of the class must guess the occupation. After the class has guessed the occupation, ask the students how this occupation uses math, reading, and writing. Repeat this until all the occupation pictures have been used.
4. Have the students draw a picture of themselves in their future career. Discuss how each will use skills they are learning now in their job.

SUMMARY POSTER OR VISUAL REMINDER:
Occupation summary poster on page 388

VARIATIONS/MODIFICATIONS/EXTENSIONS:
- Have the students write about a future career.
- Hold a career dress up day.
- Have people come into the class and discuss their occupation with the students. Ask them to wear their uniform if they have one.

JOURNAL ENTRY

Pick a subject in school that you like (math, reading, writing, science, etc.) and draw a picture of or write about a job/career that uses that subject area.

CLASSROOM GUIDANCE NEWS

Dear Parent,

If you haven't heard this question yet, you will: "Why do I have to learn this?" Children often question the relevancy of their schoolwork. They have difficulty linking what they are learning now to their future. Today in classroom guidance, we explored careers and the relationship of schoolwork to these careers.

Students had a fun time playing occupational charades. We then discussed how each occupation uses math, reading, and writing in their job. Finally, students were asked to draw pictures of themselves as grown-ups at their job.

Most likely you see your child play and pretend to be a teacher, a racecar driver, a doctor, a carpenter, etc. This type of play is to be encouraged for it is through such play that children experiment with what they are learning. Take caution that you don't discourage your child from pretending to be something just because that's not what you want him/her to be when he/she grows up.

Throughout your child's school career it will be important for you to watch as his/her strengths and talents come alive. You may be surprised to see a career in the works. You will be asked, "Why do I have to learn this? When will I ever use it?" At that time, remember to link learning to the future, and when all else fails, use the old standard line, "This teaches you to think."

It is a pleasure working with your child in classroom guidance and seeing him/her grow. As always, please feel free to contact me with any questions or concerns that you have about your child, your child's school experience, or our elementary guidance and counseling program.

Sincerely,

Firefighter

Teacher

Nurse

Scientist

Mechanic

Police Officer

Astronaut

Mail Carrier

Veterinarian

Artist

**This could be you someday.
Work hard so you'll be ready.**

Career Match-Up

GRADE LEVEL(S): 1-3

DESCRIPTION:
Students are actively involved as they match-up their career pictures and words. Students then describe their career to the rest of the class.

OBJECTIVE(S):
- Students will explore different occupations.
- Students will identify the function of various occupations.

ESTIMATED TIME: 30 minutes

MATERIAL(S) NEEDED:
- Pictures of various careers mounted on construction paper and laminated*
- Corresponding words that match career pictures
- These pictures can be found in magazines, teacher supply stores and catalogs. They are usually relatively inexpensive and worth the money.

PROCEDURES:
1. Give each student either a career picture or a career word card. Ask the students to keep their card or picture a secret until the signal is given.
2. Explain that they are to find the person who has the corresponding word to their picture or vice versa. When they find this person, they are to sit with them somewhere in the room. Give the signal to begin.
3. When all the students have matched up, ask each pair to discuss what their worker does. Have them think of 3-4 hints they could give the class about their career. Allow enough time for this and assist as needed.
4. Allow pairs to present their hints to the class. Be sure to instruct them to keep their pictures and word cards hidden as they present in order to see if the class can guess from their hints.
5. Ask the students after each presentation if they would be interested in having that career. Ask the students what they think would be important to learn in school that would help them with that job.
6. Summarize by telling the students that there are many other jobs in the world and that in order to someday choose the right one for them, they will need to think about things they like to do and things that they do well.

SUMMARY POSTER OR VISUAL REMINDER:
What Will You Be? summary poster found on page 392

Career Match-Up

VARIATIONS/MODIFICATIONS/EXTENSIONS:

• Spread the pictures out around the room and have the students stand by the career that interests them the most, then the second most, the third most, etc.
• Have some people who are in the careers you use in this lesson come talk to the class about their jobs.
• Have students cut out pictures from magazines of people in different careers.

JOURNAL ENTRY

Make a list of all of the careers that interest you.

CLASSROOM GUIDANCE NEWS

Dear Parent,

The world of work is ever changing. There are careers that exist today that did not exist when you were in elementary school. There are careers that are obsolete today that were in high demand fifty years ago. Today's lesson exposed students to some of the current careers in our society.

Students enjoyed playing a career match-up game. We discussed several different types of occupations. Students were given the opportunity to share careers in which they are interested.

When you are shopping with your child or in the community, be sure you discuss the various jobs people do. Give your child the name as well as a description of what is involved in doing that job. The more information a child has, the better choice he/she will make about a career in the future.

As always, please feel free to call me with questions or concerns that you may have about your child, your child's school experience, or our elementary guidance and counseling program.

Sincerely,

What will you be?

What's In A Name?

GRADE LEVEL(S): 2-4

DESCRIPTION:
This lesson introduces the concept that interests can be related to a future career. Using their names to make an acrostic, students list strengths and interests and then think of those strengths and interests in terms of a career.

OBJECTIVE(S):
- Students will explore different occupations.
- Students will identify individual strengths and interests.

ESTIMATED TIME: 30 minutes

MATERIAL(S) NEEDED:
Each child will need a sheet of paper

PROCEDURES:
1. Explain that who you are right now will impact who you become in the future. Things that you are good at and things that you like to do all help you practice for being an adult. Use the example of someone who wants to become a professional athlete but never practices or plays the game he/she chose.
2. Write your first or last name on the board vertically. Have the students do an acrostic of your name that describes your interests and strengths. An example is:

   R eading
   U ses good manners
   T houghtful
   H umor
   I magination
   E nthusiastic

3. After your acrostic is completed, have the students complete their own. Assist as needed.
4. After the students have completed their acrostics, go back to yours. Ask the students to name some careers that may fit with the things you wrote about yourself.
5. Have the students write a few careers that go along with their strengths and interests.
6. Share. Be sure to emphasize that as people grow and change, their interests and strengths change. Therefore, people may change their minds about their careers many times before they find the one that is best for them. This is okay.

SUMMARY POSTER OR VISUAL REMINDER:
What Will You Be? summary poster on page 396

VARIATIONS/MODIFICATIONS/EXTENSIONS:

- Have the students draw pictures of themselves as adults at their job.
- Plan a career dress-up day.
- Read aloud **When I Grow Up** by P. K. Hallinan.

JOURNAL ENTRY

Tell about some jobs/careers that may go along with your strengths and interests. Draw a picture of yourself doing one of these careers.

CLASSROOM GUIDANCE NEWS

Dear Parent,

Today's guidance lesson focused on personal strengths and interests as they relate to the future. While it may seem a little premature to discuss careers at this age, career awareness and development is important at every age. Students are beginning to excel in certain areas and are recognizing their strengths and weaknesses as well as their interests. All of these areas tie together to help a person choose a career.

In our lesson today, students thought of some words or phrases that describe themselves or their interests. Students were then encouraged to think of careers that incorporated these skills and interests. Your child completed this activity by writing an acrostic of his/her name. Then he/she listed a few careers that went along with the strengths and interests listed.

Do not be alarmed if your child's career aspirations are not what you desire. These will change over and over as your child matures. The importance of career talk is to provide an opportunity for you to encourage your child and to recognize his/her strengths. When talking with your child about careers, take the attitude of "the world is your oyster" and allow him/her to dream (big or small!)

As always, please feel free to call me with questions or concerns that you may have about your child, your child's school experience, or our elementary guidance and counseling program.

Sincerely,

What will you be?

How Are You Smart?

GRADE LEVEL(S): 3-5

DESCRIPTION:
Using a simple self-inventory, students discover their strengths. They learn that "smart" isn't just about academics. This lesson is great for building up students who may struggle with school-work but excel at other things.

OBJECTIVE(S):
- Students will identify individual strengths.
- Students will recognize and appreciate others' strengths.

ESTIMATED TIME: 30 minutes

MATERIAL(S) NEEDED:
- How Are You Smart? and What Does It All Mean? activity sheets found on pages 400-401
- Seven different intelligences posters found on pages 402-405

PROCEDURES:
1. Ask the students to define the word "smart." Write responses on the board.
2. Explain that Dr. Howard Gardner's wrote a book entitled *Frames of Mind.* In this book, Dr. Gardner identified seven different ways that people are smart. Tell the students that today they will be answering the question, "How are you smart?"
3. Have the students complete the self-inventory. Explain that they are to check all statements that they feel describe them. Have them compute their total in each box and transfer that total to the "What Does It All Mean?" sheet. Assure students that having a zero or one in some boxes is okay; as a matter of fact, no one should have all high scores!
4. Using posters, discuss the seven different intelligences. Have the students share which area(s) they feel they excel. Encourage classmates to appreciate others' strengths.
5. Explain how knowing this information can assist with study skills. If students have musical intelligence, they may benefit from making up songs or poems to help them remember mate-rial. If students have bodily kinesthetic intelligence, they may benefit from taking a 5 minute break when studying to do something like jumping jacks or jump rope.

SUMMARY POSTER OR VISUAL REMINDER:
The Seven Different Intelligences summary posters found on pages 402-405

VARIATIONS/MODIFICATIONS/EXTENSIONS:
- If you have a gifted and talented program in your school, invite the teacher to come talk to the class about the type of intelligence(s) that this program in school identifies. Students may be surprised to find that these types of programs usually target students with verbal linguistic and

logical mathematical intelligence, yet there are five other types of intelligences!
• Have the students choose one of the seven intelligences and develop a plan of how they could use that area of strength to help them with studying, listening, and learning in school. Share and display in the class.

JOURNAL ENTRY

Write about how you can use the area(s) in which you are smart to best help you with your study skills to be learning.

CLASSROOM GUIDANCE NEWS

Dear Parent,

When asked, "What is 'smart'?" most people will say something that relates to doing well in school or in jobs. Some may define "smart" as a score on an intelligence test. Students tend to associate being smart with how well one scores on a test or with grades on a report card.

In 1983, Dr. Howard Gardner published a book called *Frames of Mind* in which he identified the existence of at least seven basic intelligences. Gardner's theory broadened the scope of potential beyond the confines of an IQ score. Gardner's research suggests that intelligence has more to do with the capacity for solving problems within context.

Today in classroom guidance I posed a new question for students, "How Smart Are You?" We discussed the seven intelligences proposed by Dr. Gardner. Your child completed an inventory on him/herself. Please ask to see it. Below is a guide to the seven intelligences:

LINGUISTIC: The capacity to use words effectively either orally or in writing.

LOGICAL-MATHEMATICAL: The capacity to use numbers effectively and to reason well.

SPATIAL: The ability to perceive the visual-spatial world accurately and to act upon those perceptions.

BODILY-KINESTHETIC: Expertise in using one's whole body to express ideas and feelings and in using one's hands to produce or change things.

MUSICAL: The capacity to perceive, discriminate, and express musical forms.

INTERPERSONAL: The ability to perceive and make distinctions in the moods, intentions, motivations, and feelings of other people.

INTRAPERSONAL: Self-knowledge and the ability to act adaptively on the basis of that knowledge.

Please be sure that you check out where your child perceives his/her strengths.

We discussed that while strengths may be in a few of these areas, it is important to strive to do your best in any undertaking. Students were cautioned about using this theory as an excuse for not doing well in a school subject. We also discussed how students could use their strongest area to improve in others. For example, if a student is gifted in the bodily-kinesthetic domain, he/she may choose to study by making something, writing things down, or acting something out. If a student is strong in the linguistic domain, he/she may benefit by reading things aloud while studying.

As always, please feel free to call me with any questions or concerns that you may have about your child, your child's school experience, or our elementary guidance and counseling program.

Sincerely,

How Are You Smart?

recognizes off-key music
remembers songs and melodies
has rhythm
plays a musical instrument or sings in a choir
taps rhythmically while working
is sensitive to noises

TOTAL _____ (MS)

excels in one or more sports
moves, twitches, taps or fidgets when seated for a long time
enjoys taking things apart and putting them back together
touches new objects
expresses self dramatically
enjoys being outdoors

TOTAL _____ (BK)

questions how things work
does mental math
enjoys math activities
enjoys strategy games
enjoys logic puzzles or brainteasers
likes finding patterns

TOTAL _____ (LM)

enjoys socializing with peers
acts as a natural leader
gives advice to friends who have problems
has one or more close friends
likes to play games with others
shows concern for others

TOTAL _____ (IE)

is independent
is self-directed
prefers working alone
learns from successes and failures
has high self-esteem
knows own strengths

TOTAL _____ (IA)

tells jokes and stories
has a good memory
enjoys word games
enjoys reading and writing
has a good vocabulary
has good verbal communication

TOTAL _____ (LG)

likes to read maps and charts
daydreams more than friends
enjoys art activities
enjoys puzzles and mazes
understands more from pictures than words while reading
doodles on paper

TOTAL _____ (SP)

What Does It All Mean?

CODE	TYPE OF INTELLIGENCE	YOUR TOTAL
LG	Linguistic	
LM	Logical-Mathematical	
MS	Musical	
SP	Spatial	
BK	Bodily Kinesthetic	
IE	Interpersonal	
IA	Intrapersonal	

VERBAL-LINGUISTIC

Loves words
Hears and understands rhythms, patterns and meaning of words
Tells jokes and stories
Has a good memory

LOGICAL-MATHEMATICAL

Solves problems
Experiments
Enjoys strategy games, puzzles and brain teasers
Questions how things work

How Are You Smart?

MUSICAL

Sings

Plays a musical instrument

Speaks or moves with rhythm

Is sensitive to noise

BODILY-KINESTHETIC

Dances

Exercises

Plays sports

Enjoys taking things apart

How Are You Smart?

SPATIAL

Likes art activities
Reads maps well
Enjoys puzzles
Likes to build

INTERPERSONAL

Likes to work in groups
Considers the moods and feelings of others
Acts as a natural leader
Likes to be with friends

INTRAPERSONAL

Has the ability to understand own thoughts and feelings

Is self-directed

Prefers working alone

Is independent

Career Clusters

GRADE LEVEL(S): 3-5

DESCRIPTION:
Since it is impossible to explore all careers, this lesson gives students information on six types of careers which are grouped into clusters.

OBJECTIVE(S):
- Students will become aware of different career categories.
- Students will be aware that careers constantly change.

ESTIMATED TIME: 30 minutes

MATERIAL(S) NEEDED:
Career cluster props such as:
- Arts and Humanities: toy guitar, camera, paintbrush
- Business/Computer Technology: computer mouse, telephone, calculator
- Health Services: stethoscope, toothbrush, x-ray
- Human Services: chalk, book, fireman's hat, police badge
- Engineering Technology: toolbox, protractor, computer mouse
- Natural Resources Technology: binoculars, dolphin, microscope

(If props are not available, use pictures that are provided on pages 409-417)

PROCEDURES:
1. Have the students pretend that they are 30 years old and are at a high school reunion. Have each tell about their career at the age of 30.
2. Explain that right now students do not have to make a decision about jobs but that it is important to know interests and strengths when thinking about jobs.
3. Introduce the 6 career clusters by using tools that represent the clusters. Bring out the groups of props (or pictures if props are not available) and see if students can determine what they have in common. Describe the career cluster to students in this way:

- **ARTS AND HUMANITIES:** provide services that make our world a more enjoyable place in which to live such as photographers, entertainers, athletes, artists, musicians
- **BUSINESS/COMPUTER TECHNOLOGY:** work in a variety of business situations such as bankers, small business owners, secretaries, computer programmers
- **HEALTH SERVICES:** provide services that keep the world healthy such as doctors, nurses, radiologists, veterinarians, dentists, dieticians, EMTs, ambulance drivers
- **HUMAN SERVICES:** people helping other people such as teachers, counselors, lawyers, firefighters, police officers

- **ENGINEERING TECHNOLOGY:** provide services to construct or make existing things work more effectively such as engineers, architects, scientists
- **NATURAL RESOURCES TECHNOLOGY:** protect our environment such as forest rangers, marine biologists, scientists

As you discuss each cluster, recall what the students said they would be doing at the age of 30 and share the cluster in which they fit.

4. Explain that it is impossible to discuss every available job in the world since jobs are changing every day. Encourage students to think in terms of the job cluster in which they are most interested, especially if they are uncertain about a specific career.

SUMMARY POSTER OR VISUAL REMINDER:
Career Clusters summary poster found on page 418

VARIATIONS/MODIFICATIONS/EXTENSIONS:
- Plan a career fair. Set up exhibits by career cluster.
- Plan a career dress up day.
- Break students into six groups. Assign each group a career cluster and have them research as many careers as possible in that cluster.
- Search the internet for career sites and make these available for student use.

JOURNAL ENTRY

Choose one of the following six career clusters that interest you:
Arts and Humanities
Business/Computer Technology
Health Services
Human Services
Engineering Technology
Natural Resources Technology
Tell why that area interests you and list some jobs that may be included in this area.

CLASSROOM GUIDANCE NEWS

Dear Parent,

Today's classroom guidance lesson focused on the world of work. Your child is beginning to develop interests and strengths in certain areas and being aware of how these strengths and interests relate to careers is helpful. Today we focused on six career clusters. These clusters include:

- **ARTS AND HUMANITIES:** provide services that make our world a more enjoyable place in which to live such as photographers, entertainers, athletes, artists, musicians
- **BUSINESS/COMPUTER TECHNOLOGY:** work in a variety of business situations such as bankers, small business owners, secretaries, computer programmers
- **HEALTH SERVICES**: provide services that keep the world healthy such as doctors, nurses, radiologists, veterinarians, dentists, dieticians, EMTs, ambulance drivers
- **HUMAN SERVICES:** people helping other people such as teachers, counselors, lawyers, firefighters, police officers
- **ENGINEERING TECHNOLOGY:** provide services to construct or make existing things work more effectively such as engineers, architects, scientists
- **NATURAL RESOURCES TECHNOLOGY:** protect our environment such as forest rangers, marine biologists, scientists

Students had fun looking at some different "tools of the trade" from each career cluster and identifying jobs that belonged in each career cluster. It's never too early to begin discussing the future with your child. Although he/she does not need to make a choice now, career exploration is important. The world is open to your child. Discuss with your child the plans he/she has for the future. You may be surprised what you hear! Be cautious that you don't discourage plans, but that you listen and work to be certain that your child realizes his/her potential.

As always, please feel free to call me with any questions or concerns that you may have about your child, your child's school experience, or our elementary guidance and counseling program.

Sincerely,

Career Prop Pictures

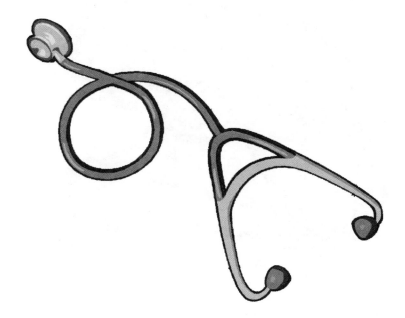

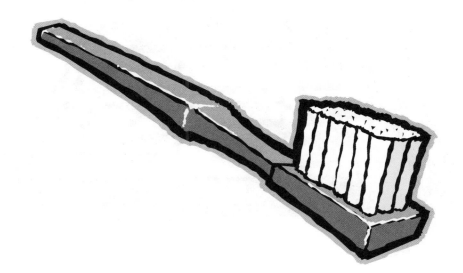

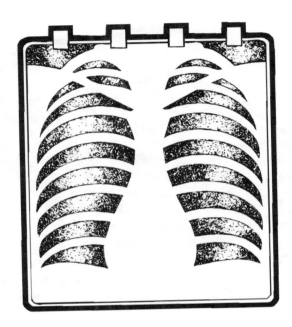

CHALK

Career Prop Pictures

Career Prop Pictures

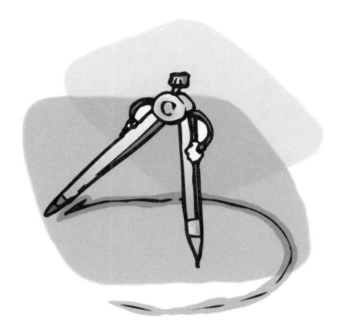

Career Prop Pictures

Arts/Humanities

Business/Computer Technology

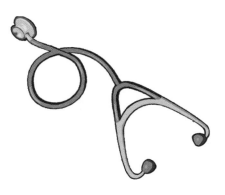

Health Services

Human Services

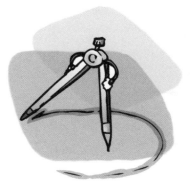

Engineering Technology

Natural Resources Technology

Give Your Dream Wings

GRADE LEVEL(S): 3-5

DESCRIPTION:
All students like to dream about the future. This lesson helps students understand that a dream is only the beginning; a plan and hard work make dreams become realities.

OBJECTIVE(S):
- Students will think about a future goal.
- Students will recognize that future dreams and goals require a plan and hard work.

ESTIMATED TIME: 30 minutes

MATERIAL(S) NEEDED:
Copies of Give Your Dream Wings and Daily News activity sheets found on pages 421-422

PROCEDURES:
1. Remind the students that a goal is something you work toward—a target.
2. Discuss that many people have dreams about things but that dreams have to be turned into goals with a plan for them to come true. Example: I can dream about owning a fancy sports car, but I must make a goal and plan for that to happen—saving money.
3. Explain that they are going to dream today. Distribute the "Give Your Dream Wings" worksheets. Ask students to complete each sentence.
4. Reemphasize that in order for a dream to become a reality, students must have specific plans. Ask each student to choose one dream from the sheet they just completed. They are to write an article in for the Daily News pretending that it is 30 years from this day. The article is to be written in third person and should state specifically how they accomplished their dream.
5. Share and discuss. This is a fun and insightful activity!

SUMMARY POSTER OR VISUAL REMINDER:
Give Your Dreams Wings summary poster found on page 423

VARIATIONS/MODIFICATIONS/EXTENSIONS:
- Choose books on various careers to share.

JOURNAL ENTRY

Draw a picture of a dream of yours. Draw a pair of wings on this dream and write on the wings the things you need to be doing now and in the future to make this dream come true.

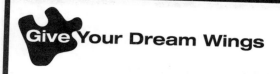
Give Your Dream Wings

CLASSROOM GUIDANCE NEWS

Dear Parent,

Today in classroom guidance students wrote some future goals. We discussed how dreams must have plans behind them to become reality. Students wrote a newspaper article for a paper thirty years in the future. The article is about him/her accomplishing a dream.

This activity allowed students to think about setting long range goals. While our long range was really LONG range and was fun to think about, the skill of long range planning is very important. The ability to plan for future goals, whether it is ten years or ten weeks, allows a child to feel some sense of control over what lies ahead. It also helps keep a child focused and organized.

Within the next several years, your child will begin selecting courses to take in school. He/she will need guidance from you and school as to which of these courses to take. Help your child understand that what he/she is doing now in school does relate to the future. As always, please feel free to call me with any questions or concerns you may have about your child, your child's school experience, or our elementary guidance and counseling program.

In partnership,

Give Your Dream Wings

Think into your future as an adult and complete each of the following sentences.

The job I would like to have is _____

_____

_____

A place I would like to travel is _____

_____

_____

A hobby I would like to have is _____

_____

_____

Something I would like to accomplish is _____

_____

_____

The Daily News

READ ALL ABOUT IT!